THE STORY OF OUR CIVILIZATION

PHILIP LEE RALPH was born in Antigo, Wisconsin. He received his B.A. from Beloit College, Wisconsin and his Ph.D. at Yale University in 1935. From 1936 to 1945 Professor Ralph taught history at Rutgers University, and since 1945 he has been Chairman of the Department of History at Lake Erie College. The Rutgers University Press published his *Sir Humphrey Mildmay: Royalist Gentleman* in 1947.

THE STORY OF OUR CIVILIZATION was first published in 1954.

THE STORY OF OUR CIVILIZATION

10,000 YEARS OF WESTERN MAN

By

PHILIP LEE RALPH

A Dutton *Paperback*

Everyman

NEW YORK

E. P. DUTTON & CO., INC.

To Marion,
George, and Mary

CONTENTS

Contents

PREFACE

THE history of the Western peoples is a vast subject to which many volumes have been devoted. The aim of this book is not to repeat or even to summarize the historical narrative as such. It is, rather, to analyze, interpret, and, so far as possible, illuminate the most salient features of the Western experience to date. The book presents a survey of the characteristics and the course of Western civilization in an endeavor to estimate its achievements, assess its strength and weaknesses, discover its persistent or recurrent objectives, and suggest areas where a more resolute application of its resources would be profitable. Examination is directed primarily to those movements and tendencies which seem most pertinent to the story as a whole and most essential to an understanding of the contemporary scene. The problems confronting civilization today are tremendous, and the author cannot claim to have solved any of them. He believes, however, that Western man, in struggling with the dilemmas that harass him, can take both warning and courage from the contemplation of his own past.

Because an interpretive work is necessarily a projection of opinion, and because this study—however erroneous the author's judgments—has grown out of years of reading and reflection, it is impossible to acknowledge the various sources which have been drawn upon in its preparation. I wish, however, to point out indebtedness in a few specific instances. For Chapter IX, material on the social and political ideals of the seventeenth-century English Puritans was found in Wilhelm Schenk's brief but very valuable study, *The Concern for Social Justice in the Puritan Revolution* (London: Longmans, Green and Co., 1948). For the reform

9

Preface

programs and international outlook of the philosophers of the Enlightenment (also in Chapter IX) use was made of Elizabeth V. Souleyman, *The Vision of World Peace in Seventeenth and Eighteenth-Century France* (New York: G. P. Putnam's Sons, 1941). The quotations illustrating the sentiments of modern imperialism in Chapter XI are taken chiefly from P. T. Moon, *Imperialism and World Politics* (New York: The Macmillan Co., 1926) and from Julius W. Pratt, *Expansionists of 1898* (Baltimore: The Johns Hopkins Press, 1936). The statistics and quoted comment on Russia's increasing industrial strength in Chapter XI are from an article by Theodore H. White, "The Challenge of Soviet Economic Growth," in *The Reporter*, May 26, 1953. Mr. C. Hartley Grattan's suggestion concerning an industrial civilization (cited in Chapter XII) appeared in his review, "New Books: Urbane Economies," in *Harper's Magazine*, August, 1952.

I am grateful to my friend, Professor Edward McNall Burns of Rutgers University, for reading the manuscript and offering constructive suggestions.

P. L. R.

THE STORY OF OUR CIVILIZATION

CHAPTER ONE

MAN

THIS story is about man and what he has done in that portion of the earth which we call the Western world. The story would be clearer if we knew what man is. It would also help if we knew where he came from and where he is going, although these questions are almost too ambitious in view of our ignorance of what man actually is now. We do not understand his essential nature, potentialities, and limitations; still less do we know whether he is unique in the cosmos or whether other worlds than ours are inhabited by humanlike beings.

This is not to say that there are no ideas about man and his station. Ever since man began to talk and think he has been fond of discussing himself, and libraries are piled high with books about human nature and behavior. But philosophers, scientists, poets, and prophets contradict one another, and the welter of theories is such as to cast doubt upon the finality of any judgment. Man has been described as but little lower than the angels, as a vile worm, as a free agent, as a helpless puppet, as good, bad, and as a mixture of all of these.

Tangible evidence on which to assess or evaluate the human stock is by no means lacking. The intention of this present survey, in fact, is to examine some of the accumulated evidence for the purpose of throwing light upon the problem of what man has been and is. The record of his activities and achievements is an ample one, although there will always be disagreement as to its implications.

In the first place, there is a great deal of scientific evidence concerning the long and gradual physical evolution of man from a simple type of life up through increasingly complex forms unto his present aspect. The process extended over thousands of millions of years and, even though the material proof for it is fragmentary, it is sufficient not only to illustrate the main outline of the successive changes but also to show that they constitute a marvelous transformation.

The record of organic change as reconstructed by scientific research is so impressive and so apparently purposeful that it may invite the drawing of rash and unwarranted conclusions. It is hard to think of the course of biological evolution without resorting to metaphors which inject a false simplicity or even a dogmatic judgment. We speak of the "tree of life," with its branches stemming forth from the common trunk at successive heights. Because evolution means change and usually toward greater complexity, we too readily assume that it is a stream of progress, from the "low" to the "high," from the imperfect to the more nearly perfect. Probably in the over-all view it is; but there is no assurance that every series of changes is a movement in the right direction. In fact it is not always clear what the right direction is. It is also evident that organic change may be such as to make a species worse off in relation to its environment; evolution can go "downward" as well as "upward"; in the former case it is called degeneration. Even when it is going "upward" and the organism is becoming better off in relation to its environment, there is no proof that all of the accompanying changes are the best conceivable. The successful species exhibits traits which are peculiarly useful in a particular environment; they may be a drawback in a different environment. We can never know, for example, how

Man

many agreeable or benevolent traits may have been squeezed out
of man in his long struggle for survival in which the race was
often to the swift and the battle to the strong. We can only
observe, gratefully, that enough altruism seems to be inherent
in human nature to make us uncomfortable in many of the patterns of social behavior to which human societies are addicted.

In the scheme of biological classification which traces lines
of descent or ascent from the earliest forms of life and demarcates
degrees of relationship among surviving types, man is placed at
the top of the list, as the highest step in the evolutionary ladder—
the "lord of creation." Many factors could be cited to explain the
basis for man's pre-eminence, but one is sufficient—it is he who
does the classifying. Perhaps his priority is actually a priori, a
subjective and arbitrary premise, although understandable in a
creature enamored not only of the mighty works he has produced
but also of his own powers of reflection and rational thought.
Certainly man is ill-advised to look down upon other organisms.
Not he alone is wonderfully made. Every form of life, even the
simplest, possesses qualities which the human brain cannot entirely
comprehend, much less create. Man's reasoning and creative
faculties are impressive; but so are the migratory instincts of birds,
the uncanny geographical memory of certain fishes, the oppressively efficient organization and the communication system of
insects. Some biologists insist that insects are, in their way, as
"high" a type of life as anything on earth. On the basis of their
great numbers both of individuals and of species, of their range
of adaptation to various environments, and of their widespread
impact upon other living creatures, the insects might lay a fair
claim to the title of "lords of creation." However, man will continue to insist on his primacy, whether or not he is able to maintain it.

The accepted scientific name used to designate our species is
in itself an indication of the high esteem with which man came to
regard his own peculiar endowments: Homo sapiens—"man the
wise." This term was invented by a European during the "Age
of Reason," and reflects the self-confident optimism of the eighteenth century. If the official tags which we append to species

had been bequeathed by some other historic period, a title with very different connotation might have been selected. Probably the mind of the early Middle Ages, obsessed by a sense of sin and frustration, would have preferred something like *Homo vermiculus* or *peccans* or *depravatus*. Romanticists of the Renaissance or the early nineteenth century might have chosen *Homo sentiens* or *heroicus*. In our own age so many different facets of human nature compete for attention that it would be difficult to agree on a key term; but *sapiens* seems less appropriate than *mechanicus*, *bellicosus*—or even *diabolicus*.

Biologically speaking, one remarkable fact about modern man is that he is widely separated both from his own evolutionary ancestors and from his extant closest of kin. In the great order of Primates—a division of the class of Mammals—the family *Hominidae* is now represented by only one surviving species, "sapiens." All living peoples, no matter how different from one another in appearance and behavior, are variations of a single species of a single genus; thus they are blood brothers in a very strict and accurate sense of the term. In the biological world as a whole there are commonly numerous species of the same genus, many genera of the same family, and so on. Paleontological evidence shows that man has been no exception. In the long course of human evolution there has been continual deviation, and man's collateral relatives in the geological time span are many. However, the peculiar fact is that all of these relatives are extinct. Man as we know him, dominant over the earth's surface, represents only one tiny surviving twig (to resort to the metaphor) in an evolutionary tree of which the roots and branches have long since disappeared.

One of the ways, then, in which man is unique, is that while he is an integral part of the organic world, he also in a sense stands apart from it because he is so distantly related to all other living creatures. Between contemporary races and their subhuman ancestors, and between them and the great apes there is not just one "missing link" but practically a whole missing chain, of which a few chance links, exciting in their significance to be sure, have been discovered.

The prehistoric human types disappeared, it is assumed, because they constituted imperfect adaptations to their environment. Modern man is also imperfectly adapted to his surroundings, but he is again peculiar in that his environment is both flexible and increasingly artificial—one that he has made himself, although not to suit himself. Contemporary man is frequently beset by doubts as to whether he will long survive, in spite of his jubilation over new sources of power which he has unlocked and in spite of the fact that he now has at his disposal resources sufficient to enrich the material content of his existence beyond anything dreamed of in the past. The solitary prominence of man in the biological world is not explained entirely on the basis that he represents the apex of evolution—that he has outstripped his nearest rivals so far that they have dropped out of sight. It is more than probable that Homo sapiens himself had something to do with the disappearance of his less gifted relatives. He has always inclined toward an uncharitable view of competing heirs to the earthly kingdom, and even the elimination of alien species has not dispelled his feeling of insecurity.

CHAPTER TWO

TOWARD CIVILIZATION

ONE of the most distinctive characteristics of man is a tendency to become civilized. Every variety of the genus, archaeological evidence reveals, had it to a degree, and with Homo sapiens, who emerged upon the scene thirty thousand or more years ago, it became a recognizable if not always potent drive. The impulse to create civilization does not entail any specific formula of action but manifests itself in innumerable ways. There is by no means universal agreement, even today, as to just what civilization is, what it must include, or when it began. The word in its literal sense means having to do with life in a *civitas* or city, but it is obvious that the process of building civilization began long before there were any cities, and some peoples have reached a relatively high degree of social development without establishing cities at all. But whatever the definition of the concept, it is clearly a state which human beings are capable of attaining, whereas other animals are not.

Man is endowed with a tendency toward civilization, but not with civilization itself. Furthermore, the tendency is commonly obscured and inhibited by other powerful and more deeply rooted impulses in his make-up, so that the attempt to become civilized calls both for a struggle against external obstacles and for war against part of his own nature. Every student of history agrees that the achievement of a high culture out of primitive beginnings is an uphill endeavor, with chances of success dubious and with the very goals obscure. This is not at all strange, because civilization is basically *unnatural;* it is an attempt to outwit nature, to lift man out of the normal setting in which he is one of a host of animals struggling to survive—a little slower of foot and clumsier than many, a little craftier than most—to lift him out of this and give him unique advantages by bending nature and her creatures to his own will. Civilization appears as an unforeseen and arbitrary invention on man's part, changing the rules of the game in his favor, a daring attempt to displace nature as final arbiter. It is artificial, contrived, and therefore extremely fragile. The primordial primitive forces are constantly hovering in the fringes, ever ready to take over again should there be any relaxation of man's vigilance. Also civilization is precarious because it is not inherent in native human equipment. It is not instinctive and not hereditary in the biological sense. Not only is it created laboriously but each successive generation must be taught to accept it and to utilize it—a task which no one has as yet discovered how to perform with very much success.

There are any number of theories as to how, when, and where civilization first began. The most puzzling question, however, is why it ever began at all. Obviously at the outset no one could foresee what was coming. Perhaps the fateful point of departure was when our ancestors began to come down out of the trees and compete for food with the animals that lived on the ground. They increased their dietary prospects by so doing but they also multiplied the dangers to which they were exposed and increased the risk of finding themselves in alien terrain where they might starve to death. If they succeeded in keeping a foothold, their numbers increased and they spread into distant regions where they encountered new enemies. As the expansion of population continued, the human beings who did not succumb in the struggle were forced to devise more ingenious methods of taking care of themselves. Each new adjustment, widening man's field of operations, inevitably necessitated another, leading the more enterprising groups ultimately in the direction of an efficiently organized society. Thus man's latent capacity for becoming civilized, as well as the painfulness of the process, was eventually revealed.

Although the task of preserving and improving a civilization is so difficult that it is usually abandoned even after a period of comparative success, it is still more difficult to originate one. The first steps are the hardest, because it is always easier to follow than to lead and easier to improve someone else's idea than to think of one yourself. Therefore, the real pioneers of human history were the nameless men and women of the stone ages who discovered how to manipulate the inert elements of their environment so as to tip the balance of nature in their favor. Their first experiments in this direction were the crudest imaginable and consisted in chipping pieces of stone slightly so that when the stone was held in the hand as a weapon it added somewhat to the formidability of its possessor. The initial poverty of human invention is shown by the fact that no improvement was made in this miserable tool over eons of time. For several hundred thousand years, perhaps half a million, man's only implement, beyond a broken tree limb such as even a gorilla might appropriate, was the eolith ("dawn stone"), so formless that it is sometimes impossible for anthropologists to determine whether a particular specimen was actually shaped by hand or simply used as found.

Finally some shaggy-browed genius invented the "fist hatchet," still a pitifully crude object, but a great advance over the eolith, not only because of its more symmetrical elongated shape but because a recognizable edge was produced by chipping off flakes with another stone used as a hammer; and it clearly shows that a technique of tool working had been acquired. Once achieved, however, the fist hatchet remained the highest example of human ingenuity for about fifteen hundred centuries, until it was replaced by knives and scrapers, still of flint but more varied in size and shape and often possessing delicately flaked edges. Again, in the Late or "Upper" Old Stone Age—a comparatively brief period, only about eight times as long as the Christian Era—the art of chipping flint reached an impressively high level, attested by a profusion of scrapers, knives, and spearheads, as well as axes. The bone and horn hooks, harpoons, and needles which date from this epoch also offer proof of the tremendous advances which had been made in toolmaking since eolithic days.

Toward Civilization

The men of the Late Old Stone Age were still savages, even though they had behind them the thrust of some half million years of human effort and groping. They did not raise any crops but depended for their food supply entirely upon the plants and animals which they found around them. They had no domestic animals, except perhaps the dog; other beasts were either their enemies or their prey. If the dog had become man's friend, this may have been as much the result of the dog's initiative as of man's; the advantages to each species in an association devoted to hunting are readily apparent. Neither men nor women wore clothing, except animal skins. There were no carts or wheelbarrows, no dishes or furniture, and no houses to put them in.

The paucity of culture was not because the Old Stone Age folk lacked intelligence. Many of their skeletons have been excavated (they buried their dead, apparently with elaborate ritual, sometimes with the limbs carefully arranged in arbitrary positions, sometimes with the bodies or naked bones smeared with paint) and from reconstructions made by trained anatomists it is possible for us to compare their appearance with that of peoples living today. The Cro-Magnon type, one of the Upper Paleolithic European races, is especially admired by anthropologists. Not only was he Homo sapiens, but he seems to have been an excellent representative of the species, with a brain fully as large as ours and a stature which sometimes exceeded six feet in the males. His skull case indicates that his brain had the same contours as that of modern man and that his speech mechanism was equally well developed. Presumably his psychosomatic equipment and even his potential for creative thought were similar to ours. If some infant of this race could have been miraculously transported through time to be reared in a modern home, there is every reason to believe that he would have become as civilized as his twentieth-century playmates and have developed into a successful or even distinguished member of our society. But in Cro-Magnon's era civilization was still embryonic, and his intelligence was doomed to dissipate itself in the wilderness. The imprint of his intelligence is seen in the beautifully carved harpoons, daggers, and gravers which he fashioned and above all in the startlingly realistic cave paintings which excite our admiration and wonder. He probably would have been as astounded at our reaction to these paintings as we are at the artistic talent which they reveal, because to him they were principally, and perhaps entirely, adjuncts to the pursuit of a food supply. The subjects consistently depicted in the paintings were bison, reindeer, and wild horses—animals which Cro-Magnon man hunted—and were executed with great fidelity to the original in order to insure success in the chase. They were not displayed in art galleries but projected on the walls of dark caves and often wantonly obliterated after they had served (or failed in) their purpose.

An ironic aspect of man's estate is that having once embarked on the course of civilization building he must continue on that course or run the risk of shipwreck. He is under a compulsion to keep on improving. There are many living species which have remained virtually unchanged for millions of years, retaining the same form and the same pattern of integration with their environment. They are, within the limits of our finite chronology, a part of the natural order, more enduring than the "eternal hills," which, after all, do come and go in successive geological eras. But with man it is different. Ever since he ceased to be content to lie in the bosom of nature and set out to devise an artificial habitat, he put himself under the necessity of zealously watching over his creation, of keeping it in repair, and of continually making it a more satisfactory ministrant to his expanding needs.

Such an imperative rests upon all peoples, but some respond more effectively than others. When one community comes into contact with another more advanced than itself, it may find its own way of life upset or displaced altogether. Apparently this is what happened when the New Stone Age races moved into Europe and the Mediterranean area about 10,000 B.C. Before the impact of the superior Neolithic culture Paleolithic man disappeared. Even if his physical stock was not entirely exterminated in Europe, his culture was extinguished.

Neolithic culture, which eventually spread over the entire world of human habitation, represents such a tremendous advance over earlier achievements that it must be regarded as one of the

great landmarks in the history of mankind. True, it is not desig-
nated as "civilization" because of the absence of certain elements
which seem indispensable to us; but at its best it provided a solution to the basic problems of nourishment, shelter, and protection.
Without the techniques which it employed and which have been
employed ever since—agriculture and irrigation; the domestica-
tion of animals; the spinning and weaving of cloth; the construction of homes, fortifications, and monuments; the manufacture of
pottery—all subsequent progress would have been impossible.
Actually there is no clearly perceptible dividing point between
Neolithic culture and civilization in the proper sense of the term.

In spite of its superiority Neolithic culture lacked some of the
picturesque traits of the preceding era. The magnificent cave art
of Paleolithic man was not continued by his successors, who
did not live in caves and did not depend upon the chase for their
sustenance and hence felt no incentive to augment the supply of
game animals by the practice of sympathetic magic. Whether
the agricultural and pastoral New Stone Age folk regarded the
cave paintings (if they ever discovered them at all) with awe or
contempt will never be known; but it is certain that they produced
nothing comparable themselves. The Neolithic approach, like all
subsequent civilized approaches to the problem of fulfilling human
needs, was fundamentally different from anything attempted
before. It involved a more elaborate and more laborious routine,
less romantic but more dependable than that of the cave dwelling
hunters. For adventure, chance, and reckless courage the Neolithic people substituted hard work. If man's lot is one of blood,
toil, sweat, and tears, the Old Stone Age folk put the accent on
blood, while their successors much preferred toil and sweat,
certainly an essential choice for the improvement of the social
order, even though it by no means eliminates tears.

One arresting aspect of Neolithic culture was its inequitable
division of labor. Inequitable not just between master and slaves
and between rich and poor—although these distinctions undoubtedly existed—but inequitable between the sexes. The
division of labor was a simple one: the women did most of the
work. They were the planters and sowers, the tillers of crops

23

and the harvesters. Probably they also cooked the meals, made and laundered the clothes, took care of the children, and did whatever house cleaning was considered necessary. (Presumably the men built houses and took a hand in the manufacture of pottery.) By long tradition the male had been warrior, hunter, trapper, and fisher; and now that agriculture had become the mainstay of the tribe his pursuits (with the exception of fighting) were transformed from a stern necessity to an economic side line, offering a convenient escape from the drudgery of domestic routine. At the same time, woman, whose duty had always been to prepare the slaughtered game for eating and to supplement it by whatever wild fruits, nuts, and grain she could gather, now found her activities enshrined as the essential ones, while they had also become far more extensive and arduous.

The pattern of culture in which women did the bulk of the work was never universal, and there were doubtless many exceptions to it (where the economic base was pastoral, men assumed more responsibility because they regarded the handling of animals as their province); but it was fairly typical of Neolithic agricultural communities. Although such a distribution of labor may shock modern feminine, and masculine, sensibilities, it is not necessarily explained in terms of subjugation or "exploitation" of the weaker by the stronger sex. By virtue of their traditional role as food gatherers, women undoubtedly were the ones who invented (or stumbled upon) the art of agriculture; and jealous pride in their discovery, reinforced by magical-religious taboos, may have been factors in their monopoly of the trade. Certainly their economic, perhaps even their social, importance was enhanced by their new function as guarantors and guardians of the food supply—breadwinners in a literal sense. Far from being a brutally oppressed class, women may have held a position of honor in these societies of feminine farmers. But whether or not such was the case, there is no denying that men got off easily. For a few centuries in the early dawn of civilization it was man's sweet privilege to devote himself wholeheartedly to pursuits which he now must indulge in only spasmodically or surreptitiously—hunting, fishing, and loafing.

This situation was only temporary, of course; but it was probably not a rebellion of women so much as man's overcleverness which proved his undoing. Once they become used to a routine, women will hold to it for generations, performing it faithfully and without much complaint. But the male is always trying to make things better; he is the everlasting tinkerer. So in due time—if speculation is permissible in the absence of direct evidence—some ill-starred reformer among Neolithic husbands must have hit upon the idea of the plow. It was a brilliant invention, but it worked havoc with the old unchivalrous division of labor. The new instrument, at first only a crude variation of the hoe, was progressively augmented both in cutting power and weight, until it was beyond the strength of feminine backs to drag it across the fields. Not wanting to pull the plow himself and unable to compel his wife to do it, man soon discovered that certain animals could be trained to perform the task with highly satisfactory results. With the substitution of the plow-and-ox for the wife-and-hoe complex, the way was opened for revolutionary improvements in agriculture. But man was now inextricably involved in the process. The subduing and training of animals was already part of his domain, and with the advent of the plow he was henceforth destined to be a husbandman.

This change in the economic functions of the sexes did not mean that woman was freed from the burden of toil, but it did mean that her mate's idyllic days were over. It is noteworthy that each advance in civilization brings with it the necessity of shouldering greater responsibilities and more numerous tasks—by both sexes—if things are to go tolerably well.

CHAPTER THREE

WESTERN ORIGINS:
THE ANCIENT NEAR EAST

A FUNDAMENTAL fact in human history is that man has had very little history in the strict sense of the term. He has inhabited the earth for something between half a million and a million years. But only during the last 6000 years or so has he possessed a highly integrated social organization, exhibited impressive intellectual attainments, and produced written records which can be perused by historians. Viewed from the standpoint of the total experience of the human race to date, civilization is an undertaking which has been entered upon only recently; and although it has already demonstrated that human nature can be modified incalculably, it has not yet taken possession of the whole of our beings. Civilized behavior is still, relatively speaking, only a veneer, the permanence and ultimate significance of which has not yet been fully proven.

THE SCOPE OF INQUIRY

Because the heritage of civilization is so recent and has occupied such a tiny portion of the life story of the genus Homo, the traditional division of chronology into "prehistoric" and historic" periods appears to be ill-proportioned and unrealistic. It is as absurd to assume that the activities of mankind were unimportant and nonhistoric until a few thousand years ago as it would be to assert that an individual's life was of no significance until the day on which he cast his first vote or began to keep a diary. In recognition of the inadequacy of the old terminology, the term "preliterate" is now preferred to "prehistoric." Nevertheless, from the standpoint of anyone who is interested in assessing man's potentialities, it is justifiable to narrow the scope of study to those eras which have left traces of significant achievement. Justifiable not only because the investigator will be shooting in the dark unless he has tangible records (including written records if he wishes to penetrate the thought life of earlier peoples), but also because these eras illustrate most fully the range of human capacity. The history of civilization is the history of a great many civilizations, showing tremendous contrasts, but all predicated upon fundamentally the same human material.

It is legitimate and proper in historical inquiry to be concerned above all else with the character and fate of civilizations. We can do very little to alter our physical heritage or our inherent mental capacity. But our social inheritance, in spite of its compelling force, is the product of man's devising and is subject to continual modification. Civilization is not fixed, like the stars in their courses; it is made by man and also unmade by him. Therefore, it may be assumed that an objective study of successive cultures will provide clues as to the factors tending to promote success and those conducive to failure.

An interest in the causes of civilization's growth and decay is nothing new. It was prominent in the speculation even of ancient thinkers. A typical notion among the Greeks was that of natural cycles, perpetually recurring. Here the theme was one of gradual but inevitable degeneration from a blissful "golden age" in the distant past, with an eventual return to the starting point and a repetition of the cycle. Somewhat comparable was the Hebrew (and Christian) tradition of an original earthly paradise, lost by man's willfulness, and to be regained only on a transcendental level. Such conceptions, naïve as they may seem, are not much more unrealistic than some which have been propounded in modern times—for example, the theory of racial determinism, or the biological metaphor which likens society to a living organism ordained to pass the climax of maturity and then to wither and decay.

While conjectures as to the probable course of civilization are old, the concept of *progress* is relatively recent. It was a corollary to the tremendous scientific advance of the sixteenth, seventeenth, and eighteenth centuries and was both stimulated and apparently documented by the Darwinian hypothesis of biological evolution in the nineteenth century. The idea of progress brought new courage, optimism, even utopianism into people's thinking. At the same time it prompted the drawing of false analogies between social institutions and biological organisms and led to unwarranted conclusions as to current and future trends. It was too easily assumed that change was inevitable, in accordance with natural "laws," and that change spelled progress. This resulted in a new kind of scientific determinism, against which liberals and humanitarians have had to wage a relentless battle.

Probably the twentieth century has witnessed a more extensive effort than ever before to understand the phenomena of social change and their significance. Increasingly this becomes a matter of diagnosing the ills of social structures in the hope that they can be restored to a greater degree of health. The reason for this is not far to seek. Alarming symptoms, uncomfortably parallel to those which have usually preceded the downfall of civilizations, can be found in abundance today. At this late hour when prophetic voices are sounding the approach of doom, historians must justify their recondite activities on the grounds that they will show us how to avoid the pitfalls of the past and save ourselves from destruction.

Unfortunately for the historians and their apologiae, the study of history has never yet saved a civilization from peril nor clearly and demonstrably contributed to its improvement. Beginning with Thucydides, if not before, reflective students have drawn some very pointed lessons from history; but it is one thing to draw a lesson and another to receive and apply it. That Western man of the twentieth century will do any better than his predecessors in this regard is almost too much to expect. However, the historian's defense must be that, no matter how slim the chances of success, there is no other alternative. Unless we ferret out the defects and errors which have proved fatal to other once vigorous civilizations, we cannot hope to strengthen our own or even to be realistic in our conception of the dangers which confront it. Ortega's dictum, that we must understand and digest the past in order to overcome it, is still valid.

In spite of mounting interest and intensive study of the subject, the "laws" which govern the success or failure, stability or impermanence of civilizations have not yet been established. Perhaps there are no such laws, inflexible and universally operative, and the most we can look for are working hypotheses which will need to be continually revised, not only as knowledge of the past is more thoroughly sifted, but as the relative urgency of contemporary problems is modified. A hypothesis may have great value even though it is only a "philosophy of history" rather than a precise and proven formula.

To say that there are no infallible laws of progress and decay is not to deny that a great deal can be discovered and in fact already has been discovered concerning the fate of previous civilizations. A careful study of any highly advanced society which has disintegrated yields much sobering insight. Except where the evidence is too fragmentary, it is possible to determine with a fair degree of assurance the causes which produced the decline of any specific historic culture, and even to recognize certain factors common in every case. The thing which cannot be—or at least has not yet been—satisfactorily explained is *why* the people concerned have allowed these causes to operate, time after time. Neither can any guarantee be provided, no matter how boldly emblazoned the warning signals, that the process won't be allowed to happen again.

A STUDY IN CONTRASTS

When Western civilization is followed back to its sources, it is found to rest upon the achievements of a large number of peoples, many of whom have passed into obscurity or lost their identity altogether. It has been erected out of the fragments and debris of civilizations which, although vanished, were once both vigorous and creative. Some of them endured much longer than the period during which ours has been in existence.

The earliest centers of civilization were not identical with any of the areas where great cultures have flourished in recent times. Europe, of course, long remained an uncivilized continent, whereas some regions in Asia, such as the Indus River Valley of India and the Yellow River Valley of China, have been continuous culture sites for a period of 4000 years or more. However, archaeological discoveries indicate that the earliest cradles of historic civilizations were in the Near East—the Nile Valley of Africa and the "Fertile Crescent" of Asia, including the Tigris-Euphrates Valley. Thus, while Western civilization is a relatively recent product, the sources from which it is derived are as old as, or older than, any which have yet been discovered.

The peoples of the ancient Near East invented and developed basic techniques, institutions, and concepts which have been in operation ever since in the Western world and beyond it. The Egyptians devised the column and colonnade; Mesopotamians the arch, vault, dome, and spire. From one or both of these areas came the foundation of mathematical knowledge and engineering skill; units of weight and measurement and the reckoning of time, including the solar calendar; some progress in astronomy and other sciences; a multitude of handicrafts and artistic patterns; forms of symbolic communication, most notably the Egyptian discovery of the principle of the alphabet and of the pen and ink method of writing. Western man is also indebted to the peoples of these areas for the territorial state and the norms of government, and, finally, for religion. Aside from the value of these and many other specific contributions, the ancient Near Eastern civilizations offer an opportunity to study the ebb and flow of human social energy over a period of more than three millenniums. If we could understand—and we cannot hope to understand fully—why these great communities failed, one after another, we should be in a better position to recognize and deal effectively with the perplexities confronting contemporary society.

In some ancient states it is fairly easy to see what went wrong. Although extremely rare, there are a few which might be called horrible examples, inculcating a negative object lesson. The Assyrian Empire offers such an illustration. Its history portrays the unenviable fate of a people who attempted a short cut to success.

The Assyrians, who had settled on an open plain in northern Mesopotamia and were exposed to attack on all sides, determined to fight their way into a secure position. In spite of initial defeats and even subjugation, they succeeded in their objective all too well. By the tenth century B.C. they had become the most formidable military force of their day. As if to compensate for their early humiliations, they made themselves a scourge to surrounding nations. From the Hittites of Asia Minor they had learned how to forge weapons of iron, and by their invention of siege machinery and heavy armaments, including a crude type of tank, they anticipated the science of mechanized warfare. To the margin of military superiority which they established over their opponents they added systematic techniques of cruelty and frightfulness. Their rapidly expanding empire covered practically the whole Fertile Crescent and Egypt and, although puny by modern standards, constituted the largest in the Western world up to that time.

But the price which the Assyrians paid for their ascendancy was ruinous. Their society was dominated by a military caste; trade and manufacture were scornfully left in the hands of foreigners; the majority of subjects were agricultural laborers and no better than serfs. Even though there is evidence of artistic talent, architectural and engineering competence, and some literary activity (Ashurbanipal's royal library at Nineveh contained about 22,000 clay tablets in cuneiform script), Assyrian culture, in contrast to the power of the state, rested on narrow and flimsy foundations. However, the costliest item of all in the balance sheet was the hatred which the Assyrian conquerors engendered among the peoples they had dominated. To overthrow the cruel tyranny became a universal passion, and as soon as their military might began to crack before the onslaught of the Chaldeans, the Assyrians found that everyone's hand was against them. Their proud fortresses were torn stone from stone, making the name Nineveh ever since a byword of desolation. Not only were the Assyrians crushed and their empire destroyed, but even as a nation they were extinguished forever. They had discovered a quick route to success—and to oblivion.

Almost opposite to the Assyrians is the case of the ancient Hebrews. Instead of forging ahead rapidly to success the Hebrews met frustration and defeat; yet out of their failure came a unique and enduring achievement. The externals of their history are commonplace. The Hebrews were one of many groups of Semitic nomads who gravitated from the Arabian desert into the Fertile Crescent, seeking a better means of subsistence, fighting to gain possession of land which various possessors had struggled over from time immemorial, and gradually absorbing characteristics of the peoples and the more mature cultures which had preceded them. Even some physical traits were acquired in the process—the "Hittite nose," for example, commonly and mistakenly regarded as a Semitic peculiarity—but more significantly the rudiments of husbandry and mechanical arts, a form of writing, and political and legal concepts. Although the Hebrews evidenced little originality in the techniques of civilization building, they developed national aspirations ambitious in scope and attempted to establish a powerful state, resplendent with the usual accouterments of Oriental monarchies. Far from being a conspicuous success, the kingdom which was founded with so much travail remained intact for scarcely a century, and the two divisions into which it separated fell prey to a succession of conquerors.

While the political debacle was working itself out, however, the Hebrews were displaying potentialities along quite a different line. They were a poetic and imaginative folk, with a keen sensitivity to social responsibilities and a remarkable insight into the mainsprings of human behavior. They gave these tendencies full play in the development of their religion, so that as their faith evolved toward an ethical monotheism it constantly received the distillation of their own experiences and of those of the other peoples with whom they had come in contact. The Hebrews borrowed—from their neighbors, rivals, and conquerors—in the field of religion as elsewhere; but they transformed, elevated, and gave a vivid stamp of originality to the elements which they as-similated. Drawing upon many strata and many centuries of tradition and speculation, they proved themselves the spiritual geniuses of the ancient world. They lifted religion from a cult to a philosophy of history—more than that, to a program of action and a message of hope for mankind.

The ancient Hebrews, however, did not fully grasp the sig-nificance of their own discoveries and intuitions. Like many other peoples, they engaged in the pursuit of mutually contra-dictory objectives. The conflicting theses of humility and service on the one hand, and vindication and power on the other, com-peted confusingly with each other. Time after time the attempt was made to re-establish dominion over that corner of the Fertile Crescent which the Jews stubbornly regarded as their Promised Land. Resiliency at the core is a quality distinguishable throughout the whole of Hebrew history. The more they were subjected the more they cherished the dream of national greatness. But each thwarting of their material nationalistic goal drove their spiritual roots deeper and also made more intense the impact of Hebraic thought upon surrounding peoples, until it became spread so widely that it could never be obliterated.

If the Hebrews had attained their desire for a mighty earthly kingdom, would they have made the same conquests in the realm of the spirit? Too high a degree of material satisfaction seems to induce deterioration of man's highest faculties—not necessarily of his intellectual faculties as a whole, but in his flexibility, re-siliency, and capacity for imaginative response to difficult situa-tions. The testimony of history on this score is so overwhelming as hardly to require citation.

Apropos of the experience of the Hebrews, the case of the an-cient Persians may be noted. Before they acquired their empire and while they were still in only the marginal stage of civilization, the Persians had come into possession of one of the most inspiring religions ever conceived. This was the belief attributed to Zoroaster (or Zarathustra), a shadowy figure of the seventh century B.C. Not only did his teaching include a practical code of personal and social ethics, but it was dynamic and cosmic in scope. In its purposeful and dramatic dualism, in its challenging appeal to the individual to dedicate his energies to the service of the universal god of Light in a struggle against the powers of Darkness, it stood head and shoulders above most of the somnolent faiths of the East. However, although Zoroastrianism was accepted by the Persians, the tremendous empire which they established through conquest was too autocratic, too lavish and materialistic to provide a favorable soil for its growth. Fortunately, some of its distinctive elements were conveyed abroad to other peoples, including the Hebrews, and became part of the religious heritage of the Western world. But the religion decayed and eventually disappeared in the country of its origin. And the Persian Empire, which lumbered along through several centuries, is far from an inspiring example of what a civilization can be.

Out of defeat, scattering, "dispersion," came the crowning achievement of the Hebrew people. It lay in nothing quantitative but in the discerning of values and the delineation of the rich possibilities inherent in every personality. They were the first to affirm confidently that man had been made in God's image, "little lower than the angels"; but that his life would be empty and meaningless, like grass that withers, unless it was brought into harmony with the impartial love of a universal God and made to exemplify justice and human brotherhood. These insights—moral, ethical, and spiritual—have been woven into the fabric of Western civilization. They persist, if only as a slumbering conscience, as long as that civilization endures, and independent of the success or failure of a Jewish national state.

The Shoddy Formula of Mesopotamia

The valley of the Tigris and Euphrates rivers, or Mesopotamia, in ancient times was the scene of the rise and fall of a long series of social and political units between the fourth millennium B.C.

and the Persian conquest in the sixth century B.C. The most obvious explanation of the instability of societies here would be the geographical setting. The lack of natural protective frontiers long delayed the political unification of the river system and kept the fertile delta and valleys continually exposed to the danger of attack. Repeatedly Mesopotamia was invaded and its cities plundered by nomadic barbarians from the hill country to the north or from the deserts to the east and south.

Actually, however, geography does not satisfactorily account for the inadequacies and eventual decline of the Mesopotamian cultures. On the whole, the physical environment was favorable to human habitation and progress, as shown by the fact that the Sumerians, who took possession of the delta not long after 4000 B.C., were able to develop vigorous communities there, founded upon agriculture and utilizing the natural waterways for purposes of irrigation and communication. Exposure to attack was, of course, a detriment; but the incursions, although disrupting and harassing, were not fatal to the institutional fabric. A successful invasion led to the imposition of foreign rule, but in the process the conquerors themselves succumbed to the way of life of the people they had vanquished. Notwithstanding the shifts in the political center of gravity and displacements in leadership, a continuity in the essential culture pattern persisted, as attested by Mesopotamian art and architecture, the cuneiform writing, political and legal systems, and religion. All of these elements can be identified with the pioneer inhabitants of the valley—the Sumerians—a people whose racial affinities, place of origin, and earliest history are largely unknown. In spite of the fact that they were swallowed up in a series of invasions beginning in the third millennium B.C. and even their language became extinct, they left an indelible stamp upon the cultures which came after them. Mesopotamian history emphasizes the cogent effect of the social environment in molding the lives of those who come in contact with it and shows that it is perfectly possible for peoples of diverse backgrounds to enter into and profit from a culture complex which none of them has originated.

The key to the ultimate failure of the Mesopotamians lies probably not in the accident of their location but in defects within their societies—in faulty emphases, wrong choices, and an inadequate scale of values. The military obsession of the Assyrians, which proved so disastrous to their survival, has already been noted. Another more characteristic and persistent motif in ancient Mesopotamia grew out of a penchant for commerce, a trait which was in itself commendable but which became magnified to the point of cupidity.

Even without the convenience of a coinage system the techniques of exchange and credit were highly developed, especially by the Old Babylonians (Amorites). The expansion of trade in the Fertile Crescent and along the Mediterranean seacoast under government encouragement and regulation and the accompanying emphasis upon personal advantage crowded into the background other more idealistic considerations. Religion, for example, never acquired much ethical or spiritual content. Not only was the belief in immortality lacking, as well as any trace of monotheism, but the gods were rarely conceived as the architects of a code of personal or social behavior.

Whereas the Hebrews, and even the Egyptians, made religion a central element in their whole pattern of living, the Tigris-Euphrates people treated it, not as unimportant, but as an auxiliary to human objectives, usually of a material sort. The stories of the Flood and the Creation were projected in elementary fashion by the Sumerians; but instead of being invested with the magnificent ethical fervor of the later Hebraic rendition, these epics in their original form portray the gods as pitiful sycophants, whiningly dependent upon man for their resuscitation after the havoc of the deluge which they had precipitated in a mood of shortsighted jealousy.

In spite of a decidedly utilitarian attitude toward religion, its operation was not casual and effortless. Its demands seemed to grow palpably and irresistibly. New and more potent deities were added to the roster from time to time and increasingly elaborate temples were erected to them. To insure their favor it was considered necessary to propitiate the gods and goddesses with expensive and socially deleterious rites, including temple prostitution. Eventually a curious reversal of relationships came about between worshipers and worshiped. The later Mesopotamians proved to be unable to control the supernatural forces which they had conceived in the role of obedient, though powerful and honored, servants. Under the Chaldeans, whose record fills the last chapter in the history of this region before the Persian conquest, religious notions took the most fantastic turn of all. More imaginative and extravagant than their predecessors, the "New Babylonians" were not content to think of the gods as earthly forces but identified them with the several planets, whence it was believed their influence radiated down upon the world. No longer subject to human manipulation, the heavenly bodies now controlled men and their destinies. The invention of astrology in the attempt to unravel decrees of fate by divining the intentions of distant star gods provided small compensation. It was a futile enterprise to try to fathom the will of deities who by definition were purposeless and irresponsible. It is not strange that among the Chaldeans a callous self-confidence was replaced by attitudes of resignation, despair, and abject submission. Such was the end result of the attempt to enroll the gods in the service of mammon.

THE VIGOR AND LONGEVITY OF EGYPT

In seeking the causes of the downfall of the ancient societies, the greatest problem is posed by the Egyptian. In its time span this civilization surpassed all the others in the Near East and it was one of the stablest known to history. The Nile Valley culture had been carried to a high point before the middle of the fourth millennium, and the period of political unity in a centralized state (with some serious but temporary interruptions) was at least as long as the whole Christian Era. The problem is why this civilization, after demonstrating such success and vigor, ever disappeared.

Even aside from its longevity, the ancient Egyptian civilization was one of the sanest and most satisfying that ever graced this planet. Certain natural advantages help explain its superior quality. The Nile Valley was a homogeneous area, reasonably safe from invasion, and conducive to unity among its inhabitants. Communication up and down the river was easy—downstream by the force of gravity, upstream by the prevailing northerly winds. The dry climate made irrigation necessary, for which the Nile not only supplied an abundance of water but also by its annual inundation of the delta renewed the fertility of the fields. It also suggested the divisions of the Egyptian calendar, prompted a study of methods of flood control, and thereby stimulated the sciences of engineering and mathematics. Quite fittingly did Herodotus call Egypt the gift of the Nile. Yet it was not a free gift by any means. The river might have gone on flowing and overflowing forever, leaving only a wilderness around it, if it had not been for the resourcefulness and the labor of the Neolithic adventurers who migrated into the valley and transformed it from a swampland into a garden spot.

The early consolidation of the entire region of Upper and Lower Egypt under the First Dynasty (about 3200 B.C.) made possible a coherent and efficiently organized society. The most outstanding Egyptian achievements reflect community effort, long-range planning, and a meticulous division of labor. To a considerable degree individual activities were channelized into projects of interest or benefit to the state as a whole, and all of society shared at least partially in the satisfaction attendant upon the completion of these enterprises. The initiative and directive force in the whole arrangement was provided by the Pharaoh, one of the most impressive figures in the world's political history. His very title—a circumlocution ("he who dwells in the great house")—suggests the awe which his office inspired. Theoretically he was the owner of all the land in the Nile Valley and stood far above even the nobles and the priests because he was supposed to be the earthly embodiment of the Sun god, not a "divine right" ruler but a god-king, a theocrat in the strictest sense of the word.

This political formula suggests an insufferably arrogant tyranny, but such was not the reality. Egyptians nourished the belief that the welfare of their state was centered in the person of the Pharaoh and depended upon his survival. To insure his immortality and

and the immortality of the state the populace dedicated an amazing amount of their energies, especially in erecting inordinately exaggerated tombs, the pyramids. For his own part the Pharaoh, who was the recipient of such elaborate honors, was bound to devote himself to the public welfare. From early youth he was trained in the economics of public administration and as heir apparent he was obliged to supervise the system of irrigation which was the mainstay of the valley people. Thus the monarch, in spite of his divine attributes, was as much a chief engineer as a supreme lord. The Pharaohs of the Old Kingdom kept no standing army with which to overrun their neighbors or quell their own subjects. Neither were they able to regard their own whims as law but were bound to respect the customs of the country. Their generally benevolent theocracy rested of course upon a naïve mythology. But it was a mythology subscribed to by the population as a whole, including the sovereign. The Pharaohs apparently had not discovered the device—so convenient to the governors of modern states—of fostering one set of myths among the populace while they adhered to quite a different set themselves.

The values upon which the Egyptians placed emphasis were stability and serenity. Their art, literature, and institutions reflect these ideals and indicate that they were attained in a large measure. It follows that the Egyptians were a peace-loving people, at least during the longest and most productive period of their history, the Old Kingdom, which endured for about a thousand years. Their society was held together not so much by force as by mutual interest. Family life was given prominence. The position of women was equal to that of men, a significant point because the treatment accorded to the less aggressive members of a community is always an index of its humaneness.

The Egyptians were deeply religious. Although their religion included many primitive and crude elements, it advanced to a high ethical and spiritual plane—comprising what Professor Breasted aptly called "the dawn of conscience"—and in its best moments approached a beneficent monotheism. A religious faith which inculcated belief both in the permanence of the state and in personal immortality constituted a rallying point and carried its adherents through many crises.

In spite of the fact that the decline of the Old Kingdom was followed by a period of feudal usurpation and a devastating barbarian invasion, the Nile Valley civilization emerged again in new splendor under the Empire to flourish for another six hundred years or so. The Empire, however, although spectacular with its colossal statues of kings and huge stone temples, is far less significant than the Old Kingdom, except to illustrate the typical degeneration of a society. It was too much like other empires before and since. Foreign conquests went hand in hand with the militarization of society, oppressive taxation, the growth of slavery, and religious cynicism and materialism. The state became more powerful than ever and less beneficial.

The decline in societal and cultural tone should not be attributed to the barbarian invasion which preceded the establishment of the Empire. The Egyptians showed themselves fully capable of recovering from the shock of this affliction, rude as it was. They not only recovered their equilibrium but absorbed their conquerors, the Hyksos, at the same time appropriating new skills which the Hyksos had demonstrated. The particular items which they learned from these barbarians were improved methods of offensive warfare; these they learned only too well and soon began to practice on a wide scale. While the Empire expanded, the Egyptians drifted farther and farther away from the ideals which they had discovered so early and fostered so long; and they paid the price in a loss of vital energy in their society. By the time the Empire was overthrown (a process repeated at intervals as long as there was anything left worth overthrowing) it had long since ceased to be creative.

Thus, as in the case of Babylonia, the real cause of decline must be assigned to unfavorable trends within the civilization itself, rather than to external forces. It was precisely when the Egyptian state became most powerful externally (and coercive internally) —as indicated by the intensity of its impact upon neighboring areas—that it proved itself to be least supple and therefore most vulnerable.

THE EVIDENCE IN PERSPECTIVE

An examination of the experiences of the peoples of the ancient Near East as a whole indicates that most of the stock theories which have been popular from time to time concerning the destiny of human societies are untenable. One of the most appealing but pernicious of such theories is that racial identity determines the character of a civilization; that "superior" races are responsible for the superior cultures which have appeared. The dogma of the role of race in history which was current in the nineteenth century and, in more exaggerated form, in the twentieth not only is unsubstantiated but is practically reversed by the evidence from the ancient world. On the basis of the record it could be argued that within the Caucasian division of mankind not the Nordic, not the Alpine, but the Mediterranean race alone showed much originative capacity. It was Mediterranean people who developed the most advanced Neolithic culture in the European theater and spread it from the Near East around both shores of the Mediterranean Sea and to the British Isles. Also the earliest historic civilizations—of the Nile Valley, of Mesopotamia, and of the Aegean Sea area—were almost entirely the product of Mediterraneans, during a time when the peoples of central and northern Europe were in a state of unpromising barbarism.

It would, however, be as unsound to pronounce for Mediterranean "supremacy" as for Nordic "supremacy." Apparently Homo sapiens everywhere has the potentiality for becoming civilized, but the stimulating leadership necessary to impel the process appears rarely and, in any case, has difficulty in perpetuating itself. Not all of the Mediterranean groups showed a proclivity for cultural inventiveness or social progress. Also, those which were successful undoubtedly contained admixtures of different physical stocks; "pure" races were as fanciful in ancient as in modern times. For example, the Egyptians, although generally of the Mediterranean type, included several other discernible strains, including Negroid.

Certainly the early Mediterranean cultures, in spite of close physical affinity among their respective protagonists, did not fall into a single pattern but differed widely from one another. Most of the Mesopotamian cultures pertained to peoples who were not only Mediterranean in race but had the additional bond of linguistic kinship; their languages belonged to the Semitic family. But this did not prevent them from developing such sharply contrasting types as the military scourges of Assyria and the star gazers of Chaldea. The common unifying elements in the successive Mesopotamian regimes were actually those derived from the Sumerians, who were definitely not Semitic and probably not Mediterranean. The ancient Hebrews, to whom in later times was imputed an avaricious zeal for financial transactions, showed little interest in or special gift along this line, even though they had settled in an area where the art of profit taking had long been cultivated. Far from being sordid materialists, they projected one of the most idealistic and spiritual conceptions of man and the universe ever known. "Race" is either a loosely conceived, symbolic, and emotion-charged term leading only to confusion, or it is a scientific concept germane to the study of man in his physical relationships. In the latter sense it deserves serious consideration; but it has little bearing upon the quality or probable success of any particular culture complex.

A factor more worthy of attention is the influence of the natural environment, the effect of geography and climate. Here, too, there is no infallible prescription. Egypt was the "gift of the Nile"; the Mesopotamians were indebted to the Tigris-Euphrates. A brilliant and distinctive "Aegean" culture was developed almost as early as the Egyptian in quite a different setting—the islands of and coastal areas surrounding a small sea. In this case, although there was no river basin to act as a magnet and mainstay, the climate and especially the impetus to communication were highly advantageous. But such conditions do not always produce social and cultural progress. Obviously not all of the world's great river deltas, even in favorable climates, have incubated high civilizations. And, although civilization apparently does not begin except where the environment is suitable, it may deteriorate even though the environment continues to be suitable. The attempts which have been made to link the decline of ancient and classical societies to climatic variations are not convincing. Undeniably, there are a few spots on the earth's surface where the weakening or abandonment of human effort can be accounted for by geographic factors (such as the Tarim Basin of Sinkiang and the Yucatán Peninsula of Mexico), but it is far more typical for decadence to outrun any betrayal on the part of nature.

Neither is the degradation of the physical stock of a once vigorous community acceptable as an explanation of its decline. Except for individuals and single or isolated communities, there is no evidence in history among any people of significant biological degeneration. Whether man as a biological organism is improving or deteriorating may be debatable; but this is something to be measured in terms of millions of years, not of centuries. When civilizations fail, it is almost always man who has failed— not in his body, not in his fundamental equipment and capacities, but in his will, spirit, and mental habits.

CHAPTER FOUR

THE CLASSICAL PATTERN: GREECE

LONG before the ancient civilizations of the Near East had run
their course, promising developments were under way farther
west. During the first millennium B.C. in the Balkan Peninsula and
the Aegean area and in the Italian Peninsula, a distinctive type of
community life was evolving, giving rise eventually to civilizations which are still referred to as "classical." The Greek and
Roman cultures are called classical because of the tradition that
the fundamental heritage of Western man owes its origin to them,
that they are the fountainhead of the European stream. The tradition is not unsupported, but it is now recognized that the real
beginnings of the Western story lie much farther back and must
be credited to the ancient peoples of the Near Orient. Moreover,
the splendors of the classical era, brilliant as they were, would
have been impossible without the great body of experience of
these non-European peoples to draw upon.

GREECE AND THE WEST

Nothing could be farther from the truth than the notion that
the Greeks, because of their peculiar creative talents, were the
discoverers of the basic ingredients of civilization. Actually civili-

zation was already old long before the Hellenic tribes had become aware of it and still longer before they contributed anything to its advancement. They crossed the threshold of history in the fullness of time—at high noon—and were the beneficiaries of innumerable folk who had preceded them in the uphill struggle.

Not only were the Greeks slow to make any contribution of their own, but they first appeared on the scene as despoilers rather than creators. The Aegean area which they made their habitat— the peninsula, the islands, and the coastal strip of Asia Minor—had been for about two millenniums the seat of a vigorous civilization, versatile, commercially active, and highly artistic. The intrusion of the Greeks destroyed it almost entirely, erasing even its language. The invaders of the Homeric Age were semipastoral barbarians. These primitive warriors had no appreciation of the culture of Mycenae, Tiryns, Knossos, and the other Aegean cities. Vexed and baffled by their stubborn powers of resistance, however, they attributed the strength of these cities to supernatural agencies. The great walls of "Cyclopean" masonry they imagined had been erected by a race of one-eyed giants; the mighty sea king of Crete, half man and half bull, was believed to live in a palace with intricate labyrinthian passageways deliberately contrived to trap his victims. But after several hundred years of assault and siege (the epic of the Trojan War represents a late chapter of the struggle) the cities were taken, pillaged, and largely abandoned. In the process the light of civilization was almost extinguished in this region. The triumph of the Greek invaders inaugurated an age of darkness.

There is a striking analogy between Hellenic and Western European history in regard to origins and early development. The Greeks came as barbarian invaders from the north and reduced a rich culture to rubble. The West-European nations sprang from northern Germanic barbarians who in the invasions of the fourth and fifth centuries A.D. overpowered and occupied the lands of the great Roman Empire. The Roman Empire had largely decayed from within before the Germanic tribes struck their fatal blows. It may also be that internal weakness and disasters in the Aegean cities contributed materially to the success of the Greek attacks.

(Records are scantier and more puzzling here than for Rome.) In both cases a severe cultural retrogression, lasting some four or five hundred years, followed the triumph of the barbarians. In both cases this decline was followed by a new and sturdy growth over the ruined foundations. Four centuries of this process of growth brought the Greeks to the highest pinnacle of their political, artistic, and intellectual evolution, celebrated as the "Golden Age" of the Athenian democracy. Almost exactly the same period of time separated the European "Dark Ages" from the climax, not of all Western history, but of the first distinctive, stable, and mature civilization which Western Europeans were to produce—the one which is awkwardly called "medieval."

Unfortunately, the Hellenic Golden Age was marked by the beginning of fratricidal warfare among the leading Greek communities, in which the corrosion of ideals and loss of political vigor were a rapid process. The budding West-European states, on the other hand, not only survived several epidemics of bloody rivalry but pressed forward into new avenues of accomplishment, embracing quite a different type of society from that surveyed by Albert the Great and St. Thomas Aquinas in the thirteenth century. The greater size, resources, and population of the European Continent as compared with the tiny world of the Greeks provided her peoples with a considerable advantage. The Peloponnesian Wars proved fatal to the independence of Athens and Sparta as well as to the lesser Hellenic cities; modern European nations could afford to quarrel among themselves and still absorb the shock of Turkish invasions, internal revolutions, and the tribulations incidental to the acquisition of overseas empires. In contrast to the internecine strife in Hellas, which ended in Roman subjugation of the entire region, the post-medieval European conflicts were a prelude to the emergence of more effective territorial states, the acceptance of which, in turn, made possible rapid material progress and a reasonable prospect of peace among Western peoples. But perhaps the tragic experience of Hellas, rather than being avoided altogether, was only postponed. The titanic struggles of the twentieth century, hardly comparable to the adolescent tussles of the early modern epoch, may prove to be the Peloponnesian Wars of the Western European era.

The analogy is by no means an exact one, and many differences can readily be detected, aside from those already mentioned. Roman and other classical elements, even though in fragmentary form, played an important part in the evolution of Western European society from the outset, whereas the characteristic Hellenic developments constituted almost a complete break with the Minoan past. The Greeks' aesthetic inclination, a few art forms, and perhaps their fondness for athletics may have been carryovers from the Aegeans; but on the whole the culture of the early seafarers was lost and remained unknown until its physical remains were unearthed by archaeologists within the last eighty years. The Greeks certainly never regarded themselves as heirs of Aegean tradition in the way Europeans looked back to imperial Rome during the Middle Ages—not to mention the Renaissance. In any case it would be discouraging to push the historical parallel too far, in view of the ephemeral character of the Greek political units, which seemed to lose their agility and succumbed to outside pressure soon after reaching the highest point of intellectual prowess. Modern nations of the West hope for a longer, if not brighter, day of glory.

THE SETTING AND THE PEOPLE

After the period of their migrations had ended, a number of environmental factors combined to facilitate progress among the Hellenic peoples. The area in which they settled offered a hospitable climate, even though meager in natural resources. The inhabitants were compelled to put forth effort to make the rocky soil moderately productive, but it was not necessary to devote all of their time or energies to the business of livelihood. They were easily attracted to the sea as a medium of trade and communication. Another advantage, far more important than the Greeks themselves acknowledged, was the proximity to other regions which had long been centers of advanced civilizations. At the same time, the insular or peninsular position of the Greek communities gave them a considerable degree of security against

47

attack. Geographic factors as a whole encouraged, and practically ensured, the development of local differences among the settlements, and the trend toward diversity became manifest in almost every aspect of Hellenic intellectual and institutional life. Thus, without any deliberate intention on the part of the people, their collective experience served as a proving ground for various ideas and, especially, political forms.

Diversity was both the bane and the blessing of Hellenic society. Limited as was the territory which they occupied, the Greeks never established an inclusive unified state. To them the state was always the city-state, the *polis*—a community overwhelmingly agricultural at the beginning and never exclusively urban, but including a town as its essential nucleus and basis of government. In spite of the acknowledged common bonds of language, culture, and religion, the individual felt no constant or compelling loyalty to Hellas as a whole.

The Greeks, of course, did not originate the city-state. It represents the most typical form whereby the transition from a tribal to a true political society (a fixed territorial unit with definable boundaries) was accomplished. However, instead of proceeding to the consolidation of their cities into a larger entity under common rule as was done so early in Egypt, Mesopotamia, and elsewhere, the Greeks preferred to exploit the possibilities inherent in a compact community of families who were able to know one another personally and to discover their common interests. Whether because of an inclination of temperament or the accident of geography and the good fortune of relative immunity from outside pressure, the Hellenic city-states, perched on their separate hilltops or nestled in their little harbors, retained their distinct individualities and developed their own peculiar institutions. The petty jealousies and animosities between these tiny sovereignties and their inability to combine promptly in the face of a common enemy eventually proved their undoing. But their independent spirit and the absence of an imposed uniformity made for a profusion of experimentation which can still be studied with profit.

48

Human beings at any given time or place are never exactly alike in their tastes, capacities, or performances. Hence it is misleading, if tempting, to generalize concerning a whole people, and especially to personify it and impute definite characteristics to the symbol. Such personifications are mere figures of the imagination, convenient both to historians and to working diplomats or politicians, but tending to produce a superficial judgment regarding the group so neatly typed. With the ancient Greeks, generalization is particularly hazardous because of the wide differences not only among individuals but among the various states.

The adjective "Greek" evokes an image of dazzling achievements in art, literature, and philosophy. Many Hellenes, however, exhibited no talent for and little interest in these matters. Some of their cities yielded no outstanding thinkers or significant works of art, and their annals are thoroughly uninspiring. The best products of Hellenic culture are rightly celebrated and admired. But it should be remembered that only a relatively small number of persons during a brief period of time took an active part in creating, or fully responded to, these treasures.

Man for man and woman for woman the Greeks were ordinary specimens of humanity. Perhaps for a while, in limited sections of their country, conditions were more favorable to the eliciting of high talent than at any other place or time in history. But there are no grounds for asserting that they were a race of geniuses, nor did they establish a society of supermen.

Still, it is permissible to evaluate a culture in the light of the best which it was able to produce, if these rare examples reflect the spirit and general direction of their time rather than being entirely at variance with it. The Hellenic qualities and achievements which seem most impressive to us, viewed from the distance of the present, were, on the whole, consistent with the character and aspirations of the society in which they appeared. They were exhibited to the greatest degree during the intellectual quickening which reached its climax in Athens in the last half of the fifth century B.C., the "Golden Age of Pericles."

DISCOVERY OF THE INDIVIDUAL

One of the most significant contributions of the Greeks was their discovery of the importance of the individual. More than most of their predecessors they glorified human personality and sought avenues through which it could express itself. For this reason they have rightly been called humanists, although this does not mean that they were humanitarians. They did not believe in equality or in the inherent sanctity of all life. Their judgments were often provincial, prejudiced, and harsh. Non-Hellenic peoples they contemptuously termed "barbarians," and they discriminated arbitrarily between one city and another and between occupants of the same locality. But they did regard their own personalities with respect and believed that they were capable of almost unlimited development. To enable the individual to realize his true potential and to live as richly and fully as possible became a prime objective as their societies progressed.

Appreciation of the value of personality led to an ardent devotion to freedom. The Greeks prized liberty, not as an abstract concept but as a necessary condition for the fulfillment of the individual's capacities and ambitions. There was something of jealousy and egoism in the pursuit of liberty; the more aggressive ones loved it so fiercely that they often denied it to less favored members of society. The ideal of freedom, always a potent force in Hellenic life, was not associated (as it has been to some degree in modern times) with equality.

Fortunately, the Greek was seldom a complete and uncompromising egoist. His individualism was tempered at some point (never determined entirely satisfactorily) by a concern for, and sense of obligation to, his community. But, again, it was not so much a case of social conscience as of enlightened self-interest. The Greek communities were small. Co-operation among the members was a necessity, most obviously in the matter of common defense against neighboring rivals, and concrete loyalties extending beyond one's own family were easily engendered. Since to the average Greek the limited, cohesive city-state appeared as the normal frame of social organization, he learned to think of his own well-being in terms of functioning in a prosperous and harmonious commonwealth, the success of which depended partly upon his own efforts and contributions. Regrettably, but understandably, his awareness of community of interest often stopped short at the borders of his own city.

The logical political corollary to these two complementary Hellenic ideals—individual freedom and a harmonious social order—was democracy. Because human beings, the Greeks not excepted, are logical only part of the time, democracy was actually established in only a few of the city-states, and in every instance it proved to be ephemeral. In Athens alone, during the fifth century B.C., was the concept given free play and made the basis not only of the machinery of government but of every type of civic enterprise and cultural endeavor.

Even at Athens democracy was never complete. Slavery was a recognized institution; foreigners were denied citizenship; and woman's place was in the home. The almost reckless faith in the common man which the Athenians displayed during the climax of their democratic experiment did not cut the bonds of all their prejudices nor lift them above the confines of a callow provincialism. But it did pretty thoroughly break down the inhibitions of the body of citizens and stimulated them to utilize their energies and talents to the fullest. It is no coincidence that the choicest specimens of artistic impulse, imagination, and intellect—with the possible exception of philosophy (reflection follows upon action and event)—were conceived and executed at Athens while the democracy was flourishing; and that during this period many of the keenest intellects from all over the Greek world were attracted to the city. The Athenian democracy offered any one a chance to be heard, and to be honored if he should merit honor. To its own citizens it provided the opportunity not merely for self-expression but for formulating the policies of the state and for creating the type of environment in which they would delight to live.

THE GREEKS AS THINKERS

The Hellenic fondness for individual freedom and self-asser-
tion manifested itself in numerous ways, not all of them entirely
commendable. In its highest form it emphasized freedom of the
mind and held forth the prospect of expanding the boundaries
of knowledge through the exercise of the untrammeled intellect.
Perhaps the greatest achievement of the Greeks was their cultivation of the art of thinking. They combined an intense curiosity
about the nature of things with a bold confidence in their own
powers of observation and deduction. They saw no reason why
man could not and should not come to a full understanding of
himself and his environment, in order to get along better in it
and enjoy it the more. "Know thyself" was a Hellenic injunction;
"Man is the measure of all things" was the cool verdict of one of
their philosophers. Aristotle taught that man is by nature a social
and political animal and that he is also rational—propositions about
both of which there has been considerable doubt in more recent
times. These articles of faith explain why the Athenians were
willing to push their democracy to such an extreme. Their government became a practical demonstration of their view of human (or
of Athenian male) nature; it was a witness to their conviction
that the citizen was politically interested, responsible, and capable
of rational judgment. And, for a time, it seemed that this confidence was not misplaced.

Much as we admire Hellenic intellectual prowess, it is hard for
us today to appreciate fully its extent and implications. Not that
our own age is devoid of the effects of thought, but the most intense and sustained thinking is usually done apart from the main
activities of living instead of being an integral part of those activities. This contemporary schism between thought and action
is a source of uneasiness to many observers. Exhortations to more
vigorous thinking are frequent; highly organized and elaborate
attempts are continually being launched to stimulate it; but the
average member of modern society can skirt by these enticements

and reproaches without getting into any immediate or obvious difficulty. If cogent and exacting thought becomes necessary, we have science and the scientists to turn to; and here there is certainly more prolific activity than ever before.

A pertinent question is whether the advance of science, momentous as its results are, has brought a more complete understanding of man and his relationship to the universe than was attained by prescientific eras. The question is complicated by the fact that science has become extremely specialized and, to a large degree, utilitarian. It is a fabulous repertory of precision instruments designed to solve specific problems or to effect tangible material changes. But in its origin and ultimate purpose science is a method of arriving at truth, and its value to mankind must be estimated in the light of how well it fulfills this function.

There are, of course, various levels of truth. From the standpoint of increasing the store of information, both factual and theoretical—and even of discovering previously unknown areas where knowledge might be forthcoming—science has put all other procedures to shame. But in regard to the more peculiarly human truths—as to man's origin and destiny and the meaning of life—the results are not so clear. The quest for this kind of truth began long before science was invented and has followed many different courses, often, to be sure, with disappointing returns. Of all the means employed to push back the curtain of ignorance, the scientific is not only the most recent but the most tedious. Practically every other method of attempting to discover truth is quicker; but the disadvantage is that ninety-nine times out of a hundred it misses the mark. In a few cases nonscientific methods have yielded results which constitute some of the most priceless attainments of the human race and which have not yet been displaced or surpassed by scientific discovery.

It has often been said that the Greeks were the first scientific thinkers. In a very broad sense this is true. The literal meaning of *science* is *knowledge*, and the classical Greeks indeed had a thirst for knowledge. They deserve to be called "lovers of wisdom," but *philosophia* did not mean to them something apart from the living experience of the individual. Actually they only dimly perceived and were little attracted to the discipline of precise factual investigation. The technique of the laboratory—the backbone of modern experimental science—was not part of their practice, and they accumulated comparatively few positive scientific data. They were at their best in a purely deductive field such as mathematics. In astronomy they went little, if any, farther than the Egyptians, Babylonians, Hindus, or Chinese. Chemistry, biology, and geology were unexplored territory. The writings of Aristotle, who represents perhaps the greatest scientific intellect of the Hellenic period, incorporate some popular superstitions and naïve pronouncements concerning the organic world. Both the content and the method of science—in the strict sense of the word—were largely unknown to the Hellenes. Their chief interest was in man and in knowledge which, arising out of his own observations and reflections, would enrich his life through ripening his understanding. Most of them had no conception of and no desire for a species of reality distinct from the world of human relationships, certainly not one which was indifferent, or potentially hostile, to that world. The Greeks, in short, were not scientists—they were thinkers.

The primary concern of the Greeks with man himself did not preclude curiosity about the external world or the nature of reality. In the course of their philosophical evolution they projected a remarkable series of guesses about the cosmos, its essence and structure. They had no device for verifying these guesses through objective tests, but they put them to the proof of argument. Exponents of different theories challenged one another's ideas. Through free discussion, with appeal both to sense experience and to reason, hypotheses in the process of being defended were also sharpened. Thus a constant corrective to sloppiness in judgment was provided. The lack of the rigorous method of induction and experimentation was undoubtedly a serious handicap; but the Hellenic thinkers went as far as possible with the tools at their disposal, and farther than most peoples have even when equipped with better tools. A striking illustration of perceptive insight is the formulation of the atomic theory of the structure of matter by Leucippus and Democritus in the fifth century B.C.

To the Greek atomists their theory of matter was largely auxiliary to psychological and ethical teachings; but the concept which they hit upon proved to be the most satisfactory hypothesis in this direction until the late nineteenth century.

SOCIAL FERMENT

Alert Hellenic minds eventually turned their attention to problems in the field of human relations and the ordering of society. Here the boldness of the Greek temper was especially in evidence, coming into conflict as it did with traditional dogmas and conventions. Sacred cows were not sacred to the Sophists of fifth-century Athens, who probed and challenged such honored usages as slavery, clannish patriotism, and the subjection of women.

As critical scrutiny became more relentless, the greatest ferment, not all of it wholesome, was produced in the Greek communities. Such disturbance was inevitable. In any society, the procedures and emotional pattern governing the intimate phases of human association are usually both strongly entrenched and unexamined. Progressive as they were in many ways, the bulk of Athenian citizens were sensitive to any attack upon established institutions or flouting of the mores. The Sophists—often bright aliens who had been drawn to the intellectual atmosphere of Athens but who retained the outsider's detachment and capacity for critical judgment—were regarded as dangerous by the pillars of society. The attempt of conservatives to discredit them was so successful that the name "sophist" has remained a term of reproach ever since.

That some of the Sophists promoted warped and superficial doctrines cannot be denied; but on the whole this group of teachers was in the Greek tradition. They carried to a logical extreme the thesis that man is a superbly endowed and self-sufficient creature, subject to limitations imposed by nature, but within those limits the judge and molder of his destiny. They were attempting to open to examination every sphere of conduct and to discover a reasoned basis for behavior and institutions. The eclipse of Hellenic self-confidence and creativeness came too soon for them to make much headway, but they were pioneers in an area which is still largely unplotted.

During and immediately following the Golden Age of Pericles, a few minds were sharp enough to discover inconsistencies and defects even in the best products of Athenian genius, including its vaunted democracy. Criticism of democracy came, figuratively speaking, both from the "left" and from the "right." The assaults of demagogues, catering to the lowest common denominator of the citizen body, were usually linked with personal ambition and typified the strenuous period of the Peloponnesian Wars. The admonitions of Socrates and Plato, on the other hand, represented a disinterested but a more conservative position. These two thinkers not only condemned abuses in practice but questioned basic assumptions of the democratic dogma, notably the maxim that all men are equally endowed with talent for understanding and directing public affairs. The ability to analyze and weigh critically their own heritage, including its most spectacular successes, is rare among any people, and is indicative of the maturity attained by the Greek intellect.

The evaluation of the Athenian democratic experiment could not, however, be carried out in an atmosphere of philosophic calm. Just as in the conflict of opposing systems in our own day, ideas became so surcharged with emotion that they lost their effectiveness as tools for sharpening the understanding. Under the devastating effects of the war between Athens and Sparta events ran faster than logic, and passions crowded deliberation into the background. Hence the most significant arguments advanced during the twilight period of Hellenic culture were not always an embodiment of actual experience, still less of majority opinion. They were more in the nature of brave hopes cast against a darkening sky.

Socrates, one of the critics of Athenian democracy, excused himself for not having taken an active part in politics on the ground that he had preferred to remain an honest man. Nevertheless, he was no cynic. He acted consistently with the belief that his fellow citizens were capable of responding to truth if they could be brought to face it—an attitude which he retained even in the hour of his trial and condemnation. He was convinced that the commonwealth could be healthy only if its members made the pursuit of virtue their sincere and foremost aim, and he dedicated his life to the mission of converting them to this worthy goal. An assembly of his compatriots heard him out but condemned him to death. (He had not really corrupted the youth, but the Athenians had just lost the war and were not in a good humor.) Plato, the discouraged idealist, went much farther in his repudiation of democracy, teaching that the common lot of humanity will never find social and political security until they are placed under the jurisdiction of the few who possess true wisdom. (He wrote these thoughts in his famous Dialogues—a much safer procedure than reciting them before an assembly.) While Aristotle's political ideal was a compromise between democracy and aristocracy and thus represents a wistful reversion to the past, both Plato and Aristotle enveloped themselves in theoretical structures sometimes far removed from contemporary conditions. Although their systems are landmarks in the history of thought, they had little impact upon the living experiences of the Greek communities. Even the Athenians were by this time moving away from democracy both in theory and practice, but neither for Socratic reasons nor in a Platonic direction.

A SPIRITUAL BLIND SPOT

The instinct for bold and untrammeled inquiry, which stirred up a storm when directed against the fabric of social custom, was equally devastating when it probed still deeper into the regions of ethics and religion. Here, however, once the barriers of conventional belief were broken through, it was not so much a matter of debate among rival theories as of laying down entirely new postulates. Hellenic religion, born of the pre-Homeric age of barbarism, offered little meat for the awakened intellect. Still less could it assist thoughtful persons who were concerned with the clarifying of values or with elevating moral standards.

This does not mean that the Greeks had no religion or that it was unimportant to them. Such an inference is contradicted by the extent to which divine homage was interwoven with all their characteristic group activities, including athletics, and by recurrent themes of Hellenic art and literature. Contemplation of the magnificent but quite approachable Olympian deities provided a rich vein for poets, sculptors, and architects. Moreover, religion prompted civic solidarity and even political progress, because an identity of interest was assumed between the city and its patron god or goddess. The Athenians assumed that Athena would share their pride not only in the Parthenon, dedicated to her, but in their victory over the Persians, in their commercial ascendancy, and in their throbbing democracy.

Nevertheless, religion, as popularly understood, remained naïve and circumscribed. Theology, to begin with, was a colorful but monstrous poetic jumble. The faith as a whole represented the symbolization of the Greeks' own achievements and wishes. The gods were themselves as they should have liked to be—more perfect in body and mind, stronger and more cunning, more irresistible, with larger passions more completely realized. The humanism of the Greeks was apparent not only in the daily satisfactions which they sought but in the underpinning of their largest hopes and aspirations. Hence, their worship was anthropocentric and earthbound, a somewhat idealized reflection of its participants' finite personalities and immediate interests. It had the great virtue of not cowing man or making him grovel in the dust, but it lacked incentive to self-sacrifice or dedicated service.

In contrast to the Hebrews, who had only to refine the religious ore which they had unearthed, the Greeks were gradually forced to abandon the shafts which they had worked for many centuries. Although ornamented with verse and song and emblazoned in marble, the Olympian cult proved impotent to deal with the problems of a mature and reflective society. Even the Homeric epics, lusty and ebullient as they are, reveal the inadequacies of the gods as cosmic principles (the splendid creatures are not really omnipotent; they are limited by the decrees of Fate—that is, by three old women with thread and scissors!). In later times numerous individuals, finding little nourishment in the public liturgies, sought solace in the Orphic and Eleusinian rites, which offered a feeling of spiritual regeneration and a promise of personal immortality—elements entirely lacking in the Olympic cult and of indifferent appeal to the typical Hellene. The great tragic dramatists of the Golden Age, while making use of familiar myths, reinterpreted the deities as moral agents which punish baseness and perfidy, thus giving quite a different cast to the popular faith. Philosophers, most emphatically of all, tended to ignore or reject the mass of religious folklore, which some found not only puerile but repulsive. In sketching his ideal state Plato proposed to ban the reading of mythological literature on the ground that it was immoral.

Condemn, ridicule, or dismiss it altogether they might, but the philosophers could do little to strengthen or ennoble the religious heritage of their people. When they sought to erect a system of ethics on a solid basis, they were forced to go far afield into uncertain ground, or else to try to convert into universal principles what had been merely rule-of-thumb devices culled from everyday experience. "Moderation," "the Golden Mean," and "Nothing in excess" were sound bits of counsel but hardly a positive foundation for a system of ethics. Neither was there much inspiration in the insipid Platonic definition of virtue as the middle ground between opposite vices. The more inviting alternative, developed so remarkably by Plato and Aristotle, was to cut free both from traditional dogma and from the world of sense experience and explore the abstract realms of epistemology, teleology, and ontology. Thus the science of metaphysics came into being, and lines of speculation were introduced which could engage philosophers for all time to come. But in taking this turn a break was made with the democratic tradition that knowledge is the province of every alert citizen; it became something esoteric and intangible. If the Sophists had "brought philosophy down from heaven to the dwellings of men," the great idealists sent it up into the clouds again, where it remained, radiating a beautiful but diffuse light.

Aristotle, it is true, displayed an omnivorous natural curiosity and the Hellenic talent for judicious compromise. But Plato, perhaps the noblest and most spiritual of Hellenic thinkers, drifted into an attitude of doubt regarding the material universe and veered toward an asceticism quite out of character with the culture of which he was a product. Thus some of the loftiest achievements of Greek genius were not only beyond the comprehension of the ordinary man but a departure from the activating principles which had been the very sinews of society. The primitivism of their religion proved a stumbling block to the Greeks, even when they shook off creed and fable and sought to define the Good in purely humanistic terms.

THE VIRTUES OF SIMPLICITY

Greek civilization was the first to declare the primacy of reason and to attempt to root a social order in this principle. The creed which affirms that reason holds the key to the secrets of the universe and is the proper guide to human conduct is a strenuous one to live by, and even the most progressive Greek communities did not entirely succeed in holding fast to it. The ideal was most fully realized in Athens, in the interval between the Persian and the Peloponnesian wars.

Strangely enough, the external aspects of life in Athens during this memorable period would seem to the man of the twentieth century as evidence of a very unreasonable and ill-ordered mode of existence. The town, with unpaved streets, neither properly drained nor lighted, could be described as a miserably primitive village, hardly a suitable abode for artists and philosophers. The citizens of this confident democracy lived in hovels of sun-dried brick, almost devoid of furniture. Both men and women wore simple clothing, and fashions rarely changed. Diet was monotonous and anything but sumptuous, consisting typically of barley cakes, dried fish, and watered wine. The celebrated banquets at which Socrates sometimes drank his friends and opponents under the table were hardly affairs to delight a gourmet. Athens of the Golden Age was definitely not the seat of material abundance or splendor.

Why such a display of poverty, such neglect of the devices which contribute to comfort and enjoyment, in a community which was obviously ingenious and sophisticated? It has been alleged that the answer lies in the institution of slavery. Primitive techniques were a matter of indifference so long as an available supply of cheap labor made it unnecessary for the prosperous freeman to bother about the mechanics of housekeeping. The argument is unsatisfactory, because many of the citizens owned no slaves, and the majority worked with their own hands or carried on a trade. Slavery was indeed an imperfection in the body politic, but not the chief reason for the lack of material progress. The slaves, although barred from political activity (one special group served as a police force entrusted with keeping order at meetings of the assembly), were almost on a plane of equality with the citizens socially and economically. Nobles and commoners, rich and poor, freemen and slaves, all shared nearly the same standard of living during the half century or so when democracy was at its height. Although this condition was an important ingredient in the successful functioning of the democracy, it was not the result of legislative enactment or of sentimental equalitarianism. It existed simply because the standard of living, provided it met a necessary minimum, was of secondary concern to the Athenians.

The simplicity, or austerity, of the Athenians in their daily living was a matter of choice and an expression of their love of leisure. It did not spring from laziness, nor from asceticism. The Greeks did not despise the flesh; they gloried in it. They regarded material objects as good, especially if employed for some significant purpose, and they were quite willing to pour forth their energies for the things which mattered most to them. But their list of the things which really matter was a unique one. It included, near the top, opportunity for discussion and reflection, for the unhurried interchange of ideas. Socrates, who represents an apex rather than the average level, went so far as to say that the unexamined life is not worth living. The Athenians had discovered, thanks partly to the beneficence of a mild climate, that cultural enrichment and even lively excitement on a high level were possible with a modest material endowment. While apparently neglecting obvious and elementary lines of progress they kept their days uncluttered by engrossing gadgets and free from the tyranny of clocked efficiency.

To comprehend the Athenian attitude more fully, it is necessary to shift one's attention from the dirty streets and unpretentious residences to the Acropolis, the elevated ground in the center of the city which was adorned by temples and was the scene of public meetings, ceremonies, and festivities. Even the temples of the Acropolis were not lavish or luxuriously appointed; they were marked by dignity and restraint. Nevertheless, they were so beautiful that Pericles could affirm unhesitatingly that to behold them was sufficient to banish sadness. The citizens found their daily delight in viewing these superb civic shrines, which with their chaste lines and perfectly fitted marble columns standing serenely against the background of the clear Mediterranean sky, seemed to offer abiding and tangible proof that man and nature can unite in harmony and that the boundless joys of the spirit can be attained in the flesh here on earth.

It was not merely for passive aesthetic satisfaction that the Athenians came to the Acropolis, but to join actively in public business and debate, and to participate in communal artistic enterprises, including musical and dramatic productions. The man who took no part in these affairs was, Pericles observed, looked upon not as one who minds his own business but as useless. In order to find time for the community activities which gave the state its distinctive character while offering the individual channels of self-expression, citizens were content to cut to a minimum their purely personal involvements. They might be compared to people attending a conference conducted by inspirational leaders and held at some site of rare natural beauty. To share in such an atmosphere the delegates will gladly live in tents for a few days. But the Athenian program was not a vacation; it was an all-year engagement.

The Road to Ruin

The pattern of life in Athens during the brief Golden Age was one of reasoned simplicity. Unfortunately, the Athenians succumbed gradually to the lure of material enticements, and the pattern was eventually broken, with disastrous effects upon all the institutions and attainments of the citizens. The particular stumbling block was a very common one—the desire for power, engendered by the coveting of an empire.

The Athenian Empire was not wrested in distant regions but was compounded out of the cities and territories of neighboring Greeks. It came into being almost imperceptibly and as a consequence of the prestige and good will which accrued to Athens from her courageous leadership in the struggle against the Persian menace. It was easy to transform the Delian League from a voluntary association of allies into a tribute-yielding organization, because Athens was not only the guiding force behind the League but, owing to her fleet, was so much stronger than any of the other members. They offered such little resistance to the sterner tone and increasing demands of Athens that her citizens, jealous as they were of their own liberties, could not resist tightening the screws upon their weaker associates. Fifty years after the defeat of the Persians at Salamis—to gain which the Athenians had had to flee to their ships and watch helplessly while their public buildings (then mostly of wood) were put to the torch—they found themselves in a position to command the northern Aegean area and had begun to treat its inhabitants as subjects.

The inevitable result of this development was the Peloponnesian Wars between the Big Two, Athens and Sparta, and their respective satellites. Athens was a liberty-loving democracy; Sparta was a garrison state. These ideological differences, though widely publicized, were by no means the sole cause of the conflict any more than they are of the struggles of our own day. The increasing arrogance and high-handedness of Athens was in itself sufficient to ensure the outbreak of war. If the Athenians were determined to preserve their freedom, then certainly the course which they took was ill-advised. The war was, and became more and more, a struggle for hegemony over people who were bred to a tradition of proud independence. It brought, slowly but inescapably, the downfall, first, of the Athenian Empire and, second, of democratic ideals and institutions. The saddest feature of the fratricidal strife was not the exhaustion of both Athens and Sparta and the eclipse of many other cities but the submersion of the basic principles which had made Hellenic civilization great.

Pericles, the elder statesman who had piloted the commonwealth into its most brilliant period and who, through his rare ability and persuasiveness, held the citizens in the palm of his hand, was shortsighted enough to regard the war as unavoidable. He hoped, however, to confine it to limited objectives. He urged his countrymen to hold fast to their empire (brushing aside any troublesome moral questions and doubts) but to seek no new conquests. After his steadying hand was removed by death, Athenian ambition expanded as the oratory of successive demagogues became more unbridled and their schemes more unprincipled. Resources were wasted, reputations ruined, and opportunities to negotiate peace neglected or deliberately sabotaged.

The Athenian historian Thucydides painted a remarkably vivid picture of these events, in the grim hope that it might serve as a warning to future generations. Actually his pages, when read today, seem almost to be giving a description of the behavior of modern nations and of the tone of international morality during the period of World War I, or of World War II and beyond. Bluntly and forcefully he reveals the ethical collapse of civilized human beings, including his own fellow countrymen, under the influence of the passions of war. These influences and their effects are uncomfortably familiar. However, if Thucydides is to be trusted, the ancient warriors were less skillful than modern belligerents in covering their wanton acts with a gloss of legality.

An unforgettable example from Thucydides' account is the hostile exchange between the Athenians and the inhabitants of the little island of Melos, who were annihilated—the men put to death, the women and children sold as slaves—when they refused to submit to Athens. The offense of the Melians was simply that they wished to remain neutral in the conflict; the Athenians were demanding that they become one of their "allies." The argument of the commissioners from Athens was, in substance: You must join us because we have the power to make you, and we'll waste no time over pretenses of right and wrong. It is our interest to compel you and it is expedient for you to submit. "Right, as the world goes, is only in question between equals in power, while the strong do what they can and the weak suffer what they must." When the Melians protested the justice of their position and said they would call upon the gods for aid, the answer was: "Of the gods we believe, and of men we know, that by a necessary law of their nature they rule wherever they can."

As the contest became more widespread, more exhausting, and more confused, involving intrigues with foreign "barbarian" powers and shifting allegiances and revolutions within the Greek cities, the character of the participants was steadily degraded. Finally, as Thucydides bitterly observed, discussion and debate ceased to serve any useful purpose because all principle had been forgotten and arguments were merely a type of psychological weapon. Words, he says, had now lost or exchanged their meanings. Honor had become stupidity, treachery astuteness, deceit success. The spiritual resources of the Greeks had always rested on a foundation of sand, and now the sands were running fast.

Imperialism, which ended the Golden Age of Athens and eclipsed an admirable way of life, was of course not invented by the Greeks—any more than it has been forsworn by modern nations. It is, unfortunately, one of the most persistent themes in history since the beginning of civilization. The temptation to seize power when it apparently is spread out before one's feet is almost irresistible. The Athenians were no worse than other people would have been (and have been) in their place, except that with their superior acumen something better might have been expected of them. Also, they had more to lose in the realm of intangibles than most political groups which have aspired to power politics, and their loss was not only a national misfortune but humanity's.

Imperialism is probably always a fatal game, but the Greeks, of all people, could ill afford to play it. They were too small a folk, too precariously situated in the vicinity of great contending powers. Divided as they were by geography, by cultural differences, and by varying political preferences, their only chance of survival was to pull together, assisting one another against common dangers but adhering rigorously to a policy of noninterference in extraneous disputes. They should have waited—like the Swiss—for the rest of the world to become as civilized as they. From the practical standpoint their bloody rivalries were suicidal. From the ideal standpoint they spelled the betrayal of their own noblest convictions, especially the affirmation that the best life is one in harmony with reason.

THE TESTAMENT OF HELLAS

The phenomenon of ancient Hellas is not a typical example of the rise and fall of a civilization. The Greeks were remarkable both in the comparative brevity and in the intensity of their performance. And decadence in their case was not so much a positive decline as a transmutation of their distinctive culture into one approximating the prevailing Near Eastern type. They did not disappear, nor revert to barbarism; but they subsided to the level of passivity which surrounded them. During the Hellenistic Age, which the conquests of Alexander the Great ushered in, while Greek idioms and clichés were being spread throughout the whole eastern Mediterranean area and beyond, Oriental influence inundated the Greek communities, with debilitating effects.

Weaknesses in Hellenism there certainly were, even in the Athenian variety at its peak. The Greek city-states seldom rose above a provincialism which would now be called narrow nationalism (although the term would have meant little to them). There was little outreaching, nothing of the missionary impulse, insufficient concern for other sections of humanity, except in so far as they could be exploited to Greek advantage. These faults and others stem directly from one deep-seated trait—an egoism which was often arrogance. Typically the Greeks were lacking in humility before their fellow men and before the mystery and majesty of the cosmos. They were children of nature, darlings of the haughty gods which their fancies had invented. They gave no quarter—neither did they demand it.

What might not have been accomplished if the eager, confident daring of the Greeks could have been combined with the sensitive social conscience of the Hebrews! An unreasonable expectation, no doubt. The most that can be hoped for from any people is that they will remain true to the best light they possess. The tragedy of human history is that few do so for any great length of time.

The Classical Pattern: Greece

No nation ever exhausts its capacity or realizes its potential in entirety. There must have been unplumbed depths not only of intellect but of moral grandeur in a people who could produce a Phidias, a Euripides, and an Aristotle. Obviously the limitations of character cited above were transcended by Democritus, who declared that to be good one must avoid even wrong desire; by Plato, who urged the seeker after wisdom to turn his eyes to heaven and, beholding, found a city in himself; and by Socrates, who said to his accusers, "I shall obey God rather than men, even if I have to die many times. . . . The difficulty is not to avoid death, but to avoid unrighteousness, for that runs faster than death."

Much has been spoken and written concerning the indebtedness of modern Western nations to Hellenic civilization. Perhaps the greatest boon of all lies simply in the demonstration of what human beings can do and in the revelation of the sweep of imagination and the mental vigor of which man is capable when conditions are favorable for the full release of his creative faculties. Greek society and culture in all their aspects would not bear repeating even if repetition were possible; but their artistic and intellectual manifestations are a challenge and a tonic to any age, particularly to one troubled by misgivings as to the worth of the species. The Greeks possessed no magic or secret formula, no biological superiority, and no lavish material resources to draw upon. They accomplished much because they believed in themselves. Men—and civilizations—live by their beliefs and die when their beliefs pass over into doubt.

CHAPTER FIVE

THE CLASSICAL FAILURE: ROME

THE case of the Romans was very different from that of the Greeks. It is true that the two peoples had much in common, and many of the external aspects of their history are similar. They included some of the same ethnic stocks; their cultural origins were comparable; they were related linguistically. The early Italic and the early Hellenic peoples, while still in a primitive stage of development, both migrated southward during the second millennium B.C. Wresting land from more civilized inhabitants who had preceded them, each came to occupy as its homeland a peninsula bathed by Mediterranean waters. The society and institutions of the Romans resembled those of the Greeks more than those of the older Oriental states. The Roman influence upon the course of European history was even greater than that of Greece and equally deserves the appellation of "classical." Furthermore, the Romans borrowed many elements of culture directly from the Greeks, and eventually their empire incorporated Hellas. Thus Rome became a medium for the diffusion of Greek influence over a wide area, although Greek culture had by then become partially Orientalized, and what the Romans propagated was Hellenistic rather than truly Hellenic.

The Classical Failure: Rome

In their later days the two peoples were closely associated for better or for worse, and each affected the other measurably. The Greco-Oriental city of Byzantium (Constantinople) was as important an administrative unit of the Empire as Rome itself and continued as the center of the remnant of the Empire after the Germanic barbarians had occupied its western portions. The downfall of the Roman state (in spite of the survival of Byzantium) closed off the stream of Hellenic influence in the West even more completely than it obliterated the Latin elements. Nevertheless, in spite of mutual interchange and the almost indissoluble linkage of the fate of the two peoples, the course and distinguishing character of their civilizations were widely separate. The Romans differed fundamentally from the Greeks in their choices, ambitions, and personality traits, and consequently in what their record affords for analysis and evaluation.

A conscientious scholar might mull over, digest, and admire the evidences of Hellenic achievement without being driven to think much about the general framework of social and political evolution and the factors conducive to progress or decay. In Roman affairs, on the other hand, it is these factors which are forced upon one's attention. The Romans, by the objectives which they pursued and the interests which they manifested, have left no other option. A Grecian urn, a fragment of funerary sculpture by an unnamed craftsman, the Parthenon, even in ruins—these speak for themselves, immediately, intimately, to any human being with a sensitive spirit. They are timeless (with all due respect to archaeologists whose painstaking labor makes it possible to date them)— things of beauty and a joy forever. The best Hellenic art and literature was indeed purposeful, but it was not subordinate to some temporary or purely individual purpose; it was not "slanted," didactic, or exhortatory. Its intention was to reveal the sublimity and potential perfectibility of human nature. Roman art was seldom conceived in this vein. It announced, commemorated, or proclaimed. It marked where the Romans had been or where they were going. It attempted to immortalize the transient aspects of a particular ruling power, or of particular individuals—recording a success or failure; qualities of heroism, nobility, or baseness;

magnificent and openhearted statesmanship; or reckless and extravagant cruelty.

The Greeks lived to enjoy life; to savor it, understand it, and fulfill it. They valued the civilized state, as they interpreted it, because it offered greater opportunity for the realization of this goal. But with the Romans the process was reversed. To perpetuate and enlarge the orbit of civilization, especially those aspects of it which can be visibly perceived and spatially extended, became their passion; the enjoyment and the refinement of living was a secondary consideration. Their hopes, talents, and creative energies were harnessed to what they conceived to be their unique destiny—the mission of civilization—and they must ultimately be judged by the measure of their success in this task. In view of the seriousness with which the Romans went about it, it is a pity that the story is not a happier one.

A DEMOCRACY WITH ARRESTED DEVELOPMENT

The early history of the Roman state shows a remarkable political evolution, with some close parallels to the contemporary development of the Greek communities. While still a rude farming people, grouped according to families and clans, the Romans deliberately converted their government from a monarchy into an aristocratic republic. This change occurred around 500 B.C., at a time when the somewhat older Athenian republic was beginning to move in a democratic direction. Although the events which launched the Roman Republic are often referred to as a revolution, in themselves they affected the character of the state hardly at all. Almost the only innovation introduced was the transfer of executive power from the king (who had never been absolute) to two consuls. Even though the consuls were elective, the new arrangement actually increased the power, not of the assembly of citizens, but of the Senate, which was the organ of the aristocratic patrician class. Thus the "revolution" of 509 B.C. was an extremely limited and conservative one, rather than a genuine popular upheaval.

The most notable feature of the first two and one-half centuries of the Republic is not the unrelenting series of wars which began as defensive operations on the part of the Romans and led, unexpectedly, to the establishment of their dominion over the Italian Peninsula. Rather, it is the gradual and, on the whole, peaceful modification of their aristocratic constitution in response to the demands of the humbler citizens, the plebeians. Political rights and opportunities were successively widened until they embraced all the free men, and the supreme legislative authority of the state was finally vested in the assembly of commoners. True, the Senate still retained great prestige and continued to exercise the initiative in formulating policies; but formally and legally the state had been transformed from an oligarchy into a democracy. Meanwhile the social barriers between patricians and plebeians had been broken through, and intermarriage between the two classes was frequent. All this had come about with some tension and commotion but almost entirely without violence, through a series of compromises, utilizing discussion and due process of law. It is a rare example among any society of intelligent and purposive adaptation of the political structure, the more notable in that it was managed during a time of external conflict. While the Romans were engaged in a long series of wars and were incorporating and organizing various sections of Italy, they groped their way determinedly to a more satisfactory balance within their own citizen body.

By 287 B.C. Rome had become, theoretically, almost as complete a democracy as Athens of the Periclean Age. But actually, in spirit and functioning her government was quite different from that of Athens and moved pretty steadily away from the democratic ideal. After the bold compromise which highlights the early centuries of the Republican period, the Romans seem to have lost their capacity for genuine political progress. This is astounding in view of the fact that their peculiar genius lay in the political and legal field. It is a discrepancy not easy to account for. The readiest although not a sufficient explanation is supplied by the compulsion of external circumstances. Soon after the readjustments in her state machinery had been completed, Rome entered upon the fierce struggle with Carthage, and this contest, regardless of its causes or outcome, opened the door to undreamed of entanglements and embarked the Romans on the course of imperialism. The succession of wars which followed, more perilous and engrossing than any the Romans had previously experienced, left the average citizen-soldier little time for political activity or reflection. He did well if he kept his farm from ruin or from being appropriated by some unscrupulous speculator.

Periods of crisis almost always induce a centralization of control, even in a democracy. In the state of continuous emergency which confronted Rome it was natural for the Senate to exercise the active direction of affairs as it had done in early times. It was also inevitable that military commanders should aspire to become a force in politics, to which end they discovered how easy it was to pit the plutocracy against the populace, conveniently and cynically using either the Senate or the assembly as a springboard to power. Hence the series of military dictators and sordid reigns of terror which blot the last century of the Republic and which reduced its traditions to rubble.

Still, external circumstances do not entirely account for the sterility of Roman statesmanship which permitted a drift toward both anarchy and dictatorship in the late Republic. The wars with Carthage, although fraught with evil consequences, were not utterly ruinous to the population of Italy or to the Roman state. However, the accession to a position of mastery in the western Mediterranean, which was the fruit of victory, and the alluring prospects of further expansion, uncovered certain traits latent in Roman character. The Romans differed essentially from the Greeks in their value preferences and especially in their concept of the significance of the individual. The Hellenic emphasis upon the primary importance of individual personality and the passion for liberty, which was a necessary counterpart, were lacking among the Tiber Valley settlers. The Romans exalted discipline, respect for authority, and unquestioning obedience. The ordinary citizen, largely because he was compelled to be a soldier so much of the time, was not keenly interested in participating in the arduous and troublesome business of making decisions determining the public weal. He preferred to leave that to duly constituted authorities, especially if their position was honored by custom. He would protest and might even revolt against flagrantly unjust treatment (slaves have done as much, in Roman and in other societies), but in general he was not inclined to challenge the *status quo*. He preferred to let things alone so long as he was not too harshly set upon, being content with a legal recognition of his rights. Consequently the citizen body as a whole never availed themselves of the opportunities opened to them by the constitutional changes which had been wrung from reluctant patricians during the youth of the Republic. The more successful plebeians, who held office, entered the Senate, and intermarried with the great families, themselves became conservative in temper and outlook. Thus they furnished new blood for the aristocracy rather than serving as agents of a rising democracy.

Perhaps this would not have been a fatal situation if the state had remained small and peaceful; but the opposite of these two conditions prevailed. The absorption of new territory and of alien peoples increased the problems of administration while it drained the energies of the citizens into military channels, dulling rather than sharpening their political acumen. At the same time the influx of wealth from the conquered provinces led to greater social and economic inequalities among the inhabitants of Italy than had ever been known before. Individual dignity and liberty, which had never been clearly understood or highly prized by the Romans, were lightly exchanged for pride in the prestige and apparent invincibility of Roman arms.

Ordinarily imperialism represents a late stage in the history of a civilization, and often it is associated with evidences of decadence. The experience of Rome seems to constitute an exception to the norm. Roman imperialism—that is, conquests and annexations beyond the natural boundaries of the Italian Peninsula—began while the state was still adolescent and its people vigorous, simple in manners and unsophisticated, anything but decadent. The ripening of their culture came later and largely as a result of expansion, which brought them into closer contact with the Greeks and other peoples to the east.

But, when viewed more carefully, it is clear that Rome is not entirely an exception to the rule. In a very real sense Roman imperialism, germinating so early and becoming more and more ineradicable, marks the beginning of decay. More precisely, it marks the end of creative efforts directed toward social adjustment and the constructing of a viable political organism. When the Romans shouldered the yoke of policing the nations (alternating sometimes with the delights of brigandage), their only partially resolved internal problems and tensions were frozen at a dead level, while their energies were deflected to external issues. Actually these internal problems could not remain at a stationary level; they became progressively worse until they were beyond solution. Thus imperialism, while by no means bringing an immediate end to Roman civilization, foreshadowed what the end would be. The process did not in itself destroy the talents or ambitions of the people. Abundant vitality, ability, even inventiveness remained long in evidence and produced a multitude of sturdy works. But these commendable qualities were not sufficiently applied toward the achieving of a more civilized, humane society for the Romans themselves.

THE ROMAN FORMULA FOR CIVILIZATION

Of culture, in the narrow sense of the word referring to the refinements and adornments of life, the Romans knew very little when they first emerged as a great power. Impetus in this direction resulted from Rome's conquests in the Eastern Mediterranean region. Thus her intellectual and artistic resources were composed largely of elements borrowed (or stolen) from her subjects and slaves. Toward the end of the Republic, culture was being imported into Italy rapidly and quite literally—by the boatload—as the Roman appetite was whetted not only for Oriental luxuries but for Greek statuary, manuscripts, clerks, and pedagogues. The impact of all this stimulated Roman intellectual life in spite of the social and political turmoil of the late Republic. When the period of anarchy had been brought to an end by Augustus, the first emperor, Latin literature came into full flower.

74

The Classical Failure: Rome

The aesthetic and literary products of the Augustan Age, even though they followed so directly in the wake of revolution, represent the high watermark of Roman culture and are a creditable accomplishment on any score. But they were not the reflection of a healthy and well-proportioned society. Only shortly before, graft and corruption had been rampant, the provinces looted, the citizens debauched. The military dictatorships and civil wars had brought an almost complete breakdown of Rome's political machinery. The only way which could be discovered out of the debacle was to establish a single authoritative ruler and entrust him with the sovereign power of the state. An autocracy, disguised with the utmost pains and fairly reeking with legality, was the means chosen to preserve order and restore the basis for normal living. The respite thus purchased proved a welcome relief, and loud were the praises of Octavian, "first citizen" (*princeps*), the revered and august one. But the populace as a whole could claim little credit for whatever improvement came about and played only a passive role in the new regime. Hence, the embellishments of the age, brilliant as they were, pertained to a small and semiofficial coterie and were not the crystallization of popular sentiments or experience.

Augustan art and literature, while not actually alien, lacked something of spontaneity and sincerity. The culture which had developed so rapidly, after a late germination, seemed to be already overripe. Sculpture was an imitation and often a mere duplication of the contemporary Greek. Even in literature, more sure-footed and independent, there were significant overtones. They are discernible in Vergil's *Aeneid*, the most celebrated masterpiece of the period. A magnificent poem and the work of a great poet, it is nevertheless contrived and artful. Not only does it subtly glorify Roman imperialism and the leadership of Augustus, but it is deliberately cast in the archaic mold of the epic, although the Romans had left the heroic age of their folk-wandering far behind, and by this time should have been ready to grapple with philosophic concepts. How successful their grappling was in this area is indicated by their failure to create a single school of philosophy of their own, and by their assimilation, not of the

75

teachings of any of the great Hellenic thinkers, but of the two popular Hellenistic creeds, Epicureanism and Stoicism, neither one of which made very heavy demands upon the intellect.

If the Romans betrayed an inadequate appreciation, bordering on contempt, for the rarest and most sensitive aspects of culture, their attitude was very different toward civilization as a whole. To defend, maintain, and extend civilization became the dominant theme of their public life.

It would be unfair to say that their obsession was purely a lust for conquest. Unlike Alexander, the Romans (a few headstrong individuals excepted) did not harbor the ambition to conquer the world. Their empire was acquired piecemeal and without deliberate design—not quite in "a fit of absence of mind" but largely through a series of errors and miscalculations. After they had destroyed the balance of power in the West by eliminating Carthage, they found themselves continually involved—sometimes reluctantly—in more remote regions. One reason for their intervention in Greece was a sincere if vague desire to protect Greece and its culture against Asiatic powers; and the first commanders sent into Hellenic territory were hailed as "liberators" by the fatuous inhabitants. Only when they discovered that the Greek communities were riven by faction, inconstant, and apparently incapable of combining for their common interest, did the Romans take a stern tone with their troublesome protégés; although when the mailed fist was revealed it made short work of Greek independence, and a city or two was sacked in the process.

Of course, provinces which had been seized were hung onto as long as possible. It is always extremely difficult to reverse the course of imperialism once it has begun and no matter how it has begun. Also, by the end of the Republican period, the idea had taken root that it was Rome's mission to uphold and disseminate civilization, in spite of the horrible botch which her citizens had made on their own home grounds. Therefore, the forceful retention of lands already occupied, and even new conquests appeared to be, if not inevitable, the easiest and most natural way to ensure the fulfillment of national destiny.

The Classical Failure: Rome

Civilization to the Romans meant order, discipline, and due process of law—plus cities. All of these items they introduced or diligently maintained in the territories under their control. The pattern which they sought to impose was faulty—inherently so because of contradictions between theory and practice at the very heart of the state, in Rome itself. But in spite of defects in conception, the remarkable system of provincial administration which the Romans developed provided the basis for the greater part of their legacy to the Western world.

After Augustus had reorganized the government of the provinces, removing unscrupulous or incompetent officials and introducing a less oppressive system of taxation, the inhabitants found their lot greatly improved and reasonably secure. This was especially notable in the West, in many parts of which primitive conditions had prevailed heretofore. During the first two centuries of the Christian Era the provincial administrators on the whole pursued a policy of flexibility, moderation, and common sense. It was the benefits conferred by this policy that explain Rome's success in empire building—rather than the invincibility of her armies or the fear which she inspired. Some provinces were obtained with little or no fighting, and during the prosperous years of the Principate revolts were few.

An asset of the Romans in dealing with provincials was their freedom from racial and national prejudice. In this particular they contrast sharply with their Greek kinsmen and just as strikingly with a good many modern powers that have aspired to world leadership. The Romans were proud of their citizenship and revered the authority of the state, but they were willing to accept as partners and even as equals all who would enter into their common loyalties. The Roman *Pax* and *Imperium* seemed to them synonymous with the highest good of mankind, but they held no theory of a master race. Hence they were tolerant not only of various religions, languages, and social customs, but of local legal traditions as well, provided they were not in conflict with the essential principles of Roman justice. In addition to allowing subject aliens to enjoy the protection of their familiar laws (administered by a Roman official whose duty it was to be versed in this

77

law as well as his own), the Romans did not hesitate to draw freely upon, and give universal application to, the customs and precepts of these aliens where they seemed to embody rational and beneficial principles. Eventually the "law of the peoples" *(jus gentium)* became one of the three recognized divisions of the great body of Roman jurisprudence, and the most vital of them all because it represented the distillation of the experience and collective judgment of so many different groups.

The peoples under Roman rule were encouraged to participate in the work of civilizing (which of course meant Romanizing) their provinces, particularly in the organizing of cities. Members of the higher class might early aspire to become voting citizens of their own municipality, and those who were capable of the responsibilities of office holding assumed the dignity of local senators and frequently were honored by a formal grant of Roman citizenship. With such inducements, the provincial gentry poured forth their energies and their substance in civic projects. Roman citizens also emigrated from Italy to the provinces, not only as administrators but as colonists, and joined with the natives in constructive undertakings.

But however sensible the Romans showed themselves in promoting stability and progress in the provinces, they could not escape from the fact that their political order was illogical and defective in principle at its very base. Rome's constitutional framework was that of a city-state, predicated upon direct participation of the citizen body in the mechanics of government; and this framework, devised in a small closely-knit area, had now been stretched over a vast territory. Obviously it was physically impossible for citizens residing in Gaul, Spain, Africa, or Illyria to take part in deliberations at Rome, and no attempt was made to allow them to do so. The provincial citizens did function effectively in managing local affairs, but always in a municipality. The self-government which gave vitality to urban communities of the West for several centuries was not conceded to a province, still less to the Empire as a whole. A representative system, based on the delegation of authority by constituents, was never used by the Romans. This was not because they were too stupid to think of

it but because, like the Greeks, they were traditionally devoted
to the city as the ideal unit; because their only experience with
self-government had been during the early days when a direct
democracy seemed both possible and practical, and finally because, by the time the imperial administration was organized,
the state at the center had been transformed into a despotism with
only the empty forms of popular sovereignty remaining.

In spite of the absence of home rule for the larger units of the
Empire, the citizens of the provinces were better off politically
than those living in Rome. The residents of the capital had been
reduced to a condition of passivity. Their brawling and butchery
had been halted by Augustus and, although the assembly was
retained during the early Principate and the Senate until the Late
Empire, both bodies were dominated or cowed by the ruler.
Assassination was still a recourse for disgruntled Senators (and
one which they did not scruple to use), but this was a desperate
remedy which revealed the hopelessness of their position. Both
the Senate and the Roman people had permanently lost all initiative in public affairs.

A factor accompanying the collapse of the democratic constitution and one of the reasons for its collapse was the tremendous
economic inequalities in Roman society. Athenian democracy
had operated most successfully during the time when its citizens,
while not all alike and certainly not coerced into a pattern of
uniformity, were on a modest and fairly equitable plane in regard
to the enjoyment of worldly goods. The Romans, similarly, had
made their most promising political advances while they were a
nation of hard-working farmers and when the gulf between
aristocrat and commoner, although acknowledged, was not so
wide as to prevent the two classes from bridging the differences
between them and co-operating for the public interest. In the
period between the Punic Wars and the end of the Republic,
however, the most extreme and invidious distinctions were created. Aside from the slaves, the status of the citizens ranged from
the penniless proletariat to the plutocracy of government con-
tractors and tax jobbers, and the landed aristocracy, whose vast
estates were run as a business enterprise and tended to drive the

small independent proprietor into bankruptcy. After the murder of the Gracchi brothers, who had striven to rehabilitate the small farmer class, no significant effort was directed toward redressing the economic balance. The reorganization under Augustus and all the reforms of the "good emperors" of the second century, well-intentioned and earnest as they were, left the lopsided social structure intact. Although slavery declined, largely because of an oversupply of cheap free labor, even during the best centuries of the Empire the gulf in Italian society between the haves and the have-nots was infinitely greater than that which had separated patricians and plebeians in the early and mid-Republic. The Roman state, then, at the very time when its influence was beginning to predominate throughout the whole Mediterranean world, was a simulating shadow-democracy, having its focal center in a society dangerously divided by rank and economic status into classes whose interests were irreconcilably opposed to one another.

TRANQUIL INTERLUDE

Why did not the projection of such a faulty political organism over a wider and wider area bring sudden collapse? Why, on the contrary, did sobriety and creative effort become more manifest, with unmistakable signs of contentment and prosperity in many quarters? Why did Edward Gibbon, surveying the scene from the heights of the eighteenth century, affirm (closing his eyes to certain factors and becoming slightly lyrical) that the middle years of the second century A.D. had been the happiest period in human experience?

The answer lies in the fact that the organizing and development of the provinces had an effect upon Roman history similar to the influence of the frontier in American history. The Roman West (Gaul, Spain, and Britain) was a frontier, which beckoned invitingly to civilizing impulses and administrative talents. The opening of new territories, ripe for the kind of work with which the Romans were most familiar, offered a challenge to their flagging spirits and released creative tendencies which had reached a dead end in Rome itself. A sense of achievement and satisfaction returned as they saw roads and cities emerging in what had been wilderness and helped bickering tribes accustom themselves to the ritual of law. Of course there were more material incentives also—opportunities to win personal distinction or financial betterment—just as there were in the American West. Retired soldiers, dispossessed farmers, and others of the unemployed settled as pioneer colonists in regions far from home, although never to the extent of emptying Italy entirely of these elements.

While serving as a safety valve for explosive forces within Roman society and providing fresh fields for the exercise of leadership, the provinces themselves received substantial gains. Economic progress was outstanding, particularly in farming, as superior methods were introduced. It is noteworthy that while agriculture was becoming more productive and profitable in the western provinces it was falling on evil days in Italy. There large tracts were being devoted to grazing or to olive and vine culture, and the small cereal farmer had abandoned his land or sunk to the position of a servile tenant, so that grains now had to be imported regularly from Africa or Sicily. Manufacture and commerce were always of secondary interest to the Romans, whose early rusticity had left a lasting imprint upon them; but these activities assumed importance in Gaul, Spain, and other regions facing the seaways, including Britain (to some extent they antedated Roman rule). By and large the western sections of the Empire were more prosperous than Rome and Italy. The products and revenues derived from them helped support the Roman government; but the provincials did not object particularly so long as their own condition was improving.

Politically and socially speaking, acquaintance with Roman techniques and standards stimulated the zeal of alert provincials, who displayed a civic spirit reminiscent of that which the Romans had evidenced in their formative period. Several phases of Roman evolution were recapitulated in the provinces. In their heyday during the mid-Empire the provincial cities of the West exhibited much the same mettle which had distinguished Rome of the mid-Republic. However, as these cities were constructed—sometimes on an ambitious scale with more space allotted than their populations could have required—they were modeled, not after the brick village on the Tiber, but after the princely city of marble which had taken its place and had almost erased its memory. Characteristic features were thick walls, arches, columns, baths, and coliseums. To make the picture complete there should also have been an idle mob, vapid and insatiable, fed and entertained at public expense. Proletarians there were, a genuinely wretched lot; but in these Western boom towns they had to work for what little bread they received. Contrary to a fairly widespread impression, not all the indigent folk of the Roman Empire were cared for by the bountiful hand of an extravagant state charity.

The vitality and long duration of the Empire were made possible by the comparatively undeveloped state of the West, which offered an outlet for energies deadlocked by the autocratic regime in Rome and which profited from the impact of these energies. Even the older and more civilized eastern provinces benefited to some extent. While the Pax Romana prevailed, avenues of communication were policed, piracy suppressed, and an intercontinental commerce encouraged.

But these favorable conditions could not continue forever. Sooner or later the problems latent in the monstrous discrepancies of Roman society—problems which had been shelved rather than solved—would have to be faced. No real attempt was ever made to solve them, although their superficial symptoms were attacked with the utmost determination. In spite of the parallel already noted between the role of the frontier in American and Roman history, there was an important difference between the two cases. In the United States the self-reliant individualism and democratic concepts which were nourished on the frontier flowed back to permeate, to a degree, the national character, and even modified political machinery. No such regeneration took place in the Roman state as a result of developments in the provinces. The imperial government was too inflexible and authoritative, too absorbed in its own ramifications to observe, let alone apply, lessons which might have been derived from this quarter. The era of constructive growth in the West furnished a breathing spell, but it only postponed the day of reckoning.

During its optimum period the well-being of the Empire resided largely in the prosperity of the middle class. While this statement is true, it perhaps implies a healthier condition than was actually the case. The "middle class" of the Roman Empire was not primarily commercial or industrial but a landed aristocracy, somewhat below the Senatorial order in rank and revenue. Its members were the backbone and nerves of the provincial cities. They organized the municipal services, manned the local offices and courts, and contributed generously from their own resources to improve and beautify their communities. However, although some of them engaged or had engaged in commerce, their income was derived chiefly from landed estates in the neighboring countryside. Hence their bias was that of country gentlemen, and they did not identify themselves with the humbler members of society—the tenants on their land or the hewers of wood and stone and drawers of water in the towns. These groups, amounting to a majority of the population, were the forgotten men and women of the Roman state. The early days of the Republic had witnessed some progress toward social, if not economic, equality. This promising stage was skipped entirely in the evolution which Roman rule inaugurated in the provinces, where class disparities were always in evidence. The provincial cities in spite of their luster were, from the economic standpoint, parasitical. They were supported by the sweat and toil of those who had no part in government and no share in the rewards of urbane living. The only benefit which the lower classes could expect was security, coupled with a condition of semiserfdom if they were country dwellers, or with the privilege of occupying wretched tenements if they were townspeople. The townsfolk might also learn to read and write, as evidenced by casually scribbled Latin inscriptions unearthed even in distant Britain.

THE LAST DESPERATE EFFORT

The over-all administrative machinery of the Roman state was a bureaucracy. Gradually but steadily, and irrespective of the personal character of the emperor, it became more ponderous, inflexible, and arbitrary. Such was the inevitable consequence of the renunciation of responsibility by the Roman citizens— bloodstained, frightened, and weary as they were—at the accession of Augustus. Bureaucracies do not prune or limit themselves; this necessary work can be done only by those who are not part of the system, and they must be uncommonly high-minded and courageous.

A notable and often remarked feature in the later years of the Empire was the expansion of the army and the increasing militarization of the whole imperial service. This was not because external dangers had become greater. Rather, it was because a military order is the most natural form for a bureaucracy to assume if it is long continued. It is easier for it to move in this direction than in any other. As signs of disturbance appear they will be suppressed; not investigated and evaluated, but smothered as promptly as possible. Military discipline provides the readiest means for such treatment. Because the bureaucracy already controls the destinies of its citizens and subjects, as it becomes militarized it transforms the state into the semblance of a vast guardhouse. The fact that eventually Rome's swollen armies were undisciplined, that her troops marauded, looted, and made and unmade emperors, does not obscure the reality that the state and society both were moving rapidly toward a regime based purely upon force. While it is natural for a bureaucracy to degenerate into militarism, the process increases rigidity, making a healthy recovery almost impossible. Thus it is always a sign of approaching catastrophe.

The last two centuries of the Empire are largely a record of failure. It is not unusual for civilizations to fail; most of them do sooner or later. None of the great human societies which the earth has known has as yet discovered the final secret of survival. Since there are tragic elements in the life process itself, reversals and defeats are inevitable. Undoubtedly there are worse things than failure, for a nation as for an individual. History discloses examples of glorious failures, as well as of inglorious successes. In the long run it is better to fail in the right things than to succeed in the wrong. The worst fate of all is to aim at a false image of good and still miss the mark, which is what happened in Rome's case. The Roman tragedy is that even if her leaders had managed to realize their objectives they would not have served the cause of civilization. Their pathetically earnest but heavy-handed efforts were merely to uphold the framework of a government which was becoming more alien and hostile to the welfare of the people among whom it operated.

In spite of the stern commands of the bureaucracy, centrifugal forces rapidly gained momentum. The anguish of the lower classes, which had been too long ignored, finally burst out in hatred of the *bourgeoisie*, their most immediate oppressors, and unleashed a fierce class struggle. During the third century A.D., when troops were recruited chiefly from the peasants and proletariat, the army became an instrument of class conflict, and soldiers pillaged the provincial cities in a furious spirit of vengeance. At the same time the rulers, in order to keep the imperial services going, increased taxation, which had always borne most heavily upon the middle class but now became a confiscatory levy. Oppressed from above and attacked from below, this supple and able middle class faced extinction. Some of its members hurled themselves down into the ranks of serfs (which was against the law), and a few escaped upstairs into the aristocracy, where they could bargain with officials on a more equal footing, buy them off, or defy them. But the class as a whole throughout the Empire was liquidated, and thus what had been the backbone of society was eaten away.

After the class wars and other calamities of the third century, one last attempt was made to rehabilitate the Empire. It was truly a desperate attempt, because it embodied the scrapping of a thousand years of tradition, not only Roman but Hellenic as well. Up to this point the fiction had been maintained that the emperor was merely "first citizen," the trustee of authority delegated by the sovereign Roman people. Now this democratic mask was dropped entirely in favor of an out-and-out totalitarianism. The totalitarianism of that day was not a dictatorship of the masses, a corporate state, nor the rule of a master race, but a device borrowed from the effete monarchies of the Near East. The ruler was presented as a god, clothed with absolute power and elevated to a position of unapproachable sanctity, far above his subjects. Emperor worship and abject submission were prescribed as the token of allegiance and bond of unity throughout the Empire.

Diocletian and his associates who carried out these "reforms," were not paranoiacs with delusions of grandeur. They were hard-headed soldiers, in whose cool judgment the body of citizens had sunk to such a despicable estate that they could be expected to respond to no other stimulus. Diocletian was determined to save the formal aspects of the Empire at no matter what sacrifice of human dignity and rationality. His reorganization was carried through with such characteristic Roman vigor (although he wasn't Roman) that the structure did actually hold together for more than another century. Its eventual collapse, however, was all the more complete. Not only was the remedy worse than the disease but it intensified the ravages of the disease.

TRANSVALUATION OF VALUES

A tremendous literature has been devoted to describing, analyzing, and explaining the Roman downfall. Justifiably so, because of the scope and implications of the phenomenon. Rome's was a great empire, with a rich civilization; a type of world government, yet framed in a European setting. Its disintegration brought the end of an epoch and led to profound alterations in society and culture in the West. A thorough appraisal of the Roman fate would, it is believed, be of inestimable help in avoiding a similar disaster in the future. But the decline of Rome was so gradual, and the relevant data so overwhelming that historians do not entirely agree as to the most effective causes. The "decline and fall" has furnished texts for almost every variety of sermon. Some investigators stress one factor, others its opposite. Among the explanations of the Roman collapse which have had considerable support at one time or another may be mentioned: a falling off in the birth rate ("race suicide"); failure to introduce a system of representative government; excessive emphasis on agriculture to the neglect of manufacture and commerce; decay of agriculture because of soil exhaustion and climatic change; militarism; decline of the Roman martial spirit; immorality and paganism; the renunciation of reason, as attested by the abandonment of the pagan but humanistic state religion in favor of Oriental mystery cults, including finally Christianity.

The assertion that Roman society suffered fatally from "Orientalization," culminating in the adoption of an otherworldly religion, calls for brief comment. There is much evidence to support the charge. Hellenistic standards of luxury and extravagance did permeate the tastes of the upper classes, while an attitude of resignation, pessimism, and fatalism became general at all levels. But the statement, particularly as to religion, is a half-truth which confuses causes with symptoms. The most damaging Oriental element incorporated by the Romans was theocratic absolutism, with its total repudiation of the concept of free and responsible citizenship, which was made the basis of government in the Late Empire. Having swallowed such a monstrosity, the people of the Empire could hardly have been made any worse by embracing an Oriental religion—especially when that faith, which happened to originate in the Near East, was among the noblest ever conceived in any portion of the planet.

The relations between the imperial government and the early Christian Church throw significant light on the nature and immensity of the Roman failure. The small and contemptuously regarded sect of Christians, recruited in the beginning from the lowest strata of society, ultimately stood in opposition to the state and its authority. Its members deliberately turned their backs on the prevailing values, compulsions, and loyalties. They could not be made to worship the emperor; their refusal to serve in the army was notorious. In the world but not of the world, they seemed to form a race apart.

In view of the increasing difficulties of enforcing bureaucratic decrees upon an apathetic populace, it is not strange that the Roman officials, after hoping vainly that the sect would prove to be a passing fad, came to regard it as a dangerous menace. They took the position which governments almost always adopt toward such nonconforming minorities, especially when the governments are hard put to it to justify their own performance. They denounced the Christians as subversives, of highly suspect allegiance, and ordered their suppression on the ground that they were "atheists" and "enemies of the human race."

Although driven underground, the Christian communities flourished with persecution. The solemnity of Roman law, the power and threats of magistrates, the discomforts of prison, the agonies of mutilation and death left their stanchest members unmoved, and "the blood of the martyrs became the seed of the Church." As attempts at extermination were systematized and extended they became all the more difficult, not only because of the growing popularity of the new faith but because of the attitude which the Christians displayed when undergoing trial or punishment. They turned the other cheek; they blessed and prayed for their tormentors, who were completely unprepared to cope with this variety of rebellion and finally abandoned their efforts to quell it. If it were not attested by indisputable record the story would be almost incredible—that the power and terror of a conquering empire could be defied successfully by an unarmed, bedraggled little group of fanatics, drawn apparently from the scum of the earth. But the spirit proved stronger than the flesh, and the state was not as formidable as it looked. Like Martin Luther's Satan: "One little word shall fell him."

Because the Christians won their battle with the imperial government, it does not follow that Christianity destroyed the state or Roman civilization. (Very typically when a government is threatened with extinction and stands frantically at bay, it lashes out at the wrong objects, overlooking its real enemies; and Rome was no exception.) Adamant in matters of conscience, the early Christians were otherwise peaceful and law abiding, quite willing to render unto Caesar the things that were Caesar's. It is true that they denounced the state as wicked and openly predicted that it would be destroyed by the wrath of God (not the most inaccurate prophecy on record). They had set their feet on new ground. They were looking beyond to a new arrangement of things—apocalyptic perhaps, but real to them—an estate which hardly bordered on the visible worldly city but which would outlast any man-made empire, enduring even though heaven and

88

earth should pass away. They did not attack the state; they simply transferred their allegiance elsewhere, feeling that the traditional Roman imperatives were no longer significant in the light of other values which they had discovered. Considering the character of society and the opacity of the ruling bureaucracy, it must be admitted that there was something to be said for the Christians' point of view.

Christianity did not destroy the Empire, but neither did it save it. Perhaps its triumph came too late in any case and the whole affair was beyond salvaging. In this connection the most valid charge to be brought against the early Christians is that while repudiating the old order they had no conception of suitable social and political instruments with which to replace it. The necessity of planning in these areas—except on an informal, temporary basis—did not occur to them because they ardently believed that the end of the world was at hand. It was sufficient to be prepared for the last days and to await the coming of the Lord, who would reveal what was in store for the faithful. Consequently, although spreading of the religion from the lower up through the higher strata of society brought balm to individuals and mitigated the harshness of human relations somewhat, it did not change the system within which they operated. Persecution was followed by toleration and toleration was succeeded by formal adoption of Christianity as the state religion to be rigorously enforced (entailing, of course, a revolution in the status, prestige, and wealth of the Church and a softening of the moral fiber which had produced martyrs). But in spite of this transformation the general condition of the Empire continued the same as before—that is it was steadily getting worse. It has been said that the Roman Empire, like many a hardened sinner, repented and was converted on its deathbed. Which perhaps explains why some aspects of it survived in spirit, long after the body had disappeared.

An examination of all the factors involved in the decline of Rome calls for, and has received, many volumes; but the gist of the matter can be stated simply. The Roman state fell because it was not worth continuing. It no longer contributed to the well-being of its members; it was not a ministrant to a fuller life either materially or spiritually; it had become a liability rather than an asset. This does not mean that Roman *civilization* was not worth saving. It is unfortunate that the civilization was so joined to and dominated by the political fabric that when this was destroyed other elements of the entire culture were inevitably damaged and dissipated.

CHAPTER SIX

TOWARD A EUROPEAN CIVILIZATION:
THE EARLY MIDDLE AGES

WITH the disintegration of the Roman Empire and its civilization
the old order, to which the early Christians had stood in determined opposition, did pass away. But that which followed was
not what these religious pioneers had expected. It was neither the
end of the world in fire and tempest nor the kingdom of heaven
on earth. Instead, what appeared was a gray, pale dawn, revealing,
as the mists cleared, a flesh-and-blood society, lusty and vigorous,
but crude, barbarous, and rough. The cement of civilization
seemed to have given way, letting primitive forces take command.

Actually this breakdown in the social structure was not only
gradual but confined to a limited area, the western half of the
Roman Empire. The eastern portions escaped the process of bar-
barization. The Byzantine Empire, centering in the almost impregnable and highly cosmopolitan city of Constantinople, continued its dignified and sumptuous existence for another thousand
years. Nevertheless, the western provinces had been the freshest
and most vital units in the Roman state. They constituted the
proving ground for Rome's organizational efforts and their relapse

into a primitive condition marks the climax and extent of her failure. Also, the barbarizing of the West entailed a separation of this region from the centers which had always been at the fore-front of civilization and from which Rome had derived so much stimulation. The Western peoples were now thrown upon their own resources, which for the time being appeared pitifully meager. Even the common bond of Christianity did little to bridge the gap between East and West, as separatist tendencies gradually drove the Roman and Greek churches farther and farther apart.

AFTER CIVILIZATION, WHAT?

Because the extinction of the Roman Empire brought a turning point in Western history, the centuries immediately following merit attention as giving an intimation of the shape of things to come. These centuries are clouded and dubious, as suggested by the somewhat extreme title of "Dark Ages" which is customarily assigned to them. But although the subject is a gloomy one it pro-vides a pertinent case study of the aftermath of a ruptured society and culture. The question as to what happens when a civilization goes to pieces is not utterly remote from the minds of many thoughtful persons today, as they reflect on the possibility that our own civilization may be threatened with annihilation.

Paradoxically, a survey of the European Dark Ages may induce an overly optimistic attitude. They offer strong evidence that the drive toward a more durable and rewarding mode of existence is never abandoned altogether—that once the process has begun man cannot free himself from the compulsion to progress, no matter what setbacks he has encountered or however discouraging the immediate prospects. Four hundred years is not long in the life of the race, yet it sufficed to allow the European peoples to find sure footing and renewed confidence. The Dark Ages were but a transitory stage, and the period which succeeded them showed not only a revival of creative effort but the attainment of previ-ously undiscovered heights. In answer to the question, the evi-dence suggests that when one civilization dies out another, in some respects superior, takes its place.

But it cannot be assumed that this will always happen. There is no assurance that after another plunge into darkness it would again be possible to catch up and reunite the broken threads of the social fabric. The pattern into which they are woven is far more complex than any known to the ancient world. The passing of classical civilization was largely a withering of leadership, a breakup of organization and social discipline, accompanied by a collapse of self-confidence and a flight from reason—a gigantic loss of nerve. The downfall of contemporary society would probably witness these same phenomena—all cultures are dependent upon man's effort and their inadequacy is chargeable to human failure. But the collapse might also encompass the physical environment to which Western peoples have become accustomed, wrecking the instruments of livelihood, distribution, and communication on which the sheer bodily existence of modern populations depends.

There is no denying the reality or the significance of the Roman decline. However, the process did not involve as much visible change as might be imagined. For many inhabitants of the Empire their condition was affected so little that they may well have been unaware that any momentous tragedy was being enacted. The tangible manifestations of regression which investigators have been able to identify were not in themselves catastrophic or dramatic. Agricultural productivity was falling off and some valuable tracts had passed out of cultivation. After the emperors had debased the currency to such a degree that it almost disappeared from circulation, a barter economy emerged in the rural areas. The *bourgeoisie* of the provincial cities, coerced into the imperial service and ground under the heel of ruinous taxation, were being extinguished *as a class;* but even the members of this unfortunate minority were not exterminated as individuals, and the cities if no longer illustrious were still standing and populated. None of these events constituted a complete breakdown in economic life or a dissolution of all societal bonds; still less a destruction or impairment of the resources of the European continent. Certainly the invading barbarians found much that was not only worth taking but worth keeping, aside from sheer loot, in the provinces which they occupied. The Roman citizen who had been a landlord continued as a landlord after his citizenship ceased to have any meaning—or else he surrendered his estate intact to a Germanic noble. In either case the cultivators of the soil held to the same routine and the same lowly status. To the depressed *colonus* it made no difference whether his master was a swarthy Latin or a blond Teuton. The majority of the population had received little benefit from the grandeur that was Rome and were little the worse for its passing.

But the wiping out of civilization today, under any circumstances which could conceivably bring it about, would be radically different. Modern societies have much more to lose and much more that could be easily destroyed. Furthermore, practically their entire membership is inextricably involved in the operative functions at one level or another and would be drastically affected by the interruption of these functions, even though most individuals have no understanding of their nature and scope and would not have the faintest notion of how to go about rebuilding them.

Contemporary civilization, in its obvious and external aspects, is an intricate mechanism. It is increasingly interdependent and all-embracing, and yet at the same time its successful operation depends upon a more and more exacting technical proficiency, beyond the reach of the majority. Back of the engineer and technologist lies the research laboratory. Beyond that lies the tenuous realm of pure science, in which a few rare spirits scrutinize the secrets of the physical universe and through their revelations—characterized by mathematical equations rather than ecstatic trances—unlock new potentials which will alter or revolutionize the workaday world. The man in the street may be as ignorant of the cogitations of the scientist as a Campanian peasant was oblivious to the meditations of Marcus Aurelius. But while the peasant could live and die without philosophy, his modern counterpart cannot escape the impact of science, which continuously reshapes the environment in which he moves. And that environment is an artificial and brittle thing, constantly exposed to the liability of injury and difficult to repair. In fact it could be smashed to fragments by instruments of destruction now known and perhaps already laid away against such an occasion. Destroy the laboratories and the whole technological mechanism will soon be off balance. Eliminate the small core of pure scientists and even the laboratories will have little meaning—the all important explaining and directive force will have been removed.

Even the immediate physical wreckage incidental to a full-scale war staggers the imagination. Without the visible presence of an enemy the inhabitants of a congested city can be rendered more pitiably helpless than primitive villagers whose fields have been exposed to the advance of a marauding host. Modern societies are separated from nature by several layers of insulation. They might be compared to a colony of explorers which has been set down on some isolated or inhospitable spot of the earth's surface. Such a group can carry on its work even at the North Pole or under the sea; but if contact with the supply bases is broken and it is left to grapple with nature in the raw, it will perish. Members of contemporary Western civilization are like occupants of a penthouse—or perhaps a cave dwelling carved high on the face of a cliff but equipped with plumbing, electricity, and elevator shafts. If these lines of service and communication are cut off, what has been a haven becomes a tomb. An increasingly perilous vulnerability is the price paid for the technological advances which we welcome so eagerly.

Another point of difference between the decline of the ancient world and of the modern (if it should come to pass) lies in the timely presence, in the former case, of the Germanic barbarians. They were a sturdy folk, energetic and prolific, whose capacities had as yet hardly been put to the test. Through long contact with the Empire they had acquired considerable familiarity with Roman institutions and were ready and able to continue—clumsily and with modifications, of course—some aspects of them. Today, on the contrary, barbarians are in short supply.

Many vociferous public statements would have it otherwise. Spokesmen on both sides of the wall of hostility and fear which divides the great political aggregations today loudly proclaim that the people on the other side of the barrier are barbarians of the most despicable variety. Unfortunately, there is a sense in which this is true, but not quite in the way intended by those who make the charge; and in so far as it is true it applies in both directions. Our mechanized, streamlined, power-driven culture does seem to be developing within itself a special kind of barbarian, a type of man who is increasingly dependent upon artificial stimulation, increasingly intoxicated with the manifestations of speed and force, and increasingly indifferent to the discipline which has made attainable the things in which he takes such fierce delight. If our civilization is weakened to the point of collapse, it probably will be from an excess of these machine-age savages, who do not think creatively and who are alternately at the mercy of, and a terrifying threat to, the directing minority entrusted with the public destiny. But this species of barbarian, so empty of resources within himself, represents the end product of a dehumanized civilization. At the opposite pole is the true barbarian—one who has never been inducted into a highly civilized society, whose nervous energies have not yet been challenged by civilization, much less been exhausted by overstimulation.

The groups which might genuinely qualify as barbarians in this proper and historic sense of the term are scattered over distant islands or hidden away in the tropics. And the invasion of the great civilization centers—to take hold if we should lay the burden down—seems to be farthest from their intentions. Rather, they are hoping that civilization will not invade them, that the world's power constellations will continue to count them out. If Western society destroys itself it will have to furnish its own barbarians for the task of reconstruction, and there is a danger that this home-bred variety, born of chaos, may lack something of vision and enthusiasm.

THE HUMAN ELEMENT

It has already been pointed out that Roman civilization did not come to an abrupt halt nor disappear entirely. Also the Germanic peoples, although primitive, were not wholly uncivilized and had begun to learn from the Romans even before the major invasions. Conceivably, if the Empire had retained its peak effectiveness, the Teutonic tribes might have been assimilated, as were the Greeks of Italy, Phoenicians and Berbers of North Africa, and the Celts of Gaul. In that event they perhaps would have become the outermost guardians of Greco-Roman culture instead of its attackers, and, among other results, the traditional and fateful enmity between the French and the Germans might never have come into being. In any case, a considerable number of the barbarian nations reached political and social maturity in what had been the western provinces of the Empire (including, also, Italy itself). They wrested control from Romans or from Romanized provincials; they settled down among these groups; they were affected in every way by contact with them. The nascent states of Western Europe reflected at the outset a fusion of Roman and Germanic elements. The blending process was so extensive that it is almost impossible to distinguish clearly between the two conjoining streams of influence. Every medieval institution (and many modern ones) partook of both, and yet in its entirety was equally far removed from the classical Roman and from the primitive Teutonic prototypes.

Because they had no fully developed system of writing at the time of the migrations, it is not strange that the Germanic tribes adopted the Roman alphabet. But those of them who settled within the confines of the Roman Empire also abandoned their native speech for the Latin which they found current. (England, where Anglo-Saxon displaced both Celtic and Latin, provides an exception.) Their crude judicial processes and legal concepts were in stark contrast to the Roman, but they were systematized and recorded with Latin as the vehicle and were soberly written out as the *Leges Barbarorum*—the Laws of the Barbarians. (Again excepting the Anglo-Saxon "Dooms." It remained for the Norman Conquerors of Britain to translate the pungent Teutonic *mundbryce* and *grithbrice* into *contra pacem domini regis*.)

The most obvious departure was in the political field, where the venerable authority of the Caesars gave way to folkright or the decrees of warrior chieftains. However, as the tribal communities passed over into territorial states, the power of the king was enlarged and took on a more magisterial character. If it had not been for the intervention of feudalism and the lively competition of ecclesiastical potentates, the kings would certainly have succeeded in arrogating to themselves not only the trappings but the substance of the old Roman imperium. Beginning with Charlemagne, some of them actually did assume the imperial title and purple from time to time—usually with unfortunate results. But it was left for the sovereigns of postfeudal Europe, the dynasts of the early modern age, to revive the maxims of Roman law and exploit to the full its emphasis upon the supremacy of the ruler— adding a few points which even the Romans had not thought of— in their drive for absolute power.

Feudalism, the typical institution of the Later Middle Ages, offers the perfect illustration of how indissolubly Roman and non-Roman elements were intermingled to produce novel and unintended effects. The Roman landed estate (*villa* or *latifundium*) with its semiservile tenants was incorporated directly by the Germanic invaders into their society. Its inhabitants were metamorphosed imperceptibly into medieval villeins and serfs. In the long process whereby the owners of these estates became a hereditary aristocracy of warriors exercising sovereignty over their domains but mutually responsible to one another through ties of homage and fealty, many Roman formulas were brought into play. Yet the spirit and emotional content of the feudal relationship was unmistakably dyed with the fighting blood of Germanic tribesmen, and the pulverization of central authority which feudalism implied was at the opposite pole from the basic principles of Roman government. In just what proportions strains from the two stocks were combined to produce the feudal plant it is impossible to say. Neither does it matter, although rival French and German scholars have used up quantities of ink in attempting to prove that feudal origins were predominantly Latin or Teutonic respectively.

A somewhat broader consideration over which controversy has centered is the question of whether early Germanic society was free or unfree. Undeniably, after the dust of the migrations had settled it appears to have been largely servile; but was this the perpetuation of a traditional class system or does it represent the debasing effects of Roman contacts? The English and Americans regard the jury system as of unique historic importance in the safeguarding and extension of individual liberties. This device, which was introduced into England in the Later Middle Ages by the Norman kings, can be traced back through the Franks to the Romans; but in the Roman administrative machinery (and in the hands of the Norman rulers, for that matter) it served quite a different purpose, as its original title—*inquisitio*—rather grimly suggests. The general conclusion must be that at the time when the early Germanic kingdoms were taking form their societies were still rough, their institutions nebulous, their destiny uncertain. They were capable of utilizing many Roman elements, but in doing so they experienced very little immediate change, either for better or worse, in their habits and prevailing concepts.

Peoples are typically conscious of, and overly sensitive about, their ancestry. The Greeks arrogantly claimed descent from gods and demigods. The Romans traced their origins to the mythical twins Romulus and Remus, and back of them to the Trojans who had battled with the Greeks before the dawn of history. (Presumably it was not a matter of embarrassment that the Trojans had lost, because the Romans were well able to even the score.) Among Europeans much has been made of the tradition that their nations sprang from a race of conquerors who vanquished the might of Rome and through the vitalizing effects of their "new blood" inaugurated another and more successful era of constructive growth.

In reality, although the Germans differed from the Romans racially, this is the least important fact about them. Their cultural peculiarities were of great consequence, but their racial identity is of no significance at all for the shaping of Western civilization. The results of the invasions might have been the same if they had been carried out by (equally primitive) Celtic tribes, or Hellenic, or Slavic, or Hunnish. There is no sound evidence that the slight biological differences between the varieties of human stock now extant determine the character of social evolution or provide an explanation of the cultural divergences between one group and another.

Also the degree of ethnic change, whether significant or not, which accompanied the decline of Rome has often been exaggerated. The term "Germanic invasions" itself suggests too drastic a substitution of one stock for another. It is true that hitherto the Nordic division of the white race had figured very little in the conspicuous centers of civilization—although there was evidently a Nordic admixture in the Greek population—and the migrations of the barbarians introduced this strain more noticeably into portions of Western and even Southern Europe. There is no reason to suppose that the Germans were all pure Nordics, any more than they are now, or that they were the only group which showed these particular physical characteristics. The so-called "Celtic" element in the British Isles today is often represented by dark-haired, dark-eyed specimens of the Mediterranean type. But in ancient literature the Celts are described as tall and blond. Thus they must have been racially similar to the Teutons, with whom they were frequently at enmity.

There may well have been a considerable admixture of blond, blue-eyed people in the western portions of the Empire before the invasions of the fourth and fifth centuries A.D. Some anthropologists believe they have discovered evidence of a tall race—Mediterranean rather than Nordic, but inclined toward blondism—which appeared in England in prehistoric times before the Celtic invasion, not to mention the Germanic. When the Anglo-Saxons became troublesome in the fifth century, the Romanized Britons opposed them not because they were objectionable ethnically but because they were marauding robbers. A few centuries later it was the turn of the blond Anglo-Saxons to defend themselves against the equally blond Vikings from Scandinavia. The piratical and still pagan Vikings were more distinctively Nordic in appearance than any of the earlier Teutonic invaders, but the conflicts between them and their now more civilized relatives—Franks, Anglo-Saxons, and so on—were as fierce as if they had belonged to separate species.

The nature of the German people and the role of the Germanic element in European history is a subject which has been highly romanticized, both by Germans and non-Germans, and has frequently led to very heated debate. Tacitus, the Roman historian of the first century, discerned in the primitive Germans qualities of integrity and honor which he found lacking among his own countrymen. Anticipating Rousseau in a very mild way, he glorified the noble savage to highlight the flaws of an effete sophisticated society. Later it was the *furor Teutonicus* which impressed and terrified the Romans. Vandal, the name of one tribe, became a synonym for wanton destroyer, as "Saxon" did among the Britons and "Dane" among the Anglo-Saxons. The fondness for exaggeration and name calling has persisted into modern times. The appellation of "Hun" which was popular during World War I is as absurd as the Nazi claim that all true Germans are Aryans. And yet, many people today—even some who intend their prejudices to be mistaken for scholarship—maintain that the German is inherently brutal, destructive, or militaristic, and incapable of developing in a democratic direction.

Because of historic rivalries, the question of Teutonic characteristics versus those of other Europeans has been a particularly hot one between the Germans and the French. Gallic logicality, spirited devotion to liberty, and genius for civilization have been arrayed against German stodginess, regimentation, and animalism—or Teutonic thoroughness, efficiency, and cultural superiority against French capricious ineptitude and irresponsibility. The British, inclined to impartiality by their insular position, have sometimes contributed to the dispute on one side or the other. It was an expatriate Englishman, Houston Chamberlain, whose monstrous racial doctrines provided much grist for the Nazi mill. On occasion, when the French seemed more likely to upset the balance of power or disturb the peace, the English have stressed their bonds of kinship with the Teutonic peoples. But any German talk of a master race has usually aroused British ire, not so much because the British considered the theory unsound as because they had their own notions as to how and to whom it should be applied. Also the French (through Count de Gobineau), even before Hitler was born, announced that they were the true Aryans and hence superior. On the whole the French have held the advantage in their argument with the Germans because they could play the game both ways. When they like, they may claim descent from the warlike Franks, the most successful of the barbarian invaders, the stock of Charles "the Hammer," who stemmed the Moorish tide, and of the illustrious Charlemagne. In another mood or to suit a different purpose they identify themselves with the Latinized Celts, the Gallo-Romans who defended civilization in ancient times and are its natural guardians. The two claims are equally valid and equally pointless. The search for distinct, fixed, and irrevocable traits of national character is a will-o'-the-wisp pursuit. There was nothing "in the blood" of the Germanic barbarian peoples which was either inherently barbaric or conducive to signal achievement. What really counted were their traditions, social institutions, and degree of political experience. And these were, at the time when they fell heir to Roman dominion, elementary and limited.

THE CHURCH'S IMPACT UPON THE BARBARIANS

For the Romans' part, although they had much to offer, their values had become weakened, adulterated, in some cases even inverted before they made full impact upon the invaders. Far and away the most potent factor emanating from Rome was Christianity and the Church. Christianity, however, was not Roman in conception or essence; it was predicated upon assumptions antithetical to the Roman (and Hellenic) view of life and the world. In the form in which it reached the Germanic peoples it was an amalgam of various elements, not entirely consistent with one another. Carrying over from Judaism an authoritative Scripture, exacting moral code, and rigorous monotheism, it had added to these the vivid personal appeal of the Oriental mystery cults with their initiation rites and emotional emphasis. This accretion had made the religion increasingly successful in competing with Mithraism and similar salvationist cults among the frustrated peoples of the Greco-Roman world. As it gained headway within the educated intellectual classes, its theology became embellished with the symbols and mystical concepts of Hellenistic philosophy. With the rise of monasticism the ascetic ideal of renouncing the natural life—on the ground that matter, the world, and the flesh are inherently evil—was enshrined as a cardinal feature. Finally, over all this the prosaic but trenchant stamp of the Roman administrative system had been imposed, ensuring tight discipline and uniformity to the institutional framework. While many of these elements were alien to Roman tradition, practically all of them were outside the experience or imagination of the primitive Teutons. Nevertheless, the barbarians who overran the Empire seemed to recognize immediately that the Church was the strongest force with which they had to contend. Their chieftains negotiated with ecclesiastics; looting bands (and they were not universal) generally respected the churches and monasteries; and in a remarkably short time the tribesmen submitted themselves to the yoke of the new faith. Just as the Church had conquered the Roman state, so it in turn conquered the barbarians.

Arresting as is this victory, it might have been better if it had not been won so easily, or if more attention had been given to instructing the initiates in the implications of the discipline which they were embracing. Perhaps the missionaries, courageous and dedicated as they were, did not fully grasp the implications themselves. Both from the Church's standpoint and that of the barbarian states, the religious affiliation of the latter was largely a strategic consideration. It so happened that a majority of the migrating nations had been converted to the heretical Arian sect of Christianity, a circumstance which not only presented a challenge to the Roman hierarchy but which promoted discord among various Germanic groups in the West. Because the Franks, luckily discovered in a state of pristine paganism, were won over for the orthodox faith, they became practically allies of the papacy. This gave them a great advantage over the Visigoths, Lombards, and Burgundians, and it also provided the popes with a powerful lever which they did not hesitate to use.

Wholesale conversions, consummated by skillful diplomacy or inspired by a chance victory in battle, did not accomplish any notable change in ingrained habits or standards of behavior. The royal household was always the crucial point to be taken. If the king could be persuaded to shift his allegiance from the old deities, his people would follow as a matter of course. (In spite of the roughness of Germanic society, its leaders were remarkably susceptible to feminine influence, and matrimony was an effective device for bringing about a religious realignment. When a king married a Christian queen, his pagan goose was almost certainly cooked.) But a mass baptism of fighting men, reputedly in batches of thousands, at the command of their chieftain, could hardly transform them into gentle soldiers of the Cross.

King Clovis, of the Merovingian dynasty, was the instrument through which the Franks were brought into the orthodox fold; and it would be difficult to imagine an example of a convert upon whom the spiritual message of Christianity was more completely wasted. When he was being instructed in the rudiments of the faith, Clovis is alleged to have exclaimed, with his hand on his sword, that if he and his Franks had been present there would have been no Crucifixion—apparently his only venture into the field of Biblical criticism. In spite of the exhortation "Adore what thou hast burned, burn what thou hast adored," Clovis continued unabashed in his career of treachery, cruelty, and assassination. Bishop Gregory of Tours, however, who records the gruesome details without wincing, apparently regarded the king's idiosyncracies as pardonable in a son of the true Church and vindicated by their consequences. "The Lord cast his enemies under his power day after day, and increased his kingdom."

The good omen of orthodoxy and the support which it ensured from the ecclesiastical hierarchy go far to explain the rapid and successful expansion of the Frankish state. "It irks me," said Clovis, "that those Arians [the Visigoths] should possess any part of Gaul. With God's aid we will go against them and conquer their lands." When the Carolingian family seized the throne from the Merovingian rulers in the eighth century, they received the blessing of the Church more emphatically and solemnly than had their predecessors. Even the institution of monasticism served a useful political purpose. A deposed or potentially troublesome royal heir could be rendered harmless by shaving his head and sending him into a cloister. (Clovis had preferred the surer method of murdering every possible rival.) The Frankish-papal alliance paved the way for the unification (although on a superficial and temporary basis) of the greater part of Western Europe under Charlemagne, dramatized at the very end of the eighth century by the pope's bestowal upon him of the imperial title.

SYNTHESIS AT TWILIGHT

The potent leaven of Christianity conveyed through the medium of a weighty ecclesiastical apparatus to the boisterous Germanic communities produced curious results — alternately moving, repulsive, laughable, and pathetic. At the very least, however, the Church offered the basis for a formal unity among the divergent and often hostile groups, especially as the Arians were won over, by force and persuasion, to the creed which was buttressed by a tougher and more coherent organization. Connecting threads still led to Rome after the roads to that city were no longer in good repair. Even the English, following the Council of Whitby of 664, were definitely linked to the Roman communion.

As already suggested, the growing prestige of the papacy throughout the West and the emergence of the outlines of a universal church among the Latin and German peoples were largely the triumph of expediency, a diplomatic and political achievement rather than evidence of social progress or deep religious commitment. Nevertheless, the Church was a repository of many treasures—uncatalogued and even unrecognized by its ministrants—besides the essential core of spiritual teachings which were too easily incrusted with ritual and formula.

In spite of her sworn determination to uproot paganism and erase its evidences, the Church had actually preserved valuable remnants of classical culture. Hidden away, gathering dust in monasteries were fragments and entire works of Latin literature and philosophy, which had been allowed to remain either through carelessness or through a natural reluctance to destroy wantonly objects of undeniable, if forbidden, beauty. Even though the public services of the Roman state had vanished, the rudiments of an educational system were still discernible. Instruction had to be provided at least to the clergy, and the meager manuals, echoing the terminology of a more humanistic age, embodied what was significantly although too generously called the "liberal arts." Finally, theology itself, by the time it hardened into dogma, had been sifted and enlivened by the supple minds of the Church Fathers.

The patristic age, occupying the twilight zone between the classical and the medieval cultures, was within the limits of its interests a period of creative thought. The stimulus of Christianity brought a quickening to still able intellects that had grown weary of picking stray nuggets out of the played-out veins of Hellenistic philosophy. As these intellects warmed to Christianity, at least a few of them did so not with the idea of abandoning reason but of employing it in areas which seemed to be still alive. However, the new wine burst the old bottles of rhetoric and metaphysics. Impassioned arguments were launched afresh over such questions as the relationship between body and spirit, the unity or plurality of divine being, the respective merits of reason and faith, the nature and true end of man. Sharply divergent opinions were expressed and defended with acumen—until the high strategic command of the Church established that thin and twisting but unbreakable line of orthodoxy which separated the almost from the not quite, and decreed that no one should step over the border into heretical ground. Thus, although the Romans produced no distinctive school of philosophy of their own, Roman and Greek thinkers in the last centuries of the Empire dipped deep into the classical heritage to enrich the intellectual equipment of the Church. They brought the light of pagan thought into a brilliant focus upon Christian teachings before that light was extinguished.

In a measure patristic thought, for those who were keenly perceptive enough to find their way through it, bridged two worlds. The nature of the synthesis is best illustrated by the most famous and influential of the Western Church Fathers, St. Augustine of Hippo. On his long and uphill road to Christianity he stopped to investigate (and usually to embrace) almost every form of intellectual or emotional allegiance which could attract a man of education and ability. He sampled with enthusiasm each competing system, and though he rejected them one after another, some of their features were indelibly impressed upon him and borne along with him into Christianity. His background in Roman law impelled him to give a legalistic cast to theology, with God depicted as an omnipotent and implacable sovereign. In his conception the Hebrew universal Father became a Roman magistrate, inflexibly condemning his subjects for the inescapable and very un-Roman crime of being descended from Adam and Eve, who by sinning in the Garden had tainted the whole human race. At the same time from other sources, including Neo-Platonism, Augustine had absorbed a powerful mysticism, which transcended formal discipline and interpreted the divine being as compassionate yearning. ("Thou hast made us for Thyself, and our souls are restless until they rest in Thee.") Endowed with a strong and full-blooded instinct for living, he had by no means overlooked the delights of the flesh; as a youth, according to his *Confessions*, he had perhaps tarried in them too long. ("Lord, make me chaste— but not quite yet.") But when his mind was made up, he went to the opposite extreme of relentless asceticism, branding matter and the physical appetites as utterly evil. ("We die when we are born; we begin to live when we die.") If he had been able, the Bishop of Hippo would have required all priests to live as monks, instead of by the compromise which enjoined them to remain celibate while "in the world." Between flesh and spirit, between the Church Invisible and the World, between the God-state and the Devil-state there could be no reconciliation. And the *visible* Church, imperfect as it confessedly was, must command the un-questioning obedience of mortals. It was the vehicle by which the small remnant—no thanks to them or to the Church but to God's inscrutable will—would be saved. All of this dogma was set forth at tedious length but with the cogent reasoning and ex-pressive power of a well-stocked mind. St. Augustine provided, moreover, a simple but compelling philosophy of history. The world was a stage on which a divine drama was being enacted. Human history was the performance of assigned parts in the cos-mic tragedy, which began with the Fall of Man and ended with the fall of civilization. This point of view, of course, made the Church all the more qualified for the roles of prompter and critic.

At no time during the early Christian era is it possible to say: Roman influence ends here and what follows is quite unrelated to it. There were so many areas of interchange between the Roman and the Germanic, and the Church was such an omnibus of institu-tional, administrative, legal, and ideational elements that no clear dividing line exists between classical civilization and the early Eu-ropean, even though the two differed profoundly both in form and spirit. Hence, the conditions attendant upon the birth of European culture were probably not typical of what is to be expected when a great civilization disintegrates and perhaps would not be du-plicated again. Not only did the barbarian peoples acquire some Roman items intact and still usable but they also were left re-minders of a past splendor which might be recovered or even exceeded. The fires were pretty steeply banked during the Dark

Ages, but fuel was available capable of producing both heat and light.

During this transitional period, however, there was little appreciation of the legacy of the past or perception of a profitable future. The Germanic princelings were too occupied in carving out larger territories for themselves to give much thought to such matters. With the strident and pointless competition among their states the center of gravity seemed not so much to have shifted to the north as to have disappeared altogether. Even the leaders of the Church were primarily concerned with the negative task of policing a turbulent society and bolstering their own powers. The patristic age had ended in the triumph of the authoritative school of thinkers and the suppression of those who advocated intellectual freedom. The definition of dogma and heresy had choked off channels of discussion. What a difference between St. Augustine and the last of the Latin Church Fathers, Pope Gregory the Great! Over Augustine's thought, terrifying as it sometimes is, the light of reason plays continuously; whereas Gregory takes righteous pride in his bad grammar, rejects critical inquiry, and mingles together with complete indifference gems of practical piety and old wives' tales. This custodian of the "Patrimony of St. Peter" looked out sadly over what he thought was a wild sea with no land in sight, and believed that his duty was to summon all hands aboard the frail ark which he was attempting to pilot through the buffeting storm.

CHAPTER SEVEN

EUROPEAN CLIMAX:
THE LATER MIDDLE AGES

VERY commonly peoples delight in glorifying their remote and faintly remembered past. Therefore it is a little odd that the recipients of the Western heritage have a tendency to despise the early stages of its evolution. Toward the Middle Ages they customarily display an attitude of indifference or even contempt, although it was this period which witnessed both the birth and the coming of age of a distinctively European society and culture.

Lack of respect for their early history by Western peoples may be proof of a commendable degree of sophistication, showing that they are less bound by tradition, less restricted in perspective than usual. It might indicate that they are determined to "live in the present," looking forward instead of backward. But no doubt in their attitude there is an element of depreciation of the past, a disdain not only for the primitive scrub growth of civilization but even for the lofty forests, if they are no longer standing. This disdain seems to be coupled in some people's minds with the notion that the records of previous ages can be disregarded and their experiences circumvented altogether in getting on with the business of living. The notion is dangerous. We cannot escape the influence of our own past even if we close our eyes to it; and only if we attempt to understand it will we be able to surmount its limitations.

What Were the Middle Ages?

The prevalence of careless impressions concerning the formative stages of European culture is seen in the term commonly applied to them—"Middle Ages." It was coined as a title of disparagement by Renaissance humanists who wished to underline the brilliance of their own "modern" age. Aside from its vagueness, the term covers too long a stretch of time and too many contrasting conditions to make it a useful designation. An abyss of credulous ignorance, and a subtle and tightly reasoned philosophy; the legalized brawling of heavily armed ruffians, and the refined code of the Christian knight; downtrodden peasants living and dying, hardly above the animal level, on the same sorry acres, and cities linked together by international associations of enterprising merchants; wretched hovels, drafty uncarpeted baronial halls, and magnificent Gothic cathedrals—all of these may with equal justice be called "medieval." Although scholars have long since demonstrated its inadequacy, the ambiguous term will probably persist.

During the larger part of the period known as the Middle Ages the great civilizations of the world were to be found outside of Europe. (The Mohammedan or Saracenic Empire included most of Spain, and the Byzantine Empire included the Balkans; but there was little contact between these areas and the Christian communities of the West.) However, although outside influences were never entirely lacking, the development of Western civilization is chiefly the story of the Northern and Western Europeans, whether they were performing brilliantly or not. As far as these groups are concerned, the Middle Ages, occupying roughly a thousand years, comprised two related but quite distinct epochs. The first of these, the Dark Ages, has already been considered. The five or six centuries following Charlemagne belong to the "Later" or "High" Middle Ages, impossible to terminate exactly and shading over into—some would say including most of—the Renaissance. This later period differed very drastically from the earlier and laid the foundation for many aspects of the modern era—although the typical exponents of medieval culture might, if they knew anything about it, be eager to disclaim this responsibility.

In general, the later division of the medieval millennium contrasts with the earlier in its tremendous cultural superiority. There were many variations and contradictions within each of these two periods, however, and neither of them was all of one piece. The Dark Ages were dark largely because of the wide cultural gap between the Romans who were relinquishing control and the barbarians who were seizing it. But while Roman influence was negligible in some areas, such as Anglo-Saxon England and Germany east of the Rhine, in others it remained paramount for a long time. In Italy perhaps it would have retained its ascendancy indefinitely if it had not been for the "reconquest" of the peninsula in the sixth century by the Byzantine "Roman" emperor Justinian—a devastating affair which did far more to hasten the decay of civilization than the inroads of Visigoths, Vandals, or Ostrogoths. Even so, much of Roman law and portions of the old institutional structure were preserved in Italian cities throughout the Middle Ages.

Although the Dark Ages witnessed a shriveling of intellectual life and political retrogression, social and economic conditions had not yet become "medieval." The economy of the West was more varied than that which prevailed several centuries later. Curiously enough, the beginning of the Later Middle Ages coincided with an economic decline. The Merovingian Frankish kings, crude as they were, had benefited from the still active commerce of the cities of Gaul and were able to maintain a gold standard for their currency. Charlemagne's landlocked empire, although impressive in size, rested on an almost purely agrarian economy, in which gold coins disappeared from circulation. The reason for this change can be very largely assigned to the rise and expansion of Islam over Northern Africa and into Spain. The Germanic invaders of the West, though they were rustics, had not destroyed the cities of the provinces. Many of the cities, especially those facing on the Mediterranean, which had been to the Romans "Our Sea," continued to exchange their products with one another and even with the cities of the Near East. But the phenomenal expansion of Arab power, which reached a climax in the eighth century, converted the Mediterranean Sea into a Mohammedan lake and blocked off Western Europe behind the Pyrenees. With the sea a defensive frontier instead of a highway, the Christian cities of the West were deprived of the commercial contacts which had been their basis of existence. They declined in population, their merchant class dwindled to a few straggling peddlers, and European society moved steadily into feudalism.

The establishment of the Saracenic Empire, reaching from the borders of India to the Pyrenees, proved to be a stimulating force rather than an impediment to civilization within its borders. But to the Western Europeans it was a severe shock. They were not included in this new melting pot of nations and were ranged against it—first defensively and later offensively—by a fierce religious animosity. They suffered from the rupture of communication lines which had been vital not only to the Romans but to the states which had preceded the Romans. They were denied access to what had always been the sustaining and nourishing centers, the great reserve areas of civilization. And to add distress to calamity, the Viking raids of the eighth and ninth centuries threw the populations facing on the North Sea and the Atlantic into confusion. In the long run, however, the forcing of the Europeans more completely upon their own resources impelled them to digest and utilize these resources more fully. Intimations of cultural progress were evident along with and in spite of the economic decline. The "Carolingian Renaissance" was a feeble affair, sponsored by an emperor who subdued the heathen Saxons after thirty-three years of fighting but who was never quite able to learn to write. Nevertheless, in its attempts to improve education, its search for literary talent, and its encouragement of scholarship it gave promise for the future.

Neither were the Later Middle Ages, inaugurated in a left-handed manner and following staggering reverses, a single and consistent entity. Their most obvious aspect was the feudal structure of society. But from the eleventh century on, trade began to revive, old cities and rapidly growing villages took on a bustling activity, and a middle class appeared. The eleventh, twelfth, and thirteenth centuries are known pre-eminently as the "Feudal Age." Yet it was then that an urban society came into being, representing only a minority of the population but aggressive and dynamic. The cities and their citizens could not be fitted into the feudal pattern, although ingenious attempts to do so were made by ecclesiastical and secular rulers. The majority of the people remained on the soil, the feudal nobility were at the height of their glory, but the towns had become centers not only of economic innovation but of political and cultural activity. It was under the stimulus of a widening prosperity and of the varied contacts incidental to the pursuit of commerce that a synthesis and coherent expression of medieval experience was finally achieved.

Slender Material Foundations

In attempting to evaluate the significance of the Middle Ages it is appropriate to raise the question as to what constituted their distinctive characteristics. It is often assumed that the medieval man was totally different from the modern—not only distinct but now happily extinct. Admittedly there were many respects in which his world was at decided variance with the present. In some cases, however, the peculiarity lies with us rather than with our medieval ancestors, and not in every instance can it be shown that the advantage is ours.

Obviously the physical conditions of medieval life were in striking contrast to those of the modern West. Luxuries were few and necessary articles were made by hand rather than by machinery. The machinery had not been invented, and science as the procreator of technological change was unknown. But this observation applies not only to medieval civilization but to all which had preceded it (with the partial exception of spasmodic scientific dabbling during the Hellenistic Age). In regard to tools, techniques, and the nature of the environment which man shapes for himself, the dividing point is not the end of the Middle Ages, nor even the scientific discoveries of the sixteenth and seventeenth centuries, but the Industrial Revolution of the late eighteenth and nineteenth centuries, which distinguishes the contemporary from all the previous conditions of mankind.

The medieval European methods applied to meeting the requirements of livelihood were typical of those found in pre-mechanical societies. In some instances they were more primitive, in others more advanced, than the average. Agriculture was notoriously inefficient—a regrettable circumstance inasmuch as it was by all odds the leading occupation. This deficiency, which retarded the growth of population and frequently led to famine, is explained largely by the unnatural attitude of the landowning class. In contrast to the Roman landlords, some of whom made a careful study of the science of agriculture, the feudal nobles evidenced not the slightest interest in the actual processes of cultivation, which they considered degrading. Among the primitive Germans farm labor had been a function of women, not of warrior freemen. After the conquests it was left in the hands of semi-servile tenants (although of course many Germans sank to that status—in every European country the dividing line between aristocracy and commoner, while a matter of birth and "blood," was not based on racial differences for any length of time). There are exceptions to every rule; but the typical noble, who might consider it an honor to hold the stirrup, pour the wine, or carve the meat for a higher ranking lord, would rather beg, steal, or starve than put his hand to the plow.

Also, the knightly owner of a manor, or of a whole county for that matter, had little to gain directly from increasing the productivity of the soil. From his free vassals, of noble blood like himself, he could demand only allegiance, honorable personal services, and occasional monetary contributions which were rigorously limited by the feudal contract. Most of his income was derived from his menial tenants, the villeins and serfs. But their value was chiefly in the labor which they rendered—so many days a week—on the lord's demesne, that portion of the manor which supplied his own table but which his high breeding forbade him from tilling in person. The tenants also had to make payments to their lord in money or commodities, classifiable as rents, taxes, fines, gifts, etc., numerous in extent and highly burdensome. But these vexatious assessments were gradually fixed by custom and on the whole did not vary greatly with the size or quality of the crops. Hence, as long as the villages remained isolated and the peasants remained ignorant and immersed in the traditional routine of the manor, there was little incentive to devise more efficient methods.

Toward the end of the Middle Ages improvements did come about, partly as a result of the efforts of the more diligent monastic foundations. Also, with the emergence of a money economy, there was a widespread tendency to commute the manorial services into cash payments. This benefited the tenants and jolted the landlords out of their complacency, as they discovered that their revenues were stationary (having been determined by long-established custom) while prices and the cost of living were steadily going up. When it became a matter of necessity, the estate owners turned with alacrity to the problem of how to increase the yield and profit from the land.

If agricultural methods were primitive, ingenuity and resourcefulness were revealed in other lines. The "arts of war," viewed from the standpoint of techniques rather than social consequences, were carried to a high point. The English long bow; the evolution of the castle from blockhouse to stone fortress; catapults and battering rams; and the fashioning of armor which was effective, flexible, and even ornamental indicate that medieval people did not lack inventiveness. Ordinary handicrafts were carried on in about the same way they had always been—by Greeks, Romans, Phoenicians, or Egyptians—since the New Stone Age. But a few specialized crafts, especially those which were essential to the perfection of ecclesiastical architecture, reached a pinnacle which has never been exceeded, before or since. The Romanesque and Gothic cathedrals were doubtless the embodiment of medieval ideals and the product of inspiration, but they could never have become a reality except for the superlative standards of workmanship which went into them. Even in its material effects the medieval achievement was hardly one to be regarded with contempt.

TOWARD A FREER SOCIETY

As for society at large, the prevailing arrangement was a hierarchy, a rigorous class system, incorporating and exalting the doctrine that men are by nature unequal (and, for the most part, unfree). What was worse, the stratification, and the privileges and burdens assigned to each group, were based not on talent but almost exclusively on the accident of birth. Against this arbitrary and irrational organization of human beings—obviously for the benefit of the minority at the top—much of the redemptive effort of modern times has had to be directed. To overthrow it revolutions have been launched, constitutions wrested from frightened monarchs, and society shaken to its roots. Yet it is true that the extension of the feudal pattern over most of Western Europe provided channels through which community sentiments could be formulated and common interests discovered. It gave coherence to the social organism at a time when disruptive tendencies threatened to tear everything apart. And it eventually provided the instruments which could be used by the victims of the system when they had reached the point of daring to hope for a better day.

The brutal aspects of feudalism stem from the distraught conditions during which it took form, from the fact that the organizers were armed fighting men while the organized were unarmed cultivators, and from the fact that the Roman institutions and formulas which were appropriated to rationalize the whole affair were the legacy of a distorted society in which the abject dependence of one man upon another was taken for granted. Considering their origins, it is remarkable to what an extent the feudal and manorial regimes were gradually modified, refined, and purged of some of their harshest features.

The medieval class system represents an improvement over that which had characterized Roman society of the Empire or of the Late Republic. It was simpler, more consistent, and more functional. Theoretically it was distinguished by three orders or "estates"—the clergy, the nobility, and the commoners. In reality, there were only two classes. (Until the resurrection of the cities brought the *bourgeoisie* into being. Theoretically this new group made no difference; actually it made all the difference in the world.) The higher clergy were recruited chiefly from the aristocracy; and in addition to their ecclesiastical functions—often vexatiously confused with them—they administered fiefs, received homage from vassals and themselves entered into vassalage to other nobles, lay or clerical. Conflicts there were, frequently bitter, between the Church and the feudal hierarchies; but so far as social distinction, privileges, and style of living went, the lords temporal and lords spiritual were ranged together, far above the common herd. On the other hand, the village priests were usually of villein birth and remained on about the same social plane as peasants. Their clerical ministrations were substituted for the normal duty of manual labor in the fields (thus reversing St. Benedict's axiom: "To work is to pray"). But though the cloth marked them as members of the "first estate," they did not share the grandeur or the prestige of the church magnates. Broadly speaking, between the eighth and twelfth centuries the social cleavage was between unprivileged, scantily provisioned, semi-servile folk who worked productively and the privileged, non-laboring aristocracy who issued commands.

Although the majority of the population was denied real freedom, out-and-out slavery became almost negligible. Freedom is a difficult quality to define. It is always limited, conditioned, and relevant to the modes of livelihood and the state of social development. In the Middle Ages no one was utterly free in the sense that he had no obligations to those above or below him in the interlocking chain of human relationships. Feudalism was, from the medieval viewpoint, an arrangement entered into by "free" men and entailing honorable services and mutual respect. But its requirements were complicated and exacting for both lord and vassal and highly resistant to willful caprice on the part of either. The peasants, of course, being serfs rather than vassals, were outside the pale of this honorable association. At the same time, their status was influenced by the force of feudal usage, sometimes in a protective way, aside from the consideration that because the serfs were valuable property it was against the lord's interests to abuse them too wantonly even if he had the right. The position gradually attained by the peasant class offers a refreshing example of how practice and experience may outrun legal definition. The "custom of the manor," originating no one knew how, hardened into a body of rules behind which the untutored and defenseless villein could stand up and resist the arbitrary demands of his lord. According to the law books the lord owned all the property and even the bodies of his serfs (did not *servus* mean *slave*?). According to fact he could demand from them only the traditional services and fees, which were comprehensive and troublesome enough, to be sure, but not unlimited. (Naturally, some lords took a cruel advantage of their position to bleed their dependents; but brutality and cruelty are known even in better societies.)

It is notable that, in almost every instance where there was an area of uncertainty, precedent and interpretation worked unobtrusively but irresistibly in favor of the tenant. The distinction between villein and serf—if there ever was any—disappeared during the Feudal Age, not because the villein had sunk in the scale but because the serf had come up to his level. Most of the villagers were not free in the legal sense, but they had a recognized right in their lands, they accumulated property which they could pass on to their heirs or sell, and some became actually prosperous. At the close of the Middle Ages the peasant populations of England, France, and the Low Countries, and in portions of Germany and Italy were far better off than they had been at the time of the genesis of feudalism or during the period of the Roman Empire.

In the stratified society of medieval Europe, based as it was on the assumption of human inequality, the concept of democracy had no place. This marks one of the gaps between medieval thinking and that of the present day, in which the democratic concept has been agitated so long that some people have even grown weary of it. Democracy is a daring concept which has been cherished only rarely in human societies. In the ancient world the Greeks were the only people who made much of it. Even among them it was confined to a few communities. In Athens at its best it was coupled with an arbitrary discrimination between the sexes, condoned slavery, and was soon tarnished by imperialistic ambitions. The Romans were so little attracted to the democratic idea that they abandoned it almost as soon as they had devised machinery with which to give it expression. Considering the background and general direction of medieval European society, it would be strange indeed if it had shown a democratic face.

Yet there is one exception to the rule which regarded class distinctions as fixed and unbridgeable, and the exception occurred in the most important of all medieval institutions—the Church. The Church was not organized on democratic principles any more than the State. The informal association of kindred spirits which had typified the early Christian communities, and their practice of electing their own officers had been shortly abandoned. As the Church appropriated the administrative system of the Roman state it assumed the form of a papal monarchy. Also, as churches and monasteries were endowed with lands, eventually to the point where they held an impressive fraction of the landed property in every country, ecclesiastical officials became enmeshed in the feudal system. They owned serfs; they granted and received fiefs. The Church *per se* did not become feudalized—thanks in large part to the belated enforcement of the rule of clerical celibacy which prevented church property from becoming hereditary. But the fact that churchmen quarreled with barons, kings, and emperors over the bounds of spiritual and temporal authority did not mean that they repudiated the principles of feudalism. They never missed an opportunity to use them when it was to their advantage. Far from preaching that all men have equal rights and equal responsibilities, the clergy put their blessing upon the hierarchical social structure which was the order of the day. If one were to judge solely on the basis of the sermons and teachings of the medieval clergy (a few iconoclastic spirits excepted), he would have to conclude that feudal institutions were the only truly Christian ones—just as slavery was Christian to many brethren in the American South before the Civil War, and as capitalism is the only Christian system according to most spokesmen of representative churches in the United States today.

Nevertheless, there was a democratic leaven within the nurture which the Church provided. The central message of Christianity has been frequently blurred, but at no time during the history of the Church, including the Middle Ages, has it been hidden entirely. The Church affirmed that all persons are equal in the sight of God, equally endowed with a soul, and that the opportunity of winning salvation is not a matter of social status. What was more significant from the practical standpoint, the Church, in contrast to the feudal governments, did not regard humble birth as a bar to promotion within its ranks. Although the great ecclesiastics were usually chosen from the noble families, it was possible for a commoner to be advanced to a position of authority if he had managed to be inducted into holy orders and had proven capable. The monasteries were frequently called upon to furnish leadership for the Church, particularly in times of crisis, and monasteries drew their recruits from every social stratum. Several of the popes were of lowly origin, proving that it was not utterly impossible for a man of the people to rise to a position which exalted him above dukes and kings. Hildebrand, who as Pope Gregory VII was one of the most colorful and famous medieval figures, is believed to have been the son either of a peasant or of a poor carpenter. Urban IV's father was a cobbler. The Church was not the apostle of democracy; but it did pierce the aristocratic shell of society in some very vital spots.

The arbitrary division of humanity into two unequal groups which prevailed in medieval Europe unintentionally prepared the way for the emergence of a freer society. Marxian theory was even more alien to medieval thought than the concept of democracy; but Marx's notion of the simplification of the class struggle through the polarization of society, which he predicted would reach a grand climax under the operation of the capitalist system, was illustrated to some extent in the preindustrial feudal era. Not that there was a class-conscious proletariat. There is little evidence of class conflict in the Marxian sense. Stratification of the community was almost universally accepted; and the Church, which tenderly nourished (and sometimes fleeced) every group and individual in turn, added the force of religious sanction to the arrangement. Revolts of the peasants, of which there were a number before the close of the Middle Ages, were protests against particular miseries, with limited objectives, rather than attempts to overthrow the social order. (The same qualification applies to the aspirations of the discontented French peasants even at the beginning of the great French Revolution.)

But long before the end of the Middle Ages the townsmen had become a force to reckon with. Many of the towns were overgrown manorial villages, and their inhabitants were largely of servile ancestry although they had won emancipation and their economic activities separated them sharply from the feudal regime. "Islands of freedom in a sea of serfdom," the towns recruited new members from runaway serfs, who, if they were able to elude their masters for the "year and a day" stipulated by the fugitive slave code of the period, could exchange the onerous routine of the manor for the more attractive life of an artisan or tradesman. Understandably but very foolishly, the jealous aristocracy refused to concede to the city folk the social recognition which their abilities and economic importance merited. In the eyes of the nobility these monied upstarts were still "third estate" —common fellows who had grown too big for their patched breeches. They were useful, even indispensable, in certain respects, but they were not to be admitted to the charmed circle of those born to rule. Consequently, even though the *bourgeoisie* had little sympathy for the peasants, as they were forced into opposition to the nobility they became inevitably an advance guard for the whole multitude of common people.

England constitutes something of an exception. Here the aristocracy, more enlightened than the average or more frightened by the steadily increasing power of the king, combined with the urban middle class to develop the instruments of parliamentary government. The result of this co-operation was, not the century of the common man, but the early end of absolute monarchy in England. Elsewhere in Western Europe, however—the process is most strikingly illustrated in France—the great nobles preferred to fight it out with the king and with one another without appealing to the common herd. The king therefore allied himself with the despised citizens, and through their help was able eventually to break the backs of the feudal rulers one after another. Since the king was left holding the field, the influence of the *bourgeoisie*, which had worked for limited government in England, promoted absolutism in France. However, even in France the people, as opposed to the magnates, had been brought into the play. And when, long after the Middle Ages, the last vestiges of feudalism were overthrown, even though this was a victory for the *bourgeoisie* and most of the immediate benefits were appropriated by them, the whole idea of class stratification had to be renounced formally and forever.

Thus the feudal society was eventually modified in the direction of according, however grudgingly and inadequately, greater opportunity to the persons at the bottom of the scale, upon whose exploitation the whole system had depended. It made possible the transition to a freer and more flexible society than had been known to the classical world. This is not to say that feudalism was a positive good. Nor does it mean that feudalism is a necessary stage in social evolution or that it was inevitable even in European development. But its history illustrates how institutions can be adapted progressively, sometimes acquiring a form and purpose very different from the original. Such elasticity is not infinite, and by the end of the Middle Ages feudal concepts had been stretched to the breaking point. Internal and external conditions were changing more rapidly than the old formulas could be accommodated to them. The attempt to discover new bonds of allegiance and sources of authority was by no means an automatic or painless process.

THE FEUDAL ANTIDOTE TO ABSOLUTISM

Besides being an economic and social arrangement, feudalism was a form of government. Its political aspect was the oddest of all because it seemed to be the repudiation of what is ordinarily understood by government. It originated under conditions close to anarchy, and it has been defined, somewhat inaccurately, as "organized anarchy." At the beginning it was a makeshift affair, fashioned amid the wreckage of the collapsing Carolingian state and while Viking raids were frightening the weak and unprotected into the arms of the strong. It was born of chaos, fear, and greed, and founded upon brute force.

Yet, very steadily, as feudalism spread over Northern and Western Europe, it took on a more regular pattern, adapting itself to the functions of peace as well as war. There was no such thing as a "feudal system," but in every region it became at least partially systematized, less capricious and unrestrained, and developed its own peculiar version of due process of law. Some feudal principalities, of course, were no better than a brigand's lair. But that the cumbersome and contradictory feudal machinery could be utilized to promote efficient government is illustrated by the case of medieval England. When William, Duke of Normandy, crossed the Channel in 1066 to become "the Conqueror," he found that England was behind France in the process of feudalization. Instead of nipping the plant in the bud, he brought it to full bloom and gave it a prominent place in his administrative system. Naturally it was the Norman, strongly centralized brand of feudalism which William imported, together with warriors and clerks, in his long-hulled boats. Building upon it as a foundation, his successors were able to establish, not an absolute monarchy, but an effective one. And the king's own feudal court became the "mother of courts and parliament" of the British nation.

The feudal concepts of government were vastly different from the modern ones. We have moved to the opposite extreme from the man of the Middle Ages in this respect. We think of power as properly concentrated in a permanent and impersonal body. He thought of it as apportioned among particular dignitaries, varying with their rank and holdings, and transferable, never irrevocably in one place. Instead of an abstract loyalty to the state, his concern was the concrete personal loyalties binding together vassal and lord, hinging upon a solemn engagement in which one swore to become another's "man," "against all persons who may live or die." We conceive of law as the enactments of public authority, apparently illimitable in quantity as the legislative wheels grind on and on. He regarded law as steadfast, something which is not made but discovered, actually the crystallization of custom but believed to be "found at the throne of God." Today we observe—with justifiable misgivings—the enlargement of the sphere of government as more and more private functions pass under its control or into its hands altogether. There may be some slight comfort in recollecting that once the shoe was on the other foot. In the Feudal Age the normal and necessary public functions were in private hands. Instead of the government being "in business," government was the business of the great property owners (including the lords of the Church). Neither of these extremes seems to be a very good arrangement, but it becomes increasingly difficult to know where to draw the line between the two spheres of activity. The Feudal Age's answer to the problem was rough and direct. Those who had the power kept it—as long as they could. Usually it was sufficient to show that they had inherited the right to exercise it, that it had resided in their family since the time "beyond which the memory of man does not run." Even the historical argument might be dispensed with, as in the case of the earl who dared say to King Edward I, the great "English Justinian": "My warrant is my sword. "

The feudal barons, however, were not free to do just as they pleased. It was not an age of unrestricted private enterprise on the part of those whose property carried with it the right to govern. One of the outstanding characteristics of medieval political concepts was their emphasis upon the limited character of government. The underlying assumption was that none but a limited type of government was possible. In feudal theory, and largely in fact, there was no absolute ruler. Every wielder of authority was hedged about by restrictions. He was bound by his obligations not only to those above him but to those beneath him. He was subjected to the weight of custom, of precedent, of what had been done before or was believed to have been done; he was compelled to reckon with the sense of the community. Typically the community whose collective judgment he had to respect was very small, a handful of aristocrats. But the principle was stoutly upheld. Usually the feudal lord was a vassal at the same time; his interests were ambivalent and required the setting up of rules of fair play. If he oppressed his vassals he would get little support in the event that his own overlord bore down too heavily upon him. And if the lord oppressed, harried, and abused the interests of his vassals they would league against him, demanding judgment in the lord's court, which was inevitably composed of themselves. If he still refused to do them justice, they would—combining business with pleasure—take up arms and fight him.

Even the king, at the top of the social and political pyramid, did not stand outside of the system. He was caught in the same contractual net. If he did not become the vassal of another man to obtain some coveted piece of land (and kings sometimes did this without staining the royal escutcheon), it was contended that, since every fief must be held of a lord, the king held his realm of God. And because God's judgments were not always clearly and speedily rendered, the king's vassals were quite willing to take matters into their own hands. In England, where feudal devices had been deliberately introduced by the king for his own convenience, their potentiality for checking tyranny soon began to be perceived. When the barons at Runnymede coerced King John into signing Magna Charta, they were not staging a revolution. They were holding the king to an acknowledgment of their rights and of his obligations as a feudal suzerain. At the end of the Charter, after a list of some sixty grievances which John promises to attend to, a guarantee is inserted. The king solemnly pledges that if he should break his word in the future and fail to satisfy a grievance committee of twenty-five barons, then "the whole community of the country" has permission to "distress and injure us in every way they can" until the wrong is righted. After the correction has been made they are requested to "devote themselves to us as they did before." This may have been hypocrisy on the king's part, but it was not comedy; neither was it anarchy. It was a statement of feudal principles of government.

The medieval Church, in spite of its demands for unswerving allegiance, on the whole upheld the principle of limited government. The principle served as a useful lever in putting restraint upon the Church's natural rivals, the secular rulers. The popes naturally claimed the right to discipline princes as well as any other Christian, cleric or lay, even to the point of dissolving a recalcitrant ruler's subjects from allegiance to him. But however extravagant and arrogant were the assertions of some ecclesiastical spokesmen, the Church was never in a position to establish a complete theocracy over Europe, even if it harbored the design. Until the monarchies became sufficiently modern to dare to defy God and the Devil, the competition of clerical authority and the deep hold which the Church had upon all classes of the people exerted a moderating influence upon them.

The insistence that sovereign power is limited and revocable rather than absolute has not been the most common one among the higher civilizations. It stands in sharp contrast to the theocracies of the ancient Near East, to the Roman concept of imperium which culminated in tyranny, to the European despotisms of the sixteenth, seventeenth, and eighteenth centuries, and to the totalitarianisms of the twentieth century. On the other hand it was a cardinal principle of the movements for social emancipation which stemmed from the French Revolution and reached a climax in the nineteenth century. Seemingly the Middle Ages would be a strange place to look for *liberal* ideas, but they did prefigure and contribute the germs of several of them. The English champions of the rights of the subject and the powers of Parliament between Magna Charta and the revolution which dethroned Charles I drew heavily (sometimes more heavily than the facts warranted) upon medieval feudal principles. The "law of nature," a fetish of eighteenth-century liberals, was given particular prominence in the teaching of St. Thomas Aquinas and other Scholastic thinkers.

Although there were enlightened and humane elements behind the rough mien of the feudal state, democracy was not the basis of medieval government any more than it was of society. The wholesale exclusion of the great majority of the population from any share in determining public policy was, from the modern point of view, not only unjust but flagrantly inefficient, as proven by the shabby record of many feudal suzerainties and the fatuous arrogance of the great lords. Certainly there was a fair proportion of stupidity among the feudal classes; there has been among those entrusted with government in every age, no matter how they are selected. Whether the feudal governments were better or worse than the average could be debated. At least they recognized the principle—still valid—that those who are permitted to govern should be trained for it. The feudal heirs were given careful training for their duties as vassals and suzerains, which were the operating political principles according to the lights of that day.

Minority rule is typical, majority rule the exception among human societies. Although the dominant medieval belief was that society is naturally hierarchical, every class had its acknowledged function and even a certain guarantee of security. The feudal practice of excluding the uneducated toilers from political responsibility was less reprehensible than the democratic pretense which the Romans labored under for so long. Even genuine and sincere modern democracies have learned—or should have learned —that the mere enfranchisement of the whole population does not automatically bring them happiness, solve the state's problems, or ensure that wisdom will be enthroned in office. If the voters are unenlightened and indifferent, if the exercise of their citizenship is confined to indicating every four years a preference between two professional political machines, then a collective judgment is neither formulated nor carried into effect. Essential as it is for citizens of a free community to prize their liberties and discharge their responsibilities, there is something pathetic in the widespread assumption that they can be most surely inspired to this high calling by the slogan: "Vote as you please, only vote!" The ballot box is not the temple of democracy—it is only the door to it; and a door permits passage in either direction.

The frankly undemocratic feudal government, while defective in conception, full of contradictions, and often badly executed, was fundamentally honest in its professions. Actually its performance was a little better than its promise, which is a rarity among governments.

THE CLASH OF ARMS

Much stress has been placed upon the warlike character of medieval society. Whether or not it should be considered especially warlike depends upon what you are comparing it with and upon your definition of war. Certainly it was profuse with military trappings and paraphernalia. The leaders of society were of knightly rank, a fraternity of fighting men, who were schooled from early boyhood to handle weapons and took pride and delight in the skill which they acquired. Conflicts between these knights were frequent, and practice bouts for sport and entertainment could be arranged during a dull season. The whole feudal relationship was based upon the acceptance of physical force as a normal regulative agency, and the prime obligation of a vassal to his lord was to furnish him with the service of so many mounted knights for so many days a year. Lord and vassal alike regarded his sword as the ultimate guarantor of his privileges.

It is easy, however, to exaggerate the effect of these factors upon community life during the Middle Ages. First of all, the fighting nobility were a small minority of the population. Instead of drafting the peasants to wage their battles for them (a possibility but very exceptional) they jealously kept the villein class from access to the skill and the equipment which would make them of much value in chivalrous warfare. Military activity was a matter for experts, not just in its planning and direction but in its actual execution. Of course the peasants sometimes suffered from having their fields ridden over or their crops burned, but the common people were not involved in the feudal combats one tenth as much as they have been in the wars of the modern period. (There are exceptions to this toward the end of the Middle Ages, but these are associated with the development of national armies under the kings and with the decline of the feudal regime.)

Secondly, feudal battles, while they could be gruesome enough, were not ordinarily very devastating. The medieval chroniclers who relate the slaying of thousands in a single encounter are known to be capable of exaggeration. Even if their figures were accepted, the casualty rate would seem extremely low by modern standards. The concept of "total war" (except perhaps against the infidel) would have been incomprehensible to the feudal knight. The object of combat was not to exterminate your opponent but to induce him to yield a point or two in some issue under dispute, such as the title to or services due from a particular fief. The heavily armored knight was a sort of floating fortress, difficult to kill before the days of gunpowder, although if he were knocked off his horse he might be rendered helpless. Also, because of the possibility of ransom, a live captive knight was more valuable than a corpse on the field.

In the third place, stronger and stronger influences were brought to bear to regulate and restrict the scope of feudal combat. The more powerful suzerains forbade, so far as they could, private brawls among their vassals, although few were as successful as the English kings in insisting that the vassals' obligation to military service meant service in the army of the king, the supreme overlord. An even more potent restraining factor was the Church. Some churchmen, it is true, showed warlike inclinations—there is the example of the bishop who wielded a huge club because canon law forbade him to shed blood. Nevertheless, the Church carried on an unrelenting campaign, usually a flank rather than frontal attack, to mitigate the roughness of the times. It propagated the ideal of the "Christian knight," who would protect the weak and defend the right—an overly optimistic undertaking, perhaps, but as successful as most attempts to refine and rationalize violence have been. More to the point were the restrictions which the Church formulated somewhat in the nature of game laws, which prescribed the quarry and limited the slaughtering season. The "Peace of God" was supposed to give immunity from attack to peasants, merchants, clerics, and other unarmed persons. The "Truce of God," which made fighting immoral over the week end and on certain holy days, was extended to cover half of each week and whole stretches of the year. If it could have been enforced it would have so interrupted the feudal conflicts as to make them impracticable. Unfortunately, however, the Church made its own contribution to the martial spirit by inciting the Crusades and, in the wake of the fanaticism which they engendered, the popes began to explore the possibilities of extending their own territories by force of arms under the banner of religion.

Members of twentieth-century society are ill-advised to reproach the Middle Ages with being warlike. Before the conflicts which we unleash, even in periods of "peace," the petty jousting of that era pales into insignificance. It would take a hundred years of medieval warfare to equal the devastation which we can encompass in a few weeks—perhaps days. There is a curious reversal of theory and practice between then and now. Feudal society originated in force and embraced warfare as a legitimate means of settling disputes. But the technique and rules of combat were carefully stipulated and its intensity circumscribed. Our modern Western societies are founded upon free consent and their objectives are peaceful. War we declare to be abnormal and reprehensible. Solemnly we "outlaw" war, and then proceed to devote the bulk of our resources to making it more destructive. Contemporary holocausts engage whole populations, they demand the services of the entire citizen body. The medieval belief was that each class should hold to its own specific function. There were the peasants to toil, the nobles to fight (and govern), and the clergy to pray (and govern). In that age the right to fight carried with it the power to govern. Now the right to govern carries with it the power to make other people fight.

THE COSMIC VIEW

Like every civilization which is worthy of the name, the medieval finally included a view of man, of society, and of the cosmos. The medieval conception of the cosmos, against the picture presented by modern science, seems childish, naïve, and oppressively restricted. The universe was a very small affair and the earth was its center—two egregious errors to start with, to which were joined false notions of the composition, size, and movements of the heavenly bodies. Actually this cosmology was not entirely invented by the people of the Middle Ages. Its essential features had been bequeathed by the Hellenistic astronomer Ptolemy of Alexandria, a rather mediocre representative of a period in which scientific curiosity was active. Contrary to a tradition which still persists, the educated minority during the Later Middle Ages believed that the earth was round; although they thought of it as stationary, an axle on which the universe revolves not by the laws of gravity and inertia but by the compulsion of divinely instituted forces.

Every view of the universe which man is capable of attaining is necessarily compounded out of traditional beliefs, convictions, and aspirations, plus sense experience. Modern cosmologies are no exception. Their chief difference is that the sense experience now utilized includes an enormous mass of data collected by artificial instruments which magnify incalculably the range and intensity of perception. Also these continually accumulating data are subjected to critical analysis, without which, indeed, they would be not only overwhelming but meaningless. Nevertheless, the final interpretation of the observed phenomena and the explanation of their interrelationship are pure inference. We cannot know what the universe really *is*, but only what it *appears* to be at the moment in the light of our experience. While we have confidence in the expert conjectures of the scientist, we cannot *see* an electron any more than the medieval man could see the angel which he thought was constantly watching over him. Actually modern scientific discovery yields not one but many, sometimes contradictory, interpretations of the nature of reality. The descriptions change repeatedly. According to Newtonian physics matter and energy were distinct entities and the universe was infinite in extent. Now mass and motion are believed to be relative, varying manifestations of the same thing (if there still is a thing), and space is not infinite but curves back upon itself.

Because every cosmic view is only tentative, its worth is to be found largely in the response which it evokes and the services to which it can be put. Modern scientific conceptions have been tremendously valuable in widening man's perspective, jarring him out of a self-centered complacency, and giving him incentive to push the frontiers of discovery further. At the same time, however, they have made his orientation appear uncertain. They have imparted a disquieting feeling that man is lost in a great congeries of matter of which he is an infinitesimal and perhaps ephemeral particle.

The world of the Middle Ages was more solid and firmly grounded and interlocked at all points with the crises of human existence. Hell was a real place, located in the bowels of the earth. Heaven was established just beyond the orbit of the farthest and most rarefied stars. The whole tightly bound and perfectly circular creation was a magnificent theater, equipped with sumptuous lighting and sound effects, on which a divine drama was being enacted with man as the central protagonist. Of course there was also the Devil, a very lively character and prominent in his villainous role. He could lie in wait at every corner to trap the unwary, and he appeared at times to be more resourceful and efficient than Providence. But although the rules under which he operated were exceedingly generous, he was not permitted to violate them; and no drama is very exciting in which virtue triumphs too easily.

The medieval world view, tinctured as it was by the "Christian Epic," may have been a romantic fancy, but it cannot be said that it lacked purpose. To the medieval thinker the universe was full of purpose, quite clear-cut and rich in implications for human motivation. The modern scientific observer, who can see so much farther, so much more accurately, and so much more critically, is not so sure that the universe has any purpose or meaning at all. It is a matter of speculation, if not among theologians, at least among philosophers, and can be treated as a subject for debate in the pages of a genteel periodical. The question may be of no concern to the scientist as such. But if the universe is held to be without purpose in its relationship to living organisms, then the question of whether or not life has meaning becomes a matter of purely individual preference.

Although the medieval cosmic scheme was inadequate, distorted, and bound to yield before the advance of knowledge, it served as the framework for some impressive outpourings of the human imagination. Standing squarely on the basic medieval assumptions, St. Thomas Aquinas, with the aid of Aristotle and other pagan and Christian worthies, surveyed the whole panorama of man and society, pronounced it good, and explained through intricate syllogisms how it could be made even better. Dante, on the threshold of a new age, found the quaint medieval astronomy an appropriate backdrop for one of the most beautiful and inspiring poems in any modern language. The newer cosmogonies have evoked a less reassuring response in the field of letters, where man is frequently depicted as a chance aggregate of atoms, swerving aimlessly through his flickering day, helpless against "the cruel unreason of the cosmic tyranny."

The medieval view of man and human nature has often been misrepresented. As a matter of fact it changed greatly in the course of the Middle Ages, becoming mellower and more optimistic. The stark Augustinian dogma of the utter depravity of mortal flesh which had prevailed during the Dark Ages was never quite abandoned, but emphasis shifted to the more redeeming—or redeemable—traits of the species. St. Thomas held that the divine spark which strengthens the reason and engenders a desire for righteousness in every man could never be completely extinguished even in the most depraved. Although the life to come was considered of paramount importance, this life was found to be good also. The great Scholastics of the twelfth and thirteenth centuries taught that political and social institutions were intended to promote the happiness of their members rather than being a punishment for their wickedness. The interpretation of man which marked the High Middle Ages, humanistic and reasoned as it was, differed materially both from that of the Dark Ages and from that of recent times. It was not individualistic nor equalitarian. The individual was expected to function—and render useful service—as a member of his order, guild, or corporate body. But it was not a cynical interpretation. The typical exponents of medieval thought would never have approved the modern tendency toward depersonalization which is carried to the nth degree in the totalitarian states but is evident in the whole of society: the tendency to treat all human life as of equal—but very little—value.

THE FUNCTION OF RELIGION

One common assumption regarding the Middle Ages which calls for examination is that expressed in such terms as "otherworldly," and the "Age of Faith." Was the medieval a distinctively religious civilization? The question is, in itself, a commentary upon the predilections of the era in which it is raised. The cultural and social norms of the contemporary Western world are so vehemently secular that the placing of any stress upon nonmaterial values is apt to seem unrealistic and "otherworldly." Actually the great majority of civilizations have been "religious," in the sense that their direction and character were influenced by assumptions as to the relationship between man and the universe, the distinction between good and evil, and the origin and meaning of life. Even the Greeks, this-worldly humanists as they were, reckoned the gods as interested observers and participants in human affairs and assigned them an important role in their civic projects. Whether a culture so predominantly secular as ours—one which substitutes science for worship and sees its highest fulfillment in the industrialization of the earth's population—can long survive remains to be seen. The evidence of history, while not decisive, is hardly encouraging. Certainly the mere retention of religious forms or the presence of spiritual yearnings do not guarantee survival. Most civilizations have disintegrated eventually whether they were highly religious or not. But almost always the disintegration has been accompanied by a weakening of or loss of confidence in spiritual incentives.

The term "Age of Faith" as applied to the Middle Ages is inaccurate and misleading. The faith of the Early Middle Ages is better described as credulity, fed on ignorance and superstition, and typified by the easy acceptance of chance bits of undigested dogma. On the other hand, the Later Middle Ages saw not only a great increase in knowledge but a quickening of intellectual curiosity and a renewal of confidence in human capacity. If there were some magnificent expressions of faith in God and His universe, there was also quite a lively faith in man. The faith of the centuries which witnessed the high tide of Scholastic philosophy was one which warmly embraced reason.

Neither is it true that medieval people were uninterested in the things of this world. They had, to be sure, inherited the doctrine that the world and the flesh are corrupt and that the highest state to which man can aspire depends upon emancipation from his physical appetites. But the full implications of this ascetic ideal they left to the "religious"—that is, to professionals, especially the monks and nuns. The monastic institutions were not erratic aberrations. They were highly utilitarian in the medieval culture complex, even aside from the concrete services which they performed. Their inmates could (although they didn't always) devote their lives to sacrifice, unselfish toil, and prayerful contemplation—being honored for their example and atoning vicariously for the worldliness of their fellows—while the rest of society went about its business.

The generally poor standard of living which prevailed during the Middle Ages was not necessarily an example of what some antimaterialist reformers mean by "spiritual poverty." Ordinary conveniences, even sanitary precautions were lacking; houses were usually either hovels or cheerless fortresses, the resources of the greatest aristocrat could command only a fraction of the items which are now considered necessities. But while the Athenians of the Golden Age may have chosen the simple life from preference, the paucity of medieval living standards was more the result of ignorance than of voluntary self-denial. Material possessions, such as were procurable, were prized; gluttony and avarice were sins as perilous to medieval moralists as to those of any other period. And when, with the revival of commerce, the towns became prosperous, there was abundant interest in the commodities which money can buy, even if few had money with which to buy them.

The economic activity of the towns, in its conduct and organization, reflected the general medieval assumptions, influenced as they were by religious teachings. The merchant and craft guilds emphasized the interdependence of their members, who were bound to co-operate for their mutual advantage, upholding requisite standards of workmanship, and buying and selling in accordance with fixed regulations. The collectivism of the guilds and the economic theories to which they adhered present some rather sharp contrasts to modern business ethics; but perhaps too much emphasis has been placed upon their seemingly idealistic character. Typical were the doctrine of the "just price" –providing a moderate reward for services rendered rather than the highest possible profit—and antipathy to any monopoly which would benefit the individual at the expense of his fellows. If such ideas seem naïve or self-effacing, perhaps it is the modern view which is out of focus. Maybe it is not unnatural to consider the welfare of the community as more desirable than the immediate advantage of the individual. Today a regime of unlimited competition and unrestricted private enterprise no longer seems either natural or desirable, even in industrial communities which were nourished in a tradition of *laissez faire*. Businessmen, and corporations large and small, usually expend considerable effort in attempting at least to make people believe that they are primarily interested in rendering a public service and only secondarily concerned with profits. The medieval businessmen made less fuss about it. Nor did they wait for the government to step in and control them. The guilds regulated themselves for several centuries quite intelligently, and in such a way that they minimized industrial strife and promoted civic improvement. They did not stand in an inimical relation either to the public or to the government. (Or to the laboring class as such, because the typical guildsman was both a laborer and a capitalist—a sensible arrangement—until the growth of large specialized industries at the end of the Middle Ages wrecked the whole guild system and tended to drive the employers and the laborers into separate camps.) Very often, in fact, the guild or a federation of guilds constituted the town government, just as the warrior nobles constituted the feudal governments.

The exercise of salutary restraint, however, does not mean that the medieval guilds were primarily philanthropic organizations or that they were not intended to promote the economic welfare of their members. The merchants were by no means monks. They welcomed the rewards of commercial enterprise, and they were quick to recognize the strength which the accumulation of capital brought to their class. Although in the Late Middle Ages society was still feudal in structure and outlook, the tradesmen became increasingly prosperous and powerful. Their wealth was exceeded only by that of the richest nobles and kings—whose assets were for the most part not liquid—and by that of the Church. Probably this medieval middle class was better off economically in relation to the rest of society than is its counterpart in the industrial age. Today the amount of wealth to be reckoned with is, of course, enormously greater. But the skilled artisans, small businessmen and other "petty *bourgeoisie*"—to which groups the medieval traders and manufacturers corresponded most nearly—do not command as large a share of the total wealth of the community as did the guildsmen in their heyday. The proof is seen in the remarkable impact which the townsmen made upon their aristocratic contemporaries. They were able to purchase exemption from many annoying impositions and humiliations, and they were frequently granted municipal charters which accorded them the right of self-government. They could buy their way into the favor of kings, who might protect them against abuse from the nobles or help them secure commercial treaties in foreign lands. Some even bought their way up into the ranks of the nobility and assumed the adornments of gentility. In the Middle Ages as in other eras, wealth was power.

It is well known that the medieval Church officially took a dim view of moneylending as an occupation. Usury, which might be highly profitable when interest rates were not fixed by law, was branded as a sin. This attitude, however, was less the result of an otherworldly mentality than of practical circumstances. Until industry and commerce began to burgeon there was little demand for capital to invest in genuinely productive enterprises and there were no great reservoirs of capital to lend. So long as borrowing was exceptional, a resort of the improvident aristocracy, it was convenient to leave moneylending in the hands of the Jews. Thus no Christian would endanger his soul (the Jews were supposed to have already lost theirs), and it was easier to repudiate an obligation to an infidel than to a fellow Christian. The arrangement was satisfactory to everyone except the Jews; and even they often did fairly well, considering the handicaps under which they worked. When the expanding economic enterprises of the towns made the contracting of loans a normal adjunct of business, the whole picture changed. The refusal of the Church to remove its ban on "usury" aroused the resentment of the burghers, but it did not stop them from developing and using the new financial devices. Moreover, the Church itself had begun to employ its reserves of wealth for banking activities on a grandly profitable scale.

Thus, if religion means something more than acceptance of a creed and submission to the authority of a church, it is inaccurate to assert that medieval society was predominantly and abnormally religious. The mass of peasants would have to be excluded from such a category. They were necessarily of the earth, earthy. In the eyes of many nobles they were no better than highly useful but offensively smelling animals; and the Church found it necessary to keep reminding the nobility that their peasants actually possessed souls. As for the feudal nobles, no one would argue that they were, by and large, shining examples of the life of the spirit. The townsmen were perhaps remarkable in that they honored religious teachings to some extent in their pursuit of a livelihood, but their activities were definitely preparing the way for a more secular culture. That leaves the clergy, an influential and impressive group, to be sure. But churchmen became deeply implicated in such worldly matters as feudal quarrels, political ambitions, and high finance. The Church was so liable to corruption that reform movements for its purification had to be launched again and again.

Yet it is true that medieval civilization was religious in its basic convictions and aspirations. The majority of people acknowledged, when hard pressed, that the highest values were nonmaterial, abiding, and independent of the accidents of fortune. They agreed that society and its institutions rested upon divine ordinance and that their sanction lay not in force or even utility but in consonance with universal laws inherent in the mind of

God. Medieval people did not by any means act upon these convictions at all times. Their fault was not in being too spiritual but in not being spiritual enough. However, they held in high regard those individuals who did mold their lives in accordance with the ideal. The Middle Ages were the only time in the history of the West in which sainthood was a recognized vocation for live men and women. There have been saintly persons in every age. They appear even in our own; and they may be admired and marveled at, or written about. In the Middle Ages they were frequently allotted not only respect but positions of influence and authority, a procedure which would seem to us impractical and dangerous. We might knowingly choose for public office a time-server or even a rogue—but never a saint. To find a parallel to the medieval practice, one would have to turn to India and the Far East.

THE STUFF THAT DREAMS ARE MADE OF

The art of a people is always an index of its motivating interests and beliefs. It may reflect a rapport with nature, the pride of conquest, delight in human creative power, or other traits of national character. Whether the techniques are primitive or advanced, the aesthetic manifestations of a society cannot fail to convey some sense of the relationship between its members and their environment, of their feeling as to where they belong or where they are going. (If they have no sense of belonging and no idea that they are going anywhere, this, too, will appear in their art—as some critics are unkind enough to say it does in the art of the present.)

Medieval art was, on the whole, religious. This in itself, however, doesn't describe it very exactly, because the same is true in a broad sense of the art of most civilizations. More specifically, the typical works of the Middle Ages suggest community effort and community sharing in the endeavors which were chiefly prized. Architecture, the most highly developed art form, invited the assistance of a large number of workmen both skilled and unskilled, and its results could be enjoyed not only by many individuals but by many generations. Humility is another characteristic to be distinguished. Much of even the best work is anonymous. Effectiveness of display is not a prime consideration. Many beautifully illuminated manuscripts were prepared as acts of pious devotion in the monasteries and not intended for the public eye at all. Pervading medieval art is an awareness of that which is greater than man, of that which lies above and beyond his grasp. Not that it portrays a spirit of despair or of contempt for the human. There is warm sympathy and playful, even boisterous, humor. But the outreaching motif is prominent. All of these qualities attained their consummation and most complete expression in the Romanesque, and especially the Gothic, cathedrals.

Various and conflicting have been the judgments rendered upon these most characteristic and obtrusive monuments of medieval culture. The architectural style itself has been in and out of favor in different epochs. Considering the fact that tastes are bound to change, the Gothic has made a good showing. It has been utilized very scrupulously in some of the most ambitious ecclesiastical projects in the United States, such as the Washington Cathedral and the Cathedral of St. John the Divine in New York; and university campuses have amply ensured its perpetuation. But Gothic architecture cannot be for our society, as it was for the late medieval, an expression of its central interests and concerns.

The function of the medieval cathedrals has often been underestimated. In addition to being places of worship and for the social services of the Church, they furthered a variety of useful ends. They brought all artistic faculties into one focus, combining the appeal of form, line, color, and sound. On the practical side, their construction provided employment, elicited the highest talents of craftsmen, and aroused civic enthusiasm. The rivalry between cities as each one strove to produce the most magnificent cathedral (plus smaller churches, chapels, guildhalls, etc.) was comparable to that sponsored by the civic "boosters" of modern urban communities, although directed to somewhat different objectives.

Still, it could hardly be said that the cathedrals were essentially utilitarian (unless one were to accept the medieval thesis that the chief end of man is to glorify God). It may even seem that they were a wasteful extravagance—that it was wrong to pour so much energy into these tremendous stone structures, full of unusable space, with spires and buttresses reaching heavenward, while squalor lay on the ground beneath them. Remembering the narrow filthy streets and crowded, unsanitary, and highly inflammable houses in which the majority of the townspeople lived, one is tempted to reproach them for not having cleaned up their cities before they launched these grandiose projects. Surely, here was a confusion of values.

A notable feature of every civilization which advances above the primitive level is that it generates a store of surplus energy beyond what is required to supply the immediate physical needs of the group. (Not that the physical needs of a population have ever been adequately met; but the accepted definition of what constitutes their fulfillment has thus far always stopped short of exhausting the productivity of labor.) To put it another way, every civilization produces leisure as a by-product—at least for some of its members—and it is always a question how best to employ this leisure. The superfluous products of any culture—which may seem of supreme importance to its adherents as the embodiment of their higher capacities and aspirations—often will be looked upon as wasteful, frivolous, or futile by the representatives of a different culture. Neolithic peoples, for reasons which are now obscure, strained their backs to arrange gigantic stones in geometrical patterns. The Egyptians devoted hundreds of thousands of man-hours to erecting pyramids in which to bury their Pharaohs. The medieval Europeans preferred to build cathedrals.

The industrial societies of the present day have at their command an infinitely greater supply of surplus energy than any which preceded them, but the uses to which they devote this surplus might not be entirely approved by the people of less favored eras. Undeniably, more has been done in recent times than ever before to ameliorate and elevate the physical conditions of existence, even for the least fortunate members of society. But the real test comes in the area which lies beyond the bread-and-butter items, in the realm of the other things which man lives by. In this region the modern preference seems to run toward the mobile and the expendable. The accent is upon speed in production, and in dissolution, of the product. Contemporary man does not covet anything as permanent as a pyramid or as a cathedral. Some medieval churches were in process of construction for several centuries; it would be impossible to calculate their monetary cost. With modern engineering facilities one of these edifices could be duplicated in a few years' time—but the result would not be a Chartres or a Reims. On the other hand, a jet-bomber, which can be produced on an assembly line for $5,000,000 or so, could destroy any number of cathedrals and be itself destroyed, all in a few hours.

Because contemporary man has such gigantic resources at his disposal, perhaps he can afford waste on a colossal scale. If he can destroy faster he can also rebuild faster, and better, than his predecessors. In spite of his destructive bent he is continually discovering new possibilities for improving at least the external condition of society. Still, it is the preference shown in the distribution of his surplus which needs to be carefully examined. For where the treasure is, there will the heart be also.

THE PROBLEM OF LEARNING

In spite of the great changes in cultural climate which have taken place during the last five hundred years, the Later Middle Ages laid the groundwork for many conspicuous features of the modern Western era. One of their most significant and direct contributions was the development of institutions of higher learning. Although educational objectives have changed profoundly, our modern colleges and universities are the direct descendants—in some cases the still living bodies—of the Western European universities which reached a flourishing state in the twelfth and thirteenth centuries. These universities represented a new departure, quite different from anything that had been known to antiquity. Typically they were not state schools, although they served the public interest. Most of them were the outgrowth of the instructional facilities which the Church had established for the training of its own officers under the jurisdiction of the bishop of a diocese. Thus their origin was in the lap of the Church, but they ceased to be purely ecclesiastical in character as the numbers of students increased and the subjects of study were broadened to include all the intellectual interests of the day.

In spite of the authoritarian administrative system of the Church, and in spite of the jurisdictional claims of kings, the universities acquired in practice a large degree of independence in regard to their government, methods of instruction, and academic standards. Their members gave impetus to the principle of academic freedom, even if they did not define the principle or perceive all of its implications. Freedom of thought for the *individual*, especially if it contradicted authority, was not encouraged (neither is it in many modern educational institutions); but the faculties insisted successfully on the right to formulate their curricula and explore areas which presented a challenge. The climax and supreme test of this came when, as a result of contact with the Saracens during the time of the Crusades, the writings of Moslem philosophers and translations of Aristotle began to circulate in Western Europe. The outcry raised against the peril of heathen and heretical books was of no avail. Scholars, including churchmen, turned eagerly to the new sources, and allowed the stimulation which they received to enliven their own teaching and writing. In the High Middle Ages the dry bones of the "seven liberal arts" which had been inherited from the Dark Ages were given the flesh of classical study, a growing interest in geography and the natural world, rational attitudes and scientific observations appropriated from the Saracens, and a maturely critical approach to theology itself, the "Queen of the Sciences."

It is unnecessary to emphasize the fact that the medieval universities set the pattern for institutions of higher learning which has persisted to the present. The academic costume; the degrees granted; such common terms as *university, college, faculty, chancellor, dean;* the fundamental distinction between the basic arts course and graduate or professional schools—all of these are visible links between the present and the past. But it is often assumed that the similarities are only in externals, and that within the archaic shell a totally different product has been devised.

The changes in subject matter, emphasis, and techniques of instruction which have come about since the Middle Ages are indeed sweeping. The most striking contrasts are in the physical equipment of the universities, with their laboratories, libraries, lecture halls, seminar rooms—to say nothing of stadiums and field houses. Methods of instruction are not so utterly different as is commonly supposed. Some modern college students are never disabused of the notion that learning is a process of memorizing, and some medieval students were encouraged to think for themselves. How best to train a student to think, and what is the most desirable kind of knowledge for him to acquire and think about are questions which have never been settled. They were controversial issues in medieval times and they still are being debated. Admittedly, every educational system falls short of its purpose, which is to enrich the living capacities of the coming generation by acquainting them with their cultural heritage and to provide society with abler, more responsible, and more forward-looking leadership. Every educational system is caught between conflicting pressures. It must serve Caesar, and God, and Mammon. It is apt to be paralyzed between a consciousness of the need for change, on the one hand, and the weight of tradition or fear of change, on the other. It would be hard to determine whether the medieval universities were more, or less, adequate to the needs of their day than are the modern universities to the needs of ours. Modern society does not seem to be suffering from a surfeit of intelligent leadership in spite of the relatively large enrollment in our collegiate institutions. The impact of a great teacher, however, is pretty much the same in any age. It transcends the limits of prescribed method and of material facilities, whether they comprise a splendidly equipped laboratory or a row of benches. And the medieval universities did produce a number of great teachers, devoted scholars, and vigorous writers, who awakened the imagination of their students and widened the horizons of thought among their contemporaries. Perhaps this is the most that can be expected of the academic profession.

European Climax: The Later Middle Ages

More important than symbolism, terminology, and quaint customs, the medieval universities bequeathed the conviction that education should be of the whole man—that is, of the whole mind (physical education was undoubtedly neglected). They were champions of what is now called—and with historic justice—the *liberal* point of view. The basic course of instruction was in the liberal arts curriculum, which a student had to complete before he could enter the graduate disciplines of law, medicine, or theology. Thus, although many young men attended the universities with no intention of qualifying for either the priesthood or the other professions, they were not given vocational training. The mastery of a craft could be acquired through apprenticeship in a guild. Even much professional training was obtained outside the university curricula. In England, for example, a student prepared for the bar by taking up residence in one of the Inns of Court, where he could associate with practicing lawyers. The particular function of the universities was to provide an opportunity for scholars to examine the accumulated store of knowledge, to interpret it, and to enlarge it if possible. How vastly it needed to be enlarged the medieval scholar had no inkling. He was forced to exercise his wits on faulty premises, second- or third-hand misinformation, and defective translations of treasured sources. But a monumental attempt was made to correlate the data at his disposal. Culminating in the thought of Albert the Great and St. Thomas Aquinas, the result was an integrated philosophy which encompassed man, society, and the cosmos, and attempted to extract the pith of both reason and faith.

In a complex industrial society higher education has necessarily come to include more and more technical and professional training. It is significant, however, that most recent attempts to reform university curricula have stressed the necessity of bringing the student face to face with the common core of knowledge and the values which have emerged in the evolution of Western culture and are indispensable to its continuance. Repeatedly the cry is sounded, and not only by members of liberal arts faculties, that the foremost duty of the college is not to impart a skill but to help people discover what things are worth living for, and that if the colleges fail in this duty the consequences will be disastrous. The warning is opportune, but it is a reassertion of a medieval conviction. A group of college students who had been struggling with St. Thomas Aquinas were mildly startled when they learned that a quotation which they had pronounced an excellent summary of a thesis of the great Scholastic was actually lifted from the Harvard Report: *General Education in a Free Society*.

To attempt to resurrect Scholastic philosophy to cope with the dilemmas of the present day would be futile. The medieval thinkers cannot solve our problems for us. They were not even able to solve adequately the problems of their own day. The resolute and neat solutions which they had put together were robbed of their relevancy as the bases of the social order shifted and as the enlarging of European contacts brought an influx of new experiences. But the questions which they grappled with are persistent and fundamental. Although the form in which they recur is never the same, they cannot be permanently evaded.

CHAPTER EIGHT

LIBERATION THROUGH DISSOLUTION: THE ERA OF THE RENAISSANCE AND REFORMATION

Toward the close of that period of European history known as the Middle Ages, significant changes were taking place, but the changes were of a very different order from those which had characterized the beginning of the period. There was a transition toward another kind of culture and this involved the breakdown of many established patterns. Still, there was no question of the whole substance of civilization being threatened with collapse. Although it is possible to speak of the "decline" or the "passing" of the Middle Ages, medieval civilization did not fail or come to a dead end as had the old Roman Empire and its classical culture. A remarkable feature of Western civilization—and one which may induce an unwarranted complacency—is that since its inception in the Dark Ages it has never been overthrown. Passing through one crisis after another, it has thus far always emerged with apparently enhanced strength. At the end of the Middle Ages the forces making for change, although stimulated by contacts with the outer world, were indigenous, arising from within European society. As a result of internal pressure and the readjustment which it necessitated, medieval habits and concepts were sloughed off little by little.

The dynamic potential of the Western world, which has been increasingly impressive throughout the whole modern era, began to be manifested, gradually and haltingly, even before the close of the Middle Ages. The first few centuries of the ensuing period, especially the fifteenth and sixteenth, provide an opportunity for observing what happens when a society, through its own growth, has burst the bonds that held it together and is faced with the necessity of re-establishing an equilibrium. Unlike the beginning of the Middle Ages, the problem was not a loss of nerve and retreat of leadership or the influx of barbarians. Rather, there was a welling up from within the community itself. New types of satisfaction which had been only dimly perceived were now beckoning, and there was a determination to push back boundaries of enjoyment and action into areas previously unrecognized or considered unattainable. This experience can be almost as harrowing as the overwhelming of a culture by the onslaught of invaders, but it is much more likely to be followed by the successful utilization of the social energies which have been unlocked.

Beginning even as early as the thirteenth century, when the medieval order was at its height, it was steadily undermined in three vital areas. First, feudalism was pressed hard both from above and from below. The landed nobles were at a disadvantage in the face of economic trends. While manorial services were being commuted into fixed money payments, the prices of commodities were steadily rising. The lords suffered a diminution in real income and many of them went heavily and hopelessly into debt. While the aristocratic classes were by no means eliminated in Western Europe and some of their members became wealthier than ever, they no longer dominated every aspect of society. The towns rivaled the feudal suzerainties as centers of government and exceeded them in financial resources. From above, the steadily growing power of the kings cut into the jurisdiction of the nobility, limiting their courts to petty cases, and dispensing with their military services, except to furnish officers for the royal armies, which were being recruited from the whole countryside and composed chiefly of commoners. As feudalism had served economic, social, and political functions, its decline involved changes in almost every aspect of community, and even individual, life.

Second, the Church's position and authority were being challenged. The tides of sentiment which were rising gradually but inexorably were certain to sweep over even the sturdiest ecclesiastical dikes. This meant that the institution which, together with feudalism, had been the great regulative agency as well as the mistress of intellectual and artistic endeavor, was on the defensive. The kings of the nation states were establishing a more direct control over their subjects even in matters of religion, disregarding or rebuffing the papal claims to universal jurisdiction. The universities, which had been to some extent intellectual arsenals for the Church, were losing their pre-eminence as arbiters of thought. Scholasticism had begun to harden into academic, repetitive formulas, with declining appeal for alert minds. Most decisive of all, the emergence of a money economy and of a capitalist psychology was loosening the hold of the Church upon the public conscience and ethical code. The medieval ideal of a harmonious and relatively stable social order was giving way before the prospect of expanding profits with unlimited rewards for the successful directors of commerce. Merchants and bankers chafed against any interference with or disapprobation of the practices which were enabling them to move steadily upward toward the front ranks. Also on the economic side, as national and sectional interests developed, there was a mounting resentment against the financial exactions which the Church imposed with such regularity, such insistence, and such catholicity, especially when it was observed that the larger part of the revenue was expended for the benefit of Rome and Italy.

The third area of stress to which the medieval institutions and standards were subjected was a wide one, including almost the whole field of physical experience. An overwhelming mass of new data, derived in large part from the expanding orbit of European contacts and communications, impressed itself upon people's consciousness. This process had begun to be significant during the time of the Crusades and reached its full proportions with the voyages of exploration and discovery in the fifteenth and sixteenth centuries. With improvements in the art of navigation, including the use of the compass and astrolabe and the development of cartography, which made possible the establishment of a direct water route to the Indies and even the circumnavigation of the globe, not only the New World but several new worlds were opened to the inhabitants of the hitherto tightly bound little continent. It would be difficult to overestimate the effects of this transformation, either upon Europe or upon the outer lands. Even the countries which were not in a position to enter directly into the the overseas commerce felt its influence and were fascinated by its possibilities. The new commodities, foodstuffs, herbs, drugs, and delicacies raised the standard of consumption of large sections of the population. Equally important with the bullion, silks, rare woods, and gems which the well-laden hulls brought into port were the enthusiasm for further discovery, dreams of colonization, and the conviction that the Western nations might extend their dominion over all the lush spots of the earth.

Even earlier than the voyages of discovery, and quite independent of them, the attempt had been made to establish a connection not with distant contemporary El Dorados but with the culture of a fabulous past—the world of classical antiquity. The monuments, the manuscripts, the ancient records of heroic deeds had been eagerly sought after, partly because they were prized for their own sake but also in order that they might serve as an inspiration and model to those who possessed them. The reversion to pagan classicism was, superficially at least, a decided departure from the Middle Ages. The enthusiasts who dug into the soil of Italy were not hunting for the Holy Grail or bones of the martyrs. They hoped to uncover not Christ but Apollo. Affected and artificial as were some of the fads of the Italian Renaissance, they did bear witness to a yearning for a more colorful and exotic atmosphere than that to which medieval man had been acclimated.

In contrast to the pessimism and discouragement which marked the decline of the ancient world, the passing of the Middle Ages was accompanied by manifestations of energy, adventuresomeness, and a zest for living. It seemed to the leaders of the dawning age that they had attained a stature which dwarfed their cultural surroundings and that they were now ready to seek out at first hand what the earth had to offer. On the whole, the modern temper has warmed toward those figures who were conspicuous in effecting a break with the past. It has even been alleged that the human spirit had been slumbering and the intellect benumbed for several centuries until a few intrepid individuals brought an awakening. Such a conception reveals a very faulty knowledge of the Middle Ages and an undiscriminating attitude toward the men and events associated with its departure. Freshness and vitality were certainly in evidence, but the channels into which they flowed were not always the most desirable nor to be held in grateful remembrance by succeeding generations. The repudiation of deeply seated restraints encouraged recklessness as well as enterprise, and obsolete loyalties which had been ruptured could not easily be replaced by more appropriate and equally effective ties. The eager Europeans did not always exhibit the clear purpose of those whose maturity has caused them to outgrow the limitations of their background. In some respects they were more like children who have suddenly escaped from parental control and, while excited by their unexpected liberty, do not quite know what use to make of it.

The Renaissance Revolt Against Humility

Basically, the transition which was taking place at the opening of modern times was from a mutually interdependent and religiously motivated society to a competitive, individualistic, and secular one. As has already been pointed out, the Middle Ages were not exclusively or extravagantly religious. They were not otherworldly to the extent of barring interest in the here and now. But their guideposts, overlying objectives, and higher incentives were derived from a religious interpretation of man and society. This condition now changed, with results which were immediately disturbing and with ultimate consequences which were unforeseeable. Religion, far from being abandoned, remained an extremely powerful force. During the period under consideration some of the most intense manifestations of religious zeal, even obsession, were evident. But at the same time religious disciplines and loyalties were being extracted and set apart from the main activities of the individual or the community. During the Middle Ages, except among the inquisitors, fanatical crusaders (by no means including all who embarked on the Crusades), and a few dedicated and selfless saints, religion was not a particularly intense affair. A general frame of reference, a mold which surrounds and gives contour to the whole gamut of experience, is pervasive but hardly intense. Now, however, the Europeans beheld in their faith the same nervous agitation which was disturbing the entire institutional fabric. It became a more pressing and a more combative issue. A man's religion was now his special badge, his shining sword, or perhaps his necessary drug. It was not, for the ordinary man, the supporting structure of his social environment nor the interpreter of his chief pursuits. The most absorbing activities were either ends in themselves, requiring no interpretation, or their ultimate significance was beyond human comprehension. Instead of providing a bond of unity, religion became a source of division, with an appropriate climax in the "Religious Wars" of the sixteenth and seventeenth centuries, which were among the bloodiest on record.

The names "Renaissance" and "Reformation" have been given to two prominent phases of this shift to a secular society. Neither term is exact, nor does it necessarily suggest the most important aspects of the period to which it is attached. But each phase illustrates in a different way the general direction of the change.

The Renaissance, which began in Italy, reached its fullest and most characteristic expression there, and some features of it were hardly operative beyond the Italian Peninsula. Its name implies, and many leaders of the movement believed, that it was a clean break with the preceding era, amounting to a rediscovery, a veritable "rebirth" of the human will and personality. Actually the Renaissance could not have come into flower if medieval culture had not prepared the soil for it. It was deeply indebted to the Middle Ages and in many ways was closer to them, not only in time but in spirit, than to the modern age.

The mediums used to give expression to Renaissance ideals were derived largely from medieval sources. The Italian humanists did, of course, revert to Roman and eventually Greek idioms, symbols, and motifs—in so far as they were able. They were not able, and probably would not have liked, to go all the way back to the ancient order of things. The late medieval influence can be seen along with the classical even in art, the field in which Renaissance talent found its fullest and happiest embodiment. Gothic sculpture in the twelfth and thirteenth centuries had reached a high level of skill and sensitivity, testified by figures and faces which are both lifelike and appealingly beautiful. In fifteenth-century Italy sculpture came into its own as an independent art, no longer subordinate to architecture, but it was able to avail itself of an already well-advanced technique. Architecture showed a deliberate and more complete break with the Gothic tradition, illustrated by the determination to use Roman arches even where none at all were necessary and they could only be applied as extraneous decoration. While the vigor and splendor of Renaissance architecture at its best is undeniable, a good deal of it serves chiefly to emphasize the greater harmony and dignity of the Gothic.

With painting, it was quite a different story, to be sure. The glories of fresco and canvas had hardly been foreshadowed by Gothic decorators; but neither were they much indebted to the work of the ancients. They represented a fresh and original creation. Music was among the arts which received tremendous impetus during the Renaissance, but in the magnificent polyphony of this golden age of *bel canto* there was not the slightest trace of return to Greco-Roman traditions. Rather, there was a culmination of an evolution which had gone on independently in Europe throughout the medieval centuries.

In literature, undoubtedly, the term "Revival of Learning" is most nearly appropriate. Humanists, beginning with Petrarch, scorned the medieval Latin for the "purer" style of Cicero, Vergil, and Ovid. However, their progress was facilitated because of the very genuine interest in Roman literature which had often intrigued scholars in the Feudal Age, especially during the twelfth century. Also, the exaggerated and eventually pedantic adulation of classical Latin and Greek could not prevent the growth of national literatures in the vulgar tongues which many humanists affected to despise; and these vernacular languages were again a medieval product.

If scholars, writers, and artists could not avoid employing instruments which had been fashioned during the Middle Ages, still less did they create the external conditions which made the Renaissance culture possible. It was not Italian humanists of the fourteenth century who instituted a money economy, invented commerce and banking, or converted the towns into populous centers. The rise of wealthy urban communities, the stimulus of commercial contacts, the accumulation of capital with which to subsidize libraries and artists—which were necessary antecedents to the ripening of culture—were all characteristic developments of late medieval society, although augmented in the period which followed.

Thus it appears that medieval society had produced the means by which its members could liberate themselves from its restrictions and tenets. Actually, the means employed were sufficient not merely to transcend the limitations but to undermine the very foundations of medieval culture. It is not uncommon for a civilization to generate the forces which will overthrow it. Indeed it is a question as to whether this is not the dilemma which confronts Western civilization at the present moment. At the dawn of the modern age, any changes which could be detected were still very gradual, and their immediate advantages seemed to outweigh any long-range risks. However, in spite of the excitement of discovery and a jubilant feeling of release, the subsiding image of the medieval world cast a long shadow, affecting the mood even of the Renaissance.

The interests and emphases of the Renaissance proved extremely variable as it spread to the north and west. Because there were almost as many Renaissances as there were countries of Europe, the term means very little—or almost anything—when applied to Western Europe as a whole. Even in Italy, where it was indigenous and where the inhabitants could fancy themselves as the heirs of the Romans, it revealed divergent tendencies and personality types. Common factors were a display of energy, intensity of feeling, and a passion for self-realization; but they by no means fell into a uniform pattern. Emancipation to some meant indulgence of all the carnal appetites. Others were absorbed in the machinations and conflicts of politics. The scholar's lamp burned late, and so did the courtesan's. Summer nights provided an en-

chanting setting for festive boating parties or a cloak of safety
for bands of assassins. To certain individuals the call to renounce
the world and its delights was the most irresistible summons of
all. The firebrand monk Savonarola was as much a man of his
time as Lorenzo de' Medici or Cesare Borgia.

In art, the most typical and seemingly uninhibited of the creative activities associated with the Renaissance, conflicting tendencies are quite evident. In spite of revolutionary developments,
the prepossessions of the medieval mind insinuated themselves
into the character of many of the greatest works, either as a positive influence or, negatively, as the element which the artist is
attempting to deny. It is not merely that religious themes were
selected or that the Church became the most lavish patron of
artists in Italy. Traditional pious themes can be represented without any religious feeling whatsoever, and frequently they were
in the Italian Renaissance. But what is remarkable is the degree to
which painters, particularly the Florentines, were gripped by religious emotion and engrossed in serious problems concerning
man's nature, destiny, and ethical responsibilities. Florentine art,
in so far as it was religious, was neither conventional nor serene.
It is marked by tension, probing, and pathos. Frequently it focuses
attention upon the antipathy between Christian and pagan ideals,
without any clear decision in favor of one or the other. Beneath
the brush of the sensitive, introspective Botticelli, both spiritual-
ity and sensuality are apotheosized. The colossal mind of Leon-
ardo, for whom most of the involvements and exalted efforts
of his contemporaries were but child's play, brooded over the
rival claims of Parnassus and Calvary. Two almost identical
figures—young, vibrant, and appealing—he named respectively "St. John the Baptist" and "Bacchus." Was he mocking
the Gospel tradition or trying to reconcile opposing currents?
His paintings of the Holy Family are scientific studies of rock
formations or experiments in perspective; yet their piety is unmistakable and eloquent. His "Last Supper" is a classic of geo-
metric design and group arrangement (also, unfortunately, an
opportunity to experiment with newly invented pigments). But
it is one of the most moving pieces of religious drama in the
whole history of art.

Undoubtedly it is in Michelangelo, however, that the religious depth of the Renaissance is most fully revealed. Michelangelo scorned sentimentality and the conventional expressions of piety which were handled so facilely by many popular artists. He has aptly been called a humanist because he was primarily interested in man, rather than nature, science, or even effective design. But although he was a master in depicting the human form from every conceivable angle, in stone, on canvas, or plastered ceiling, his real concern was with what went on inside the human breast. Increasingly he interpreted this as a titanic struggle, tragic in its implications. Man's destiny, as Michelangelo conceived it, was full of suffering and frustration because of contrary compulsions within his nature or because of perpetual failure to realize his aspirations. Just what these aspirations are, or should be, is not entirely clear, but they seem to coincide pretty closely with the ideals which were proclaimed so forcefully throughout the Later Middle Ages. That man, no matter how gifted or how favored, is not a law unto himself—that he is answerable to moral judgments—is the burden of much of the work of this great artist. Far from repudiating Christian doctrines, he embraced them with an almost ferocious intensity. That they were worn very lightly by increasing numbers of his contemporaries, including his patrons, was doubtless a factor augmenting the tragic gloom of his creations. He dedicated his ripest talents to the service of the Church. Much as he preferred the chisel to the brush, he drove himself, cramped on a high scaffold month after month and year after year, to the Herculean task of painting the Sistine Chapel frescoes, depicting the whole Christian Epic from the Creation to the terrifying and pitiless Last Judgment. He devoted the closing years of his life to supervising the construction of St. Peter's Cathedral, and for this tremendous work he refused to accept any pay.

The ultimate significance of the Renaissance in the development of Western civilization is probably not that it marked the end of the Middle Ages or the beginning of modern times, nor even that it rehabilitated classical studies, but that it witnessed a fierce and unresolved struggle between opposing views of life. The whole story is not told in the discovery of inconsistencies and contradictions. These are almost always present in some degree and may be proofs of a healthy vitality. The juxtaposition of pagan and Christian ideals was neither revolutionary nor entirely new. From its inception Christianity had incorporated many pagan elements, and all through the Middle Ages these factors, derived from the primitive German communities or from the classical heritage, exerted an influence. It is not remarkable that Petrarch, who idolized the ancients, hated Scholasticism, wrote erotic sonnets, and shamelessly pulled strings to have himself crowned with the laurel wreath, should have toyed with the idea of becoming a monk. It is more startling, but not inexplicable, that the Church in Italy should have become the greatest patron of a culture which was often frivolous and sensual; and that a Lorenzo Valla, who exposed the "Donation of Constantine" as a fraud, excoriated the papacy, and by example and teaching repudiated Christian doctrines, should have been employed as secretary by Pope Nicholas V.

Actually the issue was deeper than that of antipathy between Christian and pagan ideals. The two categories overlap as much as they conflict. The Romans, who made a fetish of legality, subscribed to the doctrine that human laws should be consonant with universal principles of justice. They embraced Stoicism, which emphasized the brotherhood of man and submission to the eternal reason of the cosmos. The pagan Greeks, in their saner moments, regarded the intellect as man's rarest attribute, exalted the pleasures of the mind above those of the body, and insisted that the individual should seek his good in relationship to the welfare of the community. None of these concepts is inimical to the Christian scheme of things; nor was the revival of classical letters or the development of painting inherently antireligious.

The real conflict was between the tradition of service, dedication, and moral responsibility—through whatever form or creed expressed—and the impulse toward unbridled egoism, indulgence, and self-sufficiency. The sudden interest in liberating the individual from irksome restraints created a temptation to overthrow all standards (except those imposed by the nature of one's chosen craft, be it sculpture or the fine art of assassination).

Christian, pagan, or mythological tags were seized upon indiscriminately in accordance with the whim or convenience of the moment. In spite of many noble and beautiful works, the riot of lawlessness which became apparent inevitably provoked a reaction, against even the wholesome and constructive forces which had been set in motion. The fleeting picture of man at his worst—civilized man, who was able to employ refinements in his cruelty and elegance in his debauchery—was an ugly one. No wonder that some of the finer spirits, even in the relatively uninhibited realm of art, struck a note of questioning, of warning, or of protest. This circumstance makes more understandable the tragic symbolism of Michelangelo, whose extraordinarily successful quest for beauty brought him no peace. Freedom without limits and undefined, he seems to say, culminates in anguish or even slavery. Hence humanity may be represented as a bound slave—naked, beautiful, but in chains.

CLOTHES TO FIT THE MAN

As the Renaissance spread into northern Europe, it gave impetus to another movement which overshadowed it and eventually extinguished it, even in Italy, its birthplace. This other affair has been traditionally called the "Reformation," of which the "Protestant Revolt" was the most conspicuous feature. To say that the Reformation was, like the Renaissance, a phase of the transition to a secular society may seem paradoxical. True, it was by definition a religious manifestation, it was characterized by intense or fanatical religious feeling, and it was directly opposed to the mood of the Renaissance. However, in its ultimate effects it promoted the triumph of such unquestionably secular forces as nationalism, commercialism, and capitalism, and it widened the breach between medieval and modern society.

The religious upheaval, which began in Germany and rocked almost all of Western Europe, had much the same set of underlying causes which had produced the Renaissance. Also, the revival of classical studies helped to prepare the way for it, and humanist scholarship became a valuable tool in the hands of Luther and other religious reformers. The Renaissance, however, in so far as it was coherent and definable, embodied as its central theme the exaltation of man. It magnified his importance; it held him up as the mirror in which the whole of nature was reflected. It crowned him with pride, even to the point of an impetuous and dangerous arrogance. The Reformation, on the other hand, lacerated man's confident self-assurance. It sought to bring him to earth, to debase him. It flayed his presumption and branded him as a vile, unworthy creature. Both movements attacked authoritative traditions of the immediate past and both made a direct appeal to the individual; but in so far as the Renaissance was "pagan," in so far as it was inspired by science or reason (which, probably, was not very much), in so far as it glorified man, the Reformers were opposed to it. They turned their heaviest guns upon the Roman center of the Catholic Church for many reasons, among which was its identification with the typical manifestations and interests of the Italian Renaissance. The excessive emotionalism and recklessness of the Renaissance undoubtedly cried out for correction. The Reformation, however, which unleashed fresh torrents of emotion, was hardly calculated to restore a proper balance. It cultivated its own varieties of extremism. While it swept away much that was questionable and obsolete, it fell short of providing society with effective integrating principles. On the whole, it eased the flow of currents which were becoming in any case almost irresistible.

Powerful and obvious incentives to the Protestant movement were furnished by political tendencies. Although nationalistic sentiment was still largely inarticulate, there was an awareness of national *interest*, to which any external authority appeared as an impediment or rival. When Luther sought the aid of the princes, he appealed to their patriotism; "Let us rouse ourselves, fellow Germans." He called upon them to remember the glories of their country's early history and not to be hoodwinked any longer by the Pope as, he said, they had been shamefully in the past. If any Roman "courtling" should come into Germany with threatening messages, he should be commanded "to leap into the Rhine, or whatever river be nearest." The successful foundation of the Lutheran Church in Germany under the protection of individual princes strengthened the power of the states, both by canceling

allegiance to the Pope and by weakening the bonds of the un-
wieldy Holy Roman Empire. Not only in Germany but in every
other country where a reformed church was established, it served
as a prop to secular authority. England provides the classic example, where the Tudor monarchs were able to shuttle their subjects from one ecclesiastical alignment to another in accordance
with the dynastic interests of the hour.

The Protestant Revolution also depended for its success upon
the support of the middle classes. Although its patrons included
nobles and kings, the movement could not have assumed wide
proportions if it had not enlisted the enthusiasm of artisans, merchants, and bankers in the urban communities of northern Europe.
The townsmen had already learned to look to the king as the pro-
tector of their commerce against pirates, foreign powers, or the
feudal nobles. They were paying heavily for what protection they
received (often very inadequate) and they no longer saw much
advantage in supporting an expensive ecclesiastical hierarchy with
headquarters in a foreign country. Naturally, the commercial classes
in Italy took a different view of the situation, especially as papal
resources were used to foster literature and art in that region and
to make Rome the splendid center of the Renaissance. To some
degree the Renaissance papacy was regarded by Italians as an
Italian institution as it was by other Europeans; but to the former
it was a source of pride—or at least a horn of plenty. Some patriots,
however, such as Machiavelli, who dreamed of an Italy united in
a secular state, hated the papacy as deeply as did the northern
Reformers.

The rise and spread of the Calvinist faith illustrates most strikingly that the middle class was ripe for the harvest of religious
change. Though Calvin was of aristocratic breeding and conceived
his doctrines as applicable to the whole human race, the emphases
and implications of his creed seemed almost tailor-made for the
hard working and enterprising common folk. In his scheme of
things the stratification of society was stripped of all spiritual
significance. The doctrine that all persons are equal in the sight
of God was by no means new, but with Calvin it was presented
in such a way as to inspire confidence—if only the confidence of
despair—among the middle class. While no one could *know*

whether or not he was of the "elect" (and the odds were against it), Calvin taught that visible and outward signs of divine grace were the ability to walk a moral tightrope, disdaining idleness and frivolous pleasures, and also the capacity for serving as a useful and productive instrument of God's will. Productivity could be measured in various ways, and God's will was inscrutable, but it seemed to include, along with personal steadfastness and zeal for propagating the faith, the encouragement of thrift and an increase in the efficiency of human labor. The profitable servant was he who doubled his talents instead of burying them in the ground. Successful endeavor and prosperity were not a virtue, nor even a reward for virtue, but an indication that one had been selected for a high calling and might be destined for eternal blessedness (though he should never rely on it complacently). Calvin neither taught nor implied that poverty is a sin or that wealth is righteousness; but he did emphasize the inherent worthiness, and possible superiority, of the qualities which were most typical of the industrial and commercial classes. Thus he inverted the traditional judgment concerning the functions of the respective social orders, making the stone which the medieval builders had rejected the head of the corner.

It is true, as has often been pointed out, that there was an intimate connection between Calvinism and the rise of capitalism and that his system provided an ethical undergirding for an economy of expanding production and profits. It is not at all strange that this religion met with a ready response among the commercially active Dutch, the thrifty Scotch, and various lower- and middle-class elements in England, Germany, and elsewhere. In France, too, it might possibly have carried the field; but the power of the king, who had little to gain and much to lose from a religious revolution, was strong enough to hold it in check, although not without letting the Huguenots exist for a time as a sort of state within the state.

In the religious struggles of the sixteenth century, as in so many conflicts, the causes and issues were more inclusive and deeper than those things most talked about in the heat of the controversy. The Reformers usually began by denouncing such objectionable practices as the sale of indulgences, went on to challenge the whole sacramental and sacerdotal system, and then in many cases finally repudiated not only the romantic humanism of the Renaissance but the rationalistic humanism of the Late Middle Ages.

In so far as logic entered into the controversy, the Reformers were fighting a modern battle with archaic weapons. In attempting to undermine the Catholic position they fortified themselves with the theology of St. Augustine and revived the pessimistic view of man which had colored the thought of the Dark Ages. The Roman Church had taught that salvation was possible by means of faith, good works, and the efficacy of the sacraments. The Protestants rejected the latter two entirely and placed their whole reliance upon faith. But they believed that faith would appear only among those in whom God had implanted it. Luther denied that it was possible for man to choose deliberately and freely between good and evil because his will is held in bondage. Neither would man's intellectual and rational faculties provide his emancipation. Reason might be helpful when used properly, but it was also a snare—"the devil's harlot." Calvin was even more uncompromising than Luther in insisting upon the worthlessness of human flesh. In his view mankind was a corrupt mass, utterly depraved, deserving damnation *in toto*. That a minority were predestined to be saved was owing to no merit or effort on their part (although if they failed to bend every effort they were obviously not of the elect) but only to the gratuitous mercy of the Omnipotent.

There were, to be sure, gentler strains in the thought of both Calvin and Luther, to say nothing of several less numerous and less publicized sects. But the remarkable fact is that the stark, somber features of the two leading Protestant faiths were not accidental accretions but essential features, which contributed much of their dynamic appeal. Seemingly, large segments of the population of Western Europe were thirsting for the announcement of their inherent vileness. They embraced the doctrines of total depravity, of the vanity of the will, and of the futility of priestly ministrations as if they were the elixir of life. The vivid revelation of man's insignificance, accompanied by all-or-nothing injunctions, apparently released their energies as nothing

had before. Enthusiastic disciples of the new creeds busied themselves in the program of their communities as well as of their
churches. If violently set upon in their own lands, they sought
other areas where they could propagate their faith and ply their
crafts; and they crossed oceans to tame the wilderness and establish settlements of the God-fearing in new continents.

Why did the grim thesis which holds human nature in contempt
triumph over the mellower, more sympathetic, and rationalistic
point of view? To some extent it was a victory of numbers, or of
sheer weight. The middle classes were determined to overthrow
the barriers which hemmed them in and to remove all stigmas
which branded them as inferior to any other groups in society.
They were inclined to support an attack upon the supremacy
of the Church and the overweening claims of the clergy, whether
the attack was directed against ecclesiastical authority as such
or against its theological foundations. As ever in battle, the enemy's
lines were carefully scanned for any spot where a breach might
be made. Yet something deeper than the mere strategy of defense
and offense was involved. There was a sense in which the new
theology (which was really a very old one) was welcomed for
itself, paradoxical as it may seem that an optimistic appraisal of
mankind should have been voluntarily exchanged for a pessimistic
one. The gloomier interpretation was more consonant with the
activities and interests which were becoming dominant.

In the pulsating sixteenth century, with its abundant vitality,
there was little likelihood that the will of Europeans would become
paralyzed through self-doubt or wither from lack of nerve.
The accent was upon action, expansion, and self-expression.
There was uncertainty, however, as to whether all the forms
of expression and all of the more popular activities were praiseworthy. Many were clearly very different from those which had
been approved during the preceding centuries. And they were
sometimes accompanied by incidents and practices which in
almost any age would have to be considered as unfortunate, if
not reprehensible. It was impossible to reconcile all of these tendencies with the conception of man as a rational creature functioning intelligently in a well-ordered society—impossible, that
is, unless the activities themselves were modulated and adapted in

accordance with this ideal. A view of man which frankly dropped out the image of his perfectibility—or which held that if he attained perfection it would be not through, but independently of, what he did in the world of actual experience—was more accommodating. If the world, the state, the economic order were irrational, this was a melancholy but inevitable verification of the dogma of human depravity and original sin. No matter what might be undertaken to improve the external condition of society, it would still bear the marks of man's inadequacy. Therefore, the individual was freed for the particular work in which he was engrossed. If he did well he had not only accomplished something in the area where it was given men to act, but he might even have secured proof of his spiritual distinction.

To say that the sights were lowered in regard to the attainable objectives of society does not mean that religious or spiritual incentives had ceased to operate. On the contrary, these incentives were very powerful and produced remarkable examples of unstinted dedication, both individual and collective. But the ideal of personal spiritual achievement was becoming more sharply separated from the context of social relationships and responsibilities. Along with the antihumanist theology of St. Augustine was being revived his notion of the irreconcilability of the outer and inner planes of human experience. The only abiding reality was the Church Invisible, which did not coincide with the whole personnel or paraphernalia of any visible church, reformed or unreformed, still less with the temporal world. The state, for example, was coming to be regarded as both purely secular and autonomous, no longer amenable to counterpressure from a church or any other agency.

Neither Luther nor Calvin had illusions about the benevolence of governments. Luther, in a forthright utterance, declared that princes "are generally the biggest fools and worst knaves on earth." Nevertheless, both Luther and Calvin taught that it was the duty of subjects to obey their rulers, whether despotic or not, up to the very limit of their consciences. (Calvin left the door open slightly to limitations on the royal power, but not to rebellion by the masses.) When ordered to violate what were clearly divine commandments, the subjects should indeed resist. This qualification was not really revolutionary nor an indication of liberal or democratic leanings, but simply a realistic acknowledgment of a desperate extreme. It has always been the duty of the Christian to accept martyrdom rather than renounce his faith. If he is forced to this choice he must obey God rather than men. But ninety-nine times out of a hundred he was expected to obey men. Government was not defined as a positive good but regarded as a necessary evil—necessary because of man's greed, arrogance, and waywardness and evil for the same reasons. Even a tyranny, while never to be admired, was unlikely to be in excess of a people's deserts.

Although the Catholics stoutly rejected the doctrines of the Protestants and refused to concede an inch to them in argument, they were nevertheless compelled to make adjustments to the spirit of the times. Even without the Protestant defection, the Catholic Church could not have maintained indefinitely the commanding position which it had enjoyed during the Middle Ages; and now it was forced into a continuous struggle to retain such allegiances as were still feasible. In the long run, it came to accept attitudes toward the physical and social environment similar to those of the leading Protestant churches. The Catholic Reformation—which was a matter of setting the Catholics' own house in order by removing abuses and improving discipline—both strengthened the Church as a purely religious society and narrowed its role in other spheres. The moral rejuvenation of the papacy was a gigantic undertaking in itself. It succeeded, but in the process effected a rupture with the humanist tradition which the Renaissance popes had embraced so warmly. The rupture was accompanied by a falling off in creative activity, notable especially in the declining quality of Italian art. The reaction led even to a guilt complex toward some of the most superb creations of the High Renaissance, as illustrated by the painting over of the mighty nudes in Michelangelo's "Last Judgment" at papal command. As Michelangelo scornfully remarked, it was an easier matter to reform a painting than to reform the world. But the probing, penetrating challenge of the artist could not be blotted out by a layer of pigment.

The Catholic Church was now too dependent upon the support of monarchs to press its claims of superiority over them. In practice, if not in theory, it accepted the trend toward absolutism and the rigid compartmentalization of European loyalties which this implied. Although it advocated the deposition of heretical princes, it exhorted subjects to obey their ruler if he upheld the true religion. The prevailing Catholic political ideal during this period was, as Preserved Smith defined it, "despotism tempered by assassination."

While the turmoil and controversies of the Reformation Era had many facets, they were closely related to the growing cleavage which was taking place in the European world view. Not the cleavage between Protestant and Catholic, but between the conception of what is ideally desirable and the awareness of what is actually attainable in the sphere of human action.

A philosophy of life and human nature must have a reasonable correspondence to the conditions under which it is formulated, and to the pursuits and operational code of those who hold it. The view which exalts man's intrinsic worth makes heavy demands upon its adherents. The classical Hellenic concept of man as a rational, discerning being called for a high degree of intelligence, balance, and self-control. Similarly, medieval Scholastic thought, with its generous estimate of human capacity, sought to extract the utmost effort and devotion from the individual. The democratic ideal, whether Athenian or modern, requires integrity and vigilant alertness from the members of society if they are to maintain, and reap the benefits of, democracy. The Renaissance intrepretation of human nature, while flamboyant and extravagant, set an extremely high goal for the development of individual personality, epitomized in the notion of the "universal man," whose sensibilities were completely awakened, whose talents were fully employed, and who was able to function creatively at every level of activity. This is a strenuous undertaking. To the ordinary mortal it seemed to exact too much. Hence large numbers of people turned with some relief to the dogma that man is not really of such heroic mold, that he is innately corrupt and unable to achieve grandeur through the guidance of his own feeble will or reason. The contemporary currents that offered greatest attraction included the acceptance of coercive, centralized, and rather brutal governments, which promised greater efficiency because unhampered by ethical imperatives; the acquisition of wealth and the swelling of profits by any conceivable means; the uninhibited gratification of individual impulse and desire. None of these tendencies was compatible with the concept of the dignity of man—whether Hellenic, Hebraic, or Christian. But they all became understandable and even inevitable once the perverse sinfulness of the species was admitted. Thus the creed was being shaped to the exigencies of the hour.

A somewhat parallel development has taken place in recent times, typified by the Neo-Orthodox School of theologians. The movement embodies a reaction against the humanist tradition, such as was exemplified in the Renaissance, developed more coherently during the Enlightenment, and kept alive by the liberal wing of modern Protestantism. Faced with the dilemma of the increasingly amoral character of a machine civilization—of the widening gap between the ideals of progress, humanitarianism, and Christian conscience on the one hand and the imminence of a cataclysmic fate for the race on the other—the exponents of Neo-Orthodoxy have had recourse to the Augustinian-Calvinistic conception of human depravity. They feel that the trend of recent history, the stark realities of the actual world, make untenable the view that man is a rational creature, capable of charting his course wisely and successfully. Their arguments cannot be lightly disposed of, certainly not by mere academic debate; although they would lose their force if society should become, or in proportion as it becomes, more rational. The definition of anything so variable as human nature must be interpreted in the light of the external social environment, upon which it is always a commentary, intentional or not. And when men of intelligence and principle find it necessary to return to wells of pessimism in order to retain their faith, or perhaps their sanity, it is evident that civilization is not in the healthiest condition.

The transitional period which marked the beginning of the modern age was one of exciting discovery and rich promise. Every new departure in the fields of culture, thought, or economic enterprise contained valuable elements and at least the seeds of productive growth. What has been said in this discussion is not intended to deny the beneficial aspects of change. It would be difficult even to list all of the benefits which were derived, directly or indirectly, from these various movements, even those which momentarily seemed to be generating only heat and strife. Nevertheless, along with the eager determination to discover and advance, there was a relaxing of the attempt to relate the various competing interests to the general objectives of a social order. There was increasing doubt as to whether they could be so related. Without being consciously formulated, the question was arising as to whether man's organizations and material accomplishments, as distinct from man himself, could be subjected to rational control. Whether civilization—as opposed to the human stuff which enters into it—can be benevolent or purposeful. And the measurable external changes taking place not only during this early modern period but in succeeding centuries seemed to indicate a negative response to the question.

TYRANNY AND INTERNATIONAL ANARCHY

One of the most obvious effects of the upheavals of this period was to sunder the cords of unity which had been extended over Western Europe during the Middle Ages in spite of the particularism, provincialism, and faulty communications of that era. The ideal that all of Christendom should form a common entity had been given concrete and sometimes effectual expression by the Church, through its services, conducted in Latin, the universal language, through its cultural agencies, and through its administration. The unification of Europe had never been adequate nor complete. To a large extent the connecting links had been artificial or illusory, and their disappearance was not in itself an irreparable loss. More serious in consequences was the repudiation of beliefs which had served as the mainsprings of social action. The revolt against authority did not free the individual or associations of individuals from dependence upon authoritative principles. It did not automatically create self-reliant communities which were able to plot an independent course under the guidance of the suddenly released collective wisdom of their members. And under the stress of conflict and the importunity of immediate urges, there was a tendency to rally around any *ad hoc* authority which seemed convenient.

The disruptive tendencies of this age of transition were by no means unheeded or allowed to pass unchallenged. Underneath the surface there was a sincere and sometimes desperate groping for principles which might constitute a nucleus for a new community of interests. In the field of government and political theory, where the general tide was running in favor of absolutism, there were strong voices of protest. While the Protestant movement intensified the force of nationalism, in the long run—especially as sects multiplied—it encouraged an examination of the foundations of civil society, sometimes with results which were very hostile to autocratic institutions. If people could stand on their own consciences, if they could defy the injunctions of priests, it was logical for them to raise questions about the limits of secular authority. The example of government which Calvin established in Geneva came close to theocracy. Nevertheless, as Calvinism spread—partly because of the democratic structure of its churches and partly because its adherents were so often a minority in their respective countries—it tended to nourish a jealousy for the liberties of subjects and even gave approval to the idea that sovereignty resides in the people and government rests upon contract. However, liberalism was usually in inverse ratio to the numerical strength or the influence of a group. The most radical concepts were found among the Anabaptists and other minority sects which derived their support chiefly from the lower classes and were universally hounded by all of the more powerful churches—Catholic or Protestant—as well as by the established governments.

Outside of Italy, the greatest humanists deplored, along with the brutal and callously materialistic aspects of the age, the chains which monarchs were busily forging for their peoples. Erasmus, the most influential man of letters in northern Europe of the early sixteenth century, set himself squarely in opposition to Machiavelli. The essential qualifications for a ruler as Erasmus saw them were, not cunning and the ability to inspire fear, but virtue, integrity, and a sincere desire to promote his people's welfare, including their intellectual needs. The just prince, accordingly, would hold taxation to a bare minimum and scrupulously avoid war, practices for neither of which contemporary rulers were noted. His basic quarrel with Machiavelli lay in Erasmus' contention that politics should be a branch of ethics rather than a separate craft and a law unto itself. Here, of course, he was standing on medieval ground, and few cared to stand with him. Modern nations have generally preferred to follow Machiavelli rather than Erasmus, in spite of the evil odor adhering to his name and although it was considered praiseworthy, even in the sixteenth century, to write treatises denouncing the plain spoken precepts of the cynical Florentine. Politics was becoming divorced from ethics and religion, as Machiavelli clearly saw, and with results which Erasmus also saw and which have become amply documented with the passing of the centuries.

The admonitions of Erasmus and others like him were bound to be ineffectual. They were in the nature of entreaties, addressed to the rulers themselves in the hope of softening their hearts. There was no mechanism for compelling the rulers to equate their functions with either the will or the welfare of their subjects. Even most of the thinkers who advocated the bold theory of popular sovereignty were doubtful as to how it could be given practical expression without jeopardizing law and order, and generally reached the reluctant conclusion that tyranny was better than anarchy. While Erasmus considered an elective republic as ideally preferable to an hereditary monarchy, he was not willing to trust the masses with political responsibility, especially after the Peasants' Revolt in Germany.

If it was impossible to bind the despotic governments to policies of humaneness in internal affairs, it was still more hopeless to try to control their relations with one another. For all the widespread fear of anarchy, so frequently confessed, this was exactly the condition which was becoming operative between states. The increasingly violent conflicts which resulted were deplored, but international sentiment was nebulous and its expression usually unrealistic. Condemnation of war may be found among the humanists and among the Reformers, although the latter certainly contributed their share to the fomenting of strife. Erasmus again was one of the most outspoken and vehement in denouncing war, which he considered a foul blemish upon his age and a repudiation of the basic principles of Christianity. He advocated the settlement of disputes by arbitration, a proposal which at any given historical moment seems to be ahead of the times. Some passages in the famous *Utopia* of Sir Thomas More illustrate the "utopian" character of the internationalism of the period. More heaps sarcasm upon the conduct of European diplomacy, which is characterized by deceit and perfidy. The Utopians he describes as adhering to a higher standard of international morality, but only through a policy of isolationism. Although they scrupulously observe their agreements, they make no alliances. They detest war but prepare zealously for it and wage it ruthlessly when they have to. They prefer to win through craft or treachery rather than force (their object being the laudable one of minimizing slaughter), and apparently they are able to become masters in the art of corrupting others without themselves becoming corrupted. A touch of naïveté—innocent in More's day, ironic in ours—is the assertion that the Utopians consider a just cause of war the obligation of liberating other peoples from tyranny. (More startling is the claim that it is an act of justice to wage war for the purpose of seizing uncultivated land so that it may be put to profitable use "according to the law of nature.")

THE LEAVEN OF SCIENCE

One of the most truly creative forces of the period, the effects of which were hardly visible as yet, was scientific discovery and experiment. The rise of modern science was not a sudden affair; actually it did not rise very far into the range of public consciousness during the fifteenth and sixteenth centuries even though it was making remarkable advances in the hands of an interested few. The roots of scientific inquiry reached back into the Later Middle Ages, where they had been nurtured by the intellectual quickening that accompanied the renewal of contacts between Western Europe and the Near East. The material improvements which laid the basis for the Renaissance were favorable to the acquisition of valuable data concerning the natural world and the stimulation of scientific studies; but the dominant cultural trends were not altogether conducive to this end. The selfless detachment, the painstaking, relentless anonymity which the scientific discipline exacts were hardly in accord with the vaulting egoism of the Renaissance. Neither did the veneration of antiquity and of classical authorities which characterized Renaissance letters inspire an experimental approach to knowledge. The Reformation was even more directly and aggressively hostile to the scientific spirit.

Science neither had its origin during this period of transition nor was it its most typical manifestation. Nevertheless, the work of discovering, observing, and interpreting went on with increasing momentum.

Aside from concrete achievements in specific fields, the most significant advance was the apprehension of the scientific *method*. Induction from observed phenomena rather than deduction from traditional dogmas or logical postulates became the accepted procedure of investigation. This meant ultimately nothing less than the repudiation of authority in favor of experience and reason. It made no difference whether the authority was that of Roman poets, Aristotle, or the Church; it must yield to the evidence accumulated by man's senses and tested experimentally. This was a change not so much in theories of knowledge as in techniques for acquiring knowledge, by means of which the orbit of experience was being broadened and deepened as never before.

The growth of a scientific attitude was undoubtedly assisted by geographical discovery, which provided an abundance of material for examination and brought a realization that the world is larger than had been supposed. Even more challenging, however, were the revelations of astronomy, necessitating a new perspective not just in the conception of the earth but of the universe.

The revolution in astronomy from the Ptolemaic to the Copernican system not only upset long-established convictions but offered the basis for a fresh interpretation of man and human affairs. Seemingly the puncturing of myth, the promise of continually expanding knowledge, and the emphasis upon the orderly, consistent, and rational structure of the physical universe might have provided a rallying point for a harassed society at a time when the older symbols of confidence were losing their potency. Actually, the response which greeted the disclosures of astronomers and physicists gave no indication that such a hopeful possibility was glimpsed. The implications of their discoveries were but dimly grasped, misunderstood, or sullenly repulsed. Undoubtedly the scientists themselves did not understand all of the implications, but their industry and courage are in bright contrast to the petty and partisan controversies of their day. While they were pioneers in new fields, they were also carrying on the tradition of a common

European culture, and were broadening it so that it might become the basis of a universal knowledge. In a sense they were the true internationalists of the age. Not deliberately or consciously so, and perhaps it was only an accident that of the four geniuses who, successively, laid the foundations for modern astronomy Copernicus was a Pole, Tycho Brahe a Dane, Kepler a German, and Galileo an Italian. But the bonds of encouragement and sympathy which buoyed up the spirits of the early scientists cut across national and religious barriers to establish a fraternity of disinterested searchers after truth.

The scientists certainly needed all the encouragement they could get from one another. If the general public was unappreciative of their findings, the influential leaders of society were, on the whole, directly hostile to them. In spite of the revolts which had been launched in many quarters against particular authorities, there was no general disposition to renounce authority completely and rely upon the unfettered reason. Naturally the ecclesiastical powers were most forward in condemning any ideas which they regarded as contradicting the principles of the faith and the explicit teachings of the Bible. Just as all dominant sects were equally intolerant of social and religious radicals, so Protestants and Catholics saw eye to eye as to the heretical implications of the heliocentric theory. Calvin and Luther roundly condemned it. Copernicus' epochal work was placed upon the Roman Catholic Index of Prohibited Books. Galileo was summoned before the Roman Inquisition and forced to recant. Although even the threat of torture could not make him change his mind, he did prudently alter his public professions.

The nature of the intellectual struggle was perhaps most dramatically illustrated by a figure who was not actually a scientist but who was affected by the new discoveries in such a way as to transform his life and to convince him that the whole conception of reality as well as of man's place in nature would have to be changed. This was Giordano Bruno, who combined a mystical temperament with a passionate devotion to objectively verifiable truth. Bruno passed from the unwelcome discipline of a monastery to an association with the northern Reformers and beyond that to the projection of a rhapsodical pantheism which burst the shell of orthodoxy completely. The magnitude, the illimitability of the universe became his fascination. But instead of feeling that this conception reduced man to trivial insignificance, he was, on the contrary, exalted by the notion that fetters had been removed from the divine being. The universe as he saw it was infinite in extent and in the number of its worlds, but God was in every part of it. And man, by increasing his knowledge, would at the same time grow in spiritual stature and insight. A man like Bruno seemed to be more dangerous even than the professional astronomers, who were not always unwilling to affirm that the laws which they proclaimed operated in a totally different realm from that of faith and should not be thought of as contradicting the dogmas of the Church. Most of the scientists, disheartened as they may have been, died in their beds. That Bruno was burned at the stake in Rome was not entirely out of keeping with the temper of the sixteenth century.

CHAPTER NINE

THE REDISCOVERY OF MAN

Of all the forces which promoted a transition to a modern type of society, by far the most potent were the physical changes—economic and geographic—taking place in the European environment. The process of readjustment, continuing over several centuries, which gradually replaced the closed and static economy of the Middle Ages with an elastic and dynamic one, intercontinental in scope, is usually called the Commercial Revolution. In its entirety this revolution was more far-reaching and permanent in its effects than all of the accompanying artistic and philosophical movements, more even than the explosive eruptions in religion. The weakest element in medieval civilization had been its limited material development, and the prospects of enriching the physical content of existence caught the imagination of European peoples with an irresistible attraction.

The Commercial Revolution was not merely a departure from the economy of the immediately preceding centuries; it was a turning point in the history of the Western world. Ancient civilizations had occupied only the fringe of the European Continent.

Even the Roman, extensive as was its dominion, centered around the Mediterranean Sea and had little effect upon the outlying areas. The Middle Ages had introduced a significant modification by bringing practically all of northern and western Europe into a common cultural orbit; but at the same time ancient communication lines were severed and the economy became localized and restricted. Until near the end of the Feudal Age not only was trade with other parts of the world at a minimum but also Europeans had no appreciation of the potentialities of their own habitat. In an overwhelmingly agrarian regime, methods of production had been stabilized at an elementary level (distribution was almost void of method), while the most sustained efforts of society were directed to matters of organization or to the strengthening of intellectual, artistic, and spiritual capacities. These efforts produced remarkable results, but the material base on which they rested was undeniably a meager one.

The unprecedented development of commerce between the fourteenth and the seventeenth centuries, which dwarfed the medieval economy, transcended the limits of all previous ones. Expansion in the theater of commerce and in modes of operation was three dimensional. The confines of the European peninsula were broken and now the great oceans, rather than an inland sea, became the connecting links of a world trade of which Europe was the focal center. A dimension of depth was contained in the dynamics of capitalism. The rise of a monetary system, given terrific impetus by the influx of gold and silver from the New World, together with the revival of the mechanisms of banking and credit seemed to forecast a perpetual and unlimited increase in wealth.

THE ENTICEMENTS OF EMPIRE

The inhabitants of Western Europe did not yet begin to utilize fully or even to recognize the resources which their own lands contained, but they saw clearly the possibility of bringing other areas under their control. For the first time they were taking the initiative in matters affecting distant regions, ultimately the whole world. On their eastern frontiers they were, it is true, on the defensive after the fall of Constantinople to the Turks in 1453 (an event for which the Westerners had helped prepare the way by their depredations against the Byzantine Empire during the Crusades). But they held an increasingly commanding position in oceanic navigation. They were occupying stretches of the continents of North and South America, seizing strategic islands, and sending their merchant ships to the Indies and the coasts of China.

While individual energies found a great variety of outlets, a large share of the efforts of the major Western European nations for some three hundred years was devoted to the procuring of overseas empires. Imperialism has been a characteristic phase of many cultures, but the European imperialism of the period of the Commercial Revolution was in several ways a new phenomenon, as well as a unique stage of Western development. In contrast to most of the ancient empires, it consisted in the acquisition of territory separated by great distances from the conquering states. In a few cases, as in Peru and Mexico, it involved the destruction of highly developed cultures. (In India an older civilization was injured without being annihilated.) In large part, however, the European colonies, unlike the conquests of ancient rulers, were established in areas which had never known a higher civilization and where the inhabitants could offer little effective resistance. There were, to be sure, massacres of settlers by natives, but the most formidable obstacles to successful colonizing, European style, were the hazard of long voyages, uncertainties of climate and terrain, ignorance as to the topography and resources of regions to be occupied, and the competition of European rivals. Also, in striking contrast to the Roman imperialists especially, the Europeans did not attempt to incorporate their colonies directly into the political and social structure of their own nations. They extended sovereign jurisdiction over the colonies—they "annexed" them— they even introduced Christianity and other aspects of European culture among the natives. But although the conquered regions were looked upon as contributing to political prestige and especially as sources of economic gain, the Europeans did not feel any responsibility for integrating them into their own societies. Consequently the Europeanization which inevitably took place in the outlying territories did not follow a rigid or uniform pattern and produced varying results. The New World received the cultural currents of the Old, but it did not entirely cease to be a New World, even where it had been peopled by Europeans.

A desire for profits, rather than any romantic or ideological urge, was the incentive underlying the establishment of colonies. European immigrants to the New World undoubtedly came for many different personal reasons, among which the economic was not always uppermost. Probably the widest assortment of motives could be found among the settlers of the English colonies, whose members ranged from aristocrats to indentured servants, from God-fearing Puritans to convicted criminals. They crossed the seas hoping to find gold or freedom from persecution; to baptize the Indians or to debauch and enslave them; to catch fish, plant corn, or establish a new Canaan in the wilderness. But however divergent were the ambitions of the immigrants, there was remarkable singleness of aim among the financial backers of colonial projects and in the minds of the officials who authorized them. Colonial outposts were intended to yield a return upon the capital invested and to enhance the economic assets of the home country. The growth of a European population in these remote spots was a secondary consideration, regarded without much enthusiasm and with almost no perception of the tremendous consequences with which it was fraught.

THE BLESSINGS OF FAILURE

European imperialism of the early modern period reflected the ebullient energy and optimism of a restive society rather than careful calculation. Although it was undertaken for profit, the costs were not counted in advance nor could they even be estimated. The results were different and more far-reaching than had been anticipated. The venture gradually became a game played for tremendous stakes, culminating in the seventeenth and eighteenth centuries in a gigantic struggle between the larger powers for control of vast sections of the globe. Although the financial returns were substantial, in some cases greater than had been dreamed of, they were mostly dissipated in the wars which grew out of imperialistic rivalries.

The outcome of the spasm of activity and conflict in which empires were won and lost can be stated in a paradox. Generally speaking, the degree of a state's well-being was in inverse ratio to its imperialistic success. The nations that entered the race belatedly and under seeming disadvantages, or that avoided it altogether, were better off than those which had achieved the most dazzling triumphs. Portugal and Spain, the sponsors of the early epochal voyages, were the first states to lay out and exercise extensive claims and quickly became the envy and goad of their neighbors. The famous papal demarcation line of 1493 which divided the non-European world between them was a challenge thrown down to other competing powers. The pre-eminence of Spain in particular was a standing affront to the Protestant nations of northern Europe, whose seamen plundered the treasure ships from Mexico and South America and harassed the commerce of the "papists" at every opportunity. More serious was the fact that the large quantities of gold and silver imported from the New World were not used to develop Spanish industries. Instead, the easier course was followed of purchasing manufactures abroad, a policy which strengthened the economies of the countries that were Spain's natural enemies. Even more than the ruthlessness and greed of her conquistadors, the sudden and enormous colonial wealth of Spain proved to be her undoing. It lessened incentive for honest productive work and encouraged idle extravagance. It helped perpetuate the obsolete feudal structure of society and bestowed a ready income upon an absolutist monarchy so bigoted and obtuse that it exterminated the Moors, one of the most enlightened middle-class populations in all Europe. The Spanish Empire, which in the sixteenth century was the mightiest in the Western world (and with its Hapsburg affiliations probably the most powerful on earth), appeared to be stunned by such relatively minor reverses as the defeat of the Armada in the English Channel and the failure of the Dutch wars. The resources of the state were still formidable (including for some sixty years, as they did, the realm of Portugal) but so little effort was made to develop them that with the loss of her American colonies in the early nineteenth century Spain subsided to the rank of a third- or fourth-rate power, a poor relation in the European family. One of the most striking object lessons in modern times of the peril inherent in too easy material success is provided by Spain's dismal transition—from conquest to parasitism to decadence.

Holland, France, and England, in contrast to Spain, found the road to empire a difficult one, but still attractive enough to induce them to waste a good deal of their substance. The Dutch were handicapped at the start by not being an independent nation. Their eventual singular success was a by-product of their struggle against their Spanish masters, in which they learned to compensate for a small territory and population by utilizing the sea in combat. When most desperately pressed by the invader they could breach their dikes to flood him out. To provide swift means both of escape and of attack they steadily expanded their fleet. Consequently, by the early seventeenth century, even before their independence had been formally recognized, they had become the greatest naval power in Europe. To complete their revenge against Spain they seized the Portuguese East Indies, which were temporarily under Spanish dominion, and which included the fabulous Spice Islands. By wisely trimming their sails in other quarters and avoiding unnecessary conflicts in the future, the Dutch were able to retain this most coveted prize of the Far East for three hundred years regardless of the vicissitudes of empire in other parts of the world.

England and France were relatively late in entering the contest, but because of the large and fairly evenly matched potential of the two countries they became the rival giants overshadowing its later stages. While lagging behind in practice, the English and French contributed much of the theory of imperialism. Their publicists emphasized the advantages of a state-directed economy which could promote a "favorable balance of trade" and attract "treasure"—that is, bullion—into the country. (The Spanish contented themselves with accumulating and spending their gold, leaving others to theorize on the logic of it.) French enthusiasts were especially zealous in trying to make the rules work and encouraged the government to bear down heavily upon its own long-suffering subjects for lack of colonials who could provide ready profits to merchants or a surplus for the national exchequer. The diligent and thrifty Colbert carried out the prevailing ideas with the greatest completeness, if not with entire consistency. He couldn't conjure into being the ideal colonial preserves which he longed for; neither could he prevent King Louis XIV from squandering the money which he garnered for the treasury; but he could and did attempt to promote the growth of population, increase manufactures, and mold the consumption habits of the nation to discourage extravagance.

Whatever benefits accrued to France from the international competition for self-sufficient empires were indirect, such as the stimulation of shipbuilding, improvements in agriculture, and the expansion of industry. The more adequate recognition accorded to the middle class made for a healthier society and a stronger internal economy, especially during the century between the Wars of Religion and the abrogation of Huguenot toleration in 1685 by the foggy-brained Louis XIV, so inappropriately known as "the Sun King." France contributed to geographical discovery through her distinguished explorers, but was not able to retain the fruits of their discoveries, which fell largely to the British and their American colonists. Economically the French would have been better off if they had scuttled their colonial claims. In the series of wars with the British which reached a climax in the later eighteenth century, they not only lost the greater part of their overseas possessions but brought their own country to the brink of bankruptcy and revolution.

Because of retarded development, miscalculation, and the prick of unexpected adversity, the British were able to bungle their way into a great measure of success. They fitted out expeditions to try to reach the Far East by a "Northwest Passage" skirting the Arctic Circle. By butting their hulls against the ice they increased their hardihood as navigators. In warmer waters the profitable piracy against Spanish shipping was also a fine school for seamen, which could be turned to advantage later against the French. When the British did acquire holdings on the North American mainland, they dreamed of mining bullion so that they could duplicate the golden harvest of Spain. Luckily for them, there was no gold or silver to be had. Prospectors were forced to become settlers, turning to such prosaic but rewarding pursuits as agriculture, fishing, the production of naval stores, and shipbuilding. Consequently, sturdy and expanding communities came into being along the whole eastern seaboard.

The British East India Company hoped to annex the lucrative trade with the Spice Islands, but here the British were thwarted by the Dutch, who had moved into this Spanish-Portuguese preserve just ahead of them. Reluctantly and as a second choice, the company concentrated its efforts upon India, thus unintentionally preparing the way for the extension of British dominion over one of the world's richest empires, commanding a subcontinent, with resources which to this day have not been fully estimated. From the few bare footholds which the British had secured on the Indian coast enormous profits poured in almost immediately. During the latter part of the seventeenth century the company was able to pay dividends averaging twenty-five per cent annually, and between 1669 and 1683 East India stock almost tripled in market value. The on-the-spot opportunities for sharp individuals were practically unlimited. In 1757 after he had maneuvered the Nawab of Bengal into a position of dependence upon the company, Robert Clive laid hands upon a large personal fortune, but later remarked that when he remembered the gold, silver, and jewels in the Nawab's treasury he was astonished at his own moderation.

The French agents in India attempted to establish political influence in strategic areas. The British, left free to follow the dictates of commerce, amassed sufficient financial reserves to be able to match the French with political intrigue when that was necessary and also to raise their own armies and put them in the field. The ousting of the French garrisons from India by 1763 was accomplished by company men and their native auxiliaries at practically no expense to the British government except for a little naval support.

Some other European states which were not in a position to establish colonies or compete for distant trading posts managed to get along remarkably well. Prussia (Brandenburg), a minor German state at the beginning of the age of imperialism, had advanced to the rank of a first-class power by its close, without adding a square foot of overseas territory. Frederick the Great kept his eyes on Europe and his mind on the main chance, ready to pounce on his neighbors at any sign of weakness. When his phenomenal success against Austria frightened France into a general alliance aimed at crushing the upstart, it seemed that Frederick's ambitions ınight cost him too dearly. But fortunately for him, England and France were moving into the final phase of their semiglobal struggle. England was bound to support any enemy of France, and her victory in the Seven Years' War was also a triumph for Prussia. France's desperate attempt to retain her empire—which she lost to her rival across the Channel—had proved a boon to her rival across the Rhine.

Still the mistrust and enmity which Prussia incurred was a considerable price to pay for a larger space on the map of northern Europe. More secure in the long run were the nations that avoided both the virus of imperialism and the enticements of power politics. In an age when blood and money were being spent freely for the procuring of empire, the Swiss were trying to extricate themselves from one. By the close of the fifteenth century they had wrung from the Hapsburg Holy Roman Emperor a precarious independence which they were determined to maintain against that or any other outside power. It was a difficult undertaking, not only because of the smallness of the country but because the Swiss were subject to all the cross currents and tensions which were disturbing European society. The religious controversy fell squarely into their midst. Zwingli, one of the great names in the Protestant Revolt, was a native son, and Calvin chose Geneva as the site from which to hurl his thunderbolts. The Catholic and Protestant cantons were equally unshakable in their resolution, and there were enough points at issue between the two factions to plunge the little country into a ruinous civil war, the more venomous because of the inclination of each side to seek outside support. After a few bitter clashes, however, the Swiss resolved their dilemma by a rare stroke of rationality. They agreed to disagree, leaving each canton to manage its internal affairs and mode of worship but forswearing foreign alliances and pledging mutual support to protect their common liberties. In an age of extreme intolerance they demonstrated that tolerance was possible and, still more distinctive, that community-mindedness could be achieved among people who differed in language and in fundamental beliefs and practices. They have continued to give a demonstration of this down to the present day.

The Swiss were not saints or gifted with superlative wisdom.

The Confederation which they established was hampered by an unwillingness to trust the central government with adequate powers, and most of the thirteen cantons were oligarchic republics rather than democracies. (It was not until the nineteenth century that they thoroughly revised their constitution and then became a school for the Western world in democratic reform.) Perhaps if the Swiss had been differently located, if they had commanded fine ports on the Atlantic instead of Alpine passes, they might have developed insatiable ambitions. Even in their mountain fastness they were not unaffected by the tumults around them. They participated in many, needlessly and gratuitously, by hiring out their scanty manpower to serve in foreign armies, thus making profit and sometimes fame out of other people's misfortunes without jeopardizing their national existence. Eventually the public conscience became disgusted with this gory traffic (Zwingli had denounced it in his day), and after the Napoleonic wars the exporting of mercenary soldiers was prohibited, a measure which lent greater firmness and consistency to the Swiss policy of neutrality in European—or World—wars. But in domestic affairs the Swiss Confederation, as early as 1531, offered an example of cohesion without suppression of differences, of mutual co-operation without a dead level of uniformity, which unfortunately is almost unique.

The Scandinavians, likewise, waited out the contest for empire of the seventeenth and eighteenth centuries, although they were historically qualified to give lessons to others in that department. In earlier times they had bred seafaring bands of pirates, marauders, merchants and colonizers to wrest strongholds from the Saracens in the Mediterranean and penetrate into unexplored northern latitudes. These exploits, however, had been the work of individuals or groups on their own. Whether successful or not they had left unaffected the status of the mother lands, and the northern peoples from which the Vikings had sprung did not commit their national fortunes to a competition with the resources of Spain, France, or England. Throughout the seventeenth century Sweden was still a major power, as emphasized by the exploits of Gustavus Adolphus in the Thirty Years' War and by the brilliant, though futile, victories of Charles XII at the close of the century. Her imperialistic prospects, however, were largely confined to the Baltic region, and here she yielded ground after defeat by Russia and as the Hohenzollern design for Prussia began to unfold. The international prestige of the northerners was speedily eclipsed, and the acceptance of this fact saved them from certain disillusionment and disaster. They were not as successful as the Swiss in avoiding the entanglements and bruises of European rivalries, but they moved more and more determinedly toward a policy of alert and benevolent neutrality.

On first thought it may seem that Great Britain's experience refutes the thesis that a nation's ultimate well-being stood in inverse ratio to the prospering of its imperialistic undertakings. In the sixteenth century England had been on the defensive against Spain and France and narrowly escaped invasion. By 1763 she was mistress of the sea and commanded an enormous domain, a substantial part of which had just been acquired from France by the fortunes of war. And in the nineteenth century she became both the richest and the most powerful state in the world.

Actually, however, the case of England substantiates the thesis. It was the defeats and frustrations which she suffered in the early part of the struggle for empire which stimulated the resourcefulness of her people and the diversification of her economy, promoting especially the steady and phenomenal growth of her maritime enterprise. The commercial superiority which she built up in this way was more valuable and less ephemeral than the profits which could be extracted from colonial overlordship. At any rate, almost on the heels of their victorious but grueling struggle with France, the British lost the most important of their New World possessions through the American Revolution. The vain attempt to suppress the colonists brought a constitutional crisis in England, involved the country in a fresh war with her old rivals Spain and France (who had to be compensated in the peace settlement), jeopardized her naval strength, and decimated her trade. Furthermore it necessitated a re-examination of Britain's colonial policy, which resulted in the scrapping of the basic principles of imperialism. Her English-speaking colonies were granted more and more generous degrees of self-government, enabling them to evolve into free commonwealths, unhampered by coercive restrictions of crown or British parliament. They remained bound to Britain by ties of sentiment—the more so as coercion was removed—but empires are maintained by other forces than the reciprocal flow of sentiment. The British Dominions became entities reminiscent of the ancient Greek settlements in Sicily and southern Italy; they ceased to be colonies in the modern European sense of the term. Thus Britain's failures were in the professed objectives of imperialism and her greatest successes in the areas where she repudiated the pattern. Regrettably, other nations and the British themselves did not learn the lesson as well as they might have.

It is true that even with the loss of the thirteen colonies and the subsequent initiation of the Dominion concept, Britain's empire was still large and still retained with determination and occasional ruthlessness. But it is unrealistic to argue this as the basis for England's prosperity and unique pre-eminence in the nineteenth century. The Industrial Revolution, which originated in England and from there set the pace for the rest of the Western world, provides the true explanation. This revolution in technology and society was not the offspring of empire (it could never have begun in Spain, for example). It was the result of a complex variety of factors—natural, political, and economic—operating directly in England and among her own population. Furthermore, the new industrial development gave impetus to the antimercantilist laissez-faire school of thought which was in opposition to the whole logic of imperialism. England's productivity and financial strength seemed to increase as she moved in the direction of free trade, which she finally embraced unreservedly. As the Industrial Revolution spread to the continent of Europe it had the affect there also, although in varying and lesser degrees, of diverting attention from expansionist schemes to mechanical progress at home. Only in the late nineteenth century, when a serious drop in the prosperity curve was discernible, did the siren call of empire again become compelling, with more alluring promises and more disastrous consequences than the age of mercantilism had known.

The fact that England retained and extended her position in India during the ebb tide of European imperialism may seem to be such a monumental exception to the trend indicated as to refute the argument that it really was a trend so far as the major power, Great Britain, was concerned. With the British entrenched in a subcontinent, one of the most populous and richest regions of Asia, against the will of the inhabitants, how could it be alleged that they had renounced imperialism? Logic and consistency are not always to be expected in the policies of any people, certainly not in those of the British. Their position in India, while important and real enough, was to some extent anomalous. The victory over the French in 1763 had not bestowed India upon Great Britain or even given her a trade monopoly. It merely determined that the British would be the only one of the foreign trading powers there who might, if they chose, engage in military and political activities. (The French tried to revive the practice themselves during the Revolutionary and Napoleonic wars.) The East India Company was still interested almost exclusively in revenue, although it was becoming more difficult to distinguish between the profits of legitimate commerce and the subsidies, taxes, and perquisites which accrued to the company through its extralegal position as a sovereign power in the regions where it operated. The British authorities in Westminster were reluctant to acknowledge or assume responsibility for the political role of the company, while aggressive governors, carrying on the tradition of Warren Hastings (whose impeachment trial had ended in acquittal), negotiated treaties, waged wars, and annexed native states right and left. Except for ineffective temporizing measures, the home government did not squarely assume the rule even of the "British" portions of India until the Great Mutiny of 1857 had revealed the reckless ineptitude of the company's system and by endangering the lives of British subjects had shocked the entire nation.

Aside from the fact that the Indian Empire was acquired only gradually and through the back door, it would be difficult to prove that it was essential to England's nineteenth-century prosperity. The capital derived from India may have had more to do with the progress of the Industrial Revolution than Englishmen have ever acknowledged, but it was not the decisive factor. At the time when the technological revolution was getting under way in England, the East India Company's revenues had fallen off because of the expensive wars in India and adjacent regions for which the company was directly or indirectly responsible. The cost of its blunders, including the Great Mutiny, was, to be sure, charged largely against the Indian people, thus increasing the burdens of this dejected folk and retarding their economic growth. Their depressed condition, however, was hardly beneficial to England; in fact as she became interested in India as a market for her cotton manufactures, the extreme poverty of the Indian population was a disadvantage. Individual and family fortunes—far too many and usually ill deserved—were made in India, but it is questionable whether they had a salutary effect upon either English society or English economy. And the distrust which Britain's Indian policy fostered among the Asiatic peoples as a whole was a heavy price to pay for a surplus of sterling credits. By the late nineteenth century the British were clinging to the "Jewel of Empire" from strategic considerations and for reasons of prestige rather than economic necessity.

IN SEARCH OF A NEW SOCIAL ORDER

The early modern period had begun with the discovery of new interests which promised a high degree of personal satisfaction. A spirit of restlessness, impatience, and even reckless arrogance was a natural accompanying factor. The sweep of material forces was so compelling that it threatened to suspend or overwhelm values which had been deeply rooted and carefully cultivated, as illustrated by the changing climate in religion. It became an easy matter for people to embrace a shabby view of human nature, so eager were they to remove restraints upon activities which were immediately appealing. Man was to be taken, so to speak, at a large discount, in the hope of quick and profitable returns upon the investment of his efforts. It was inevitable that misgivings should follow the adoption of such a rash attitude.

The enlarging sphere of opportunity and the material improvements embodied in the Commercial Revolution held great possibilities for the enrichment of civilization. As time went on, however, it became apparent that they were not automatically contributing to such an end, that they were not living up to expectations even in terms of personal reward. The expansion of commerce had brought an unprecedented increase in wealth, an influx of new and highly desirable commodities, and a consequent growth in the population of Western Europe. But incomes were very unevenly distributed and the condition of the lower classes, especially in the cities, was if anything worse than before. The era which proclaimed the right of man to develop his talents to the full, to probe without inhibitions his innermost feelings, and to oppose the dictates of his conscience to ecclesiastical authority also witnessed the revival of slavery and the recognition of the trade in human bodies as a major business enterprise. The voyages of discovery had opened avenues of commerce which made possible a wider exchange of goods than ever before, offering substantial benefits to all peoples. But almost immediately the gates were slammed shut by jealous governments determined to keep outsiders from sharing in the exploitation of regions to which they had staked a claim. Although monopolistic regulations could not always be enforced in the face of the natural pressures of supply and demand, they intensified feelings of envy, frustration, and belligerence among the nations.

The replacing of the feudal by a capitalist economy seemed at first to be a process of emancipation. With the decline of the guilds and similar agencies of collective restraint, a premium was placed upon private initiative in venturing into areas which combined risk with high remuneration. Essentially, modern capitalism began as the vindication of private ownership, with special emphasis upon the right of the owner of wealth to dispose of his goods as he pleased and to invest and reinvest his earnings for the purpose of increasing his wealth ad infinitum. Yet the most alluring and obvious profits were those derivable from commerce, and commerce became an object of meticulous regulation by the state governments. The system of mercantilism, which was the economic dogma and practice almost universally approved in Western Europe during the Commercial Revolution, stressed the necessity of a national economy, tightly controlled, and directed to enhancing the wealth and military strength of the state. It called for minute prescription of industry, agriculture, and especially commerce, typified by the erection of tariff barriers and the bestowing of rewards and penalties in the form of subsidies or heavy taxation. In the heyday of mercantilism, even in such a

relatively liberal country as England, governments did not scruple
to regulate prices, wages, the movement of people from one community to another, and even their diet and apparel. Consequently,
the early age of European capitalism was anything but a regime
of free enterprise.

In the semicollectivist economy of the Later Middle Ages, pro-
ducers and distributors had been restrained by codes which they
formulated and enforced upon themselves and which reflected the
generally approved standards of their day. Now they were hedged
and bludgeoned by rules imposed upon them by a political authority not amenable to their control and chiefly interested in magni-
fying its own power. The middle class in its eagerness to shake off
the grip of the nobility and of the Church had bolstered centralized monarchical governments which were approaching the stage
of unlimited despotism. The middle class also found that the revenues of trade and industry were being consumed in wars, in-
decisive in outcome and more and more exhausting. The pursuit
of commerce had turned into the battle of empires, in which national economies were crippled, resources wasted, and human
values reduced. A series of revolts—artistic, religious, and economic—had been launched on behalf of the individual, yet
the majority of individuals were more hopelessly bound than ever.

At all times, however, part of the resources of the European
intellect was directed against the objectionable features of the prevailing trends. The desire for freedom had been a powerful stimulus from the beginning and one which could not be obliterated
entirely. Many protests and concrete programs, some of them of
heroic proportions, made the securing of a wider freedom their
goal. These usually did not rest on sheer expediency but were
buttressed by ideal considerations, often derived from religious
conviction. An example is the Dutch struggle for independence
against Spain, which, as already pointed out, was at the same time
an incident in the competition for empire. In this contest sincere
religious feeling and aversion to tyranny were intermingled in-
separably with commercial ambition and national pride, and not
all those who supported the Dutch cause were high-minded
idealists. The effect of their final success was marred by the vindictive jealousy which the Dutch exhibited toward the neighbor-

ing provinces of the southern Netherlands, whose inhabitants remained Catholic and loyal to Spain. Also, although the Dutch worked so devotedly to procure freedom, they were not overly zealous in extending political privileges to the humbler members of their own communities, and their thoroughgoing Calvinism kept them from being tolerant of all divergent opinion. In spite of these qualifications, however, the new nation was born into an atmosphere much freer than that of most European countries, and the Dutch achievement represented a notable contribution to the cause of human liberty.

Wider in its implications than the struggle which gave birth to the Dutch Republic was the ferment contributed by the left-wing religious groups in England during the first half of the seventeenth century. This ferment was something more than the final phase of the religious controversies that had rocked much of Europe in the course of the preceding century. The Reformation had aimed at overthrowing restrictions and repudiating authority rooted in the medieval heritage. It had succeeded in its immediate objectives without, however, establishing a sure basis for a harmonious society. On the contrary, it was becoming apparent that the general sweep of events was not a procession toward this ideal goal. Hence, the proponents of the ideal were of necessity a restless minority, frequently dissenting and warning, if not lone voices crying in the wilderness. Nevertheless, they tried to meet the challenge presented by environmental change; and they believed for a time that it would be possible to bring the majority to their point of view and to ground their proposals in the collective wisdom of mankind.

Puritanism is the term which covers the reforming and dissenting English movements in the broadest sense, and Puritanism was a force both inside and outside of the established Church. To describe its several facets simply as variant forms of Calvinism is inadequate. Its origin was of Calvinist inspiration, but it not only adapted itself to changing conditions and to the strongly felt needs of the groups that embraced it but also drew into a common center many influences from the near and remote past. At the outset in the sixteenth century, English Puritanism was part of an international Protestant movement (understandably so because its leadership was supplied largely by men who had spent years of exile on the Continent). In the beginning, however, it was hardly cosmopolitan in attitude and its intellectual foundations were rather meager. Its primary aim, aside from what it did to the individual, was to transform the character of the English Church. It sought to effect a more complete break with the Roman Catholic tradition, to liberalize the hierarchy so as to allow greater discretion to the individual clergyman, and to emphasize discussion and discourse as opposed to ceremony and sacrament. In keeping with the genius of Calvinism, it exalted individual responsibility, the obligation incumbent upon each personality to prove its worth and seek its fulfillment. It was an activist creed, burning to express itself in the sphere of everyday affairs, yet impelled by nonmaterial standards. For these reasons it not only came to be a powerful current of protest but bade fair to make over English society and institutions. Puritanism in its most dynamic phase in England was not restricted to the urban middle and lower classes. It gained a following among the country gentry, men of breeding and education, who were able to contribute a breadth of outlook and intellectual maturity to the debates which were carried on privately and publicly during the closing years of the Elizabethan Era. It secured a stronghold in the University of Cambridge; it was viewed sympathetically by members of the queen's council; it found an increasing voice in Parliament.

Under the early Stuart monarchs the Puritan concern for reform of the Church attached itself to a campaign to preserve popular liberties against encroachments by the king and to defend the rights of citizen and Parliament in the face of the Stuart doctrine of divine right. The persecution by Charles I and Archbishop Laud stimulated a great migration of Englishmen to America; but those of the Puritans who remained in England were prominent in all areas of resistance to the government of the dissembling but inflexible Stuart and constituted the backbone of the parliamentary party.

During the period of the civil wars and the interregnum the forces of Puritanism attained their greatest momentum, attracted the widest popular support, and were directed most searchingly to the problems of the social order. Having achieved ascendancy in the state, the more radical Puritan elements seemingly found the way open to them to build a commonwealth in the image of their hearts' desire. The reformers had definite ideas as to what needed to be done, in many fields besides that of ecclesiastical discipline. While under the spell of a foreshortened but powerful cosmic view of human destiny, and while earnestly seeking to ready themselves for the life hereafter, they were eager to transform the realities of the present life in the material world. They outlined a simple but positive political philosophy, which called for government by consent of the governed, the abolition of hereditary privilege, the enlargement of the franchise —even to the point of universal manhood suffrage. In spite of wide differences of opinion on these matters, among the groups most directly involved in overthrowing the monarchy there was general agreement as to the need for political reform. The so-called Levelers, who numbered in their ranks army leaders and gentlemen of standing as well as untutored common folk, were advocates of democracy. Nor were the reformers blind to social and economic evils. While rarely approaching communism (in spite of the charges of their opponents), they condemned the extreme and increasing inequalities of contemporary society. They championed the poor, who were being driven from their lands by the inexorable enclosure movement and afflicted by rising prices. The Puritan conscience was especially incensed at the entanglements, delays, high cost, and outright injustice of the law courts and advocated their drastic overhauling (something not accomplished until two centuries later). Although frequently depicted as stern visaged and strait-laced, many Puritans of the mid-seventeenth century actually showed strong traces of humanitarianism. They demanded penal reform, pointing out the iniquity and the folly of hanging poor wretches for petty thefts. At least a few far-seeing spirits of this tradition reflected critically on the moral issues raised by the pushing of commercial enterprise among the unresisting natives of India and cried out against the slave trade.

Undeniably, religious enthusiasm was sometimes attached to fantastic schemes and to wild individuals; but the bulk of the program propounded by the most boldly experimental wing of Puritanism was not wild or fantastic. The "Praise-God Barebone Parliament" (the nominated Parliament of 1653) has frequently been regarded as an example of the pathetic impracticality of the zealots who predominated in the Independent churches at the time and as a *reductio ad absurdum* of attempted rule by the saints. Yet foremost among the proposals of the Barebone Parliament were the abolition of tithes and the reform of legal procedures in the interest of speed and economy—measures which were neither utopian nor rabidly sectarian. This ill-fated Parliament did not fail because of incompetence; it was dissolved through the calculated strategy of its conservative members, who were eager to circumvent any encroachment upon vested property rights.

The religious reformers who pursued the goal of social and economic justice at the height of the English revolution had absorbed ideas from various sources and attempted to bring them together in focus upon the central problems of contemporary society. In many ways their preconceptions were medieval rather than typically Reformationist. This is seen especially in their economic views, which generally condemned usury and excessive profits, clung to the notion of a just price, and not only deplored extremes of inequality but tended to regard material wealth with suspicion. Obviously, they assumed that politics was not an end in itself but to be taken in the context of ethical and spiritual functions. Although as heirs of Calvin they placed great emphasis upon individual responsibility, they displayed a strong sense of community and warmly supported the concept of human brotherhood. Another remarkable aspect of their position is the frequent appeal to reason, and the exalting of reason as an essential trait in man and the basis for social organization. In harmony with the late medieval thinkers, some insisted that reason and faith were allies and that to oppose reason was to deny, rather than to obey, God. At the same time they were doubtful about identifying divine wisdom with any particular ecclesiastical foundation and were typically anticlerical. To a medieval framework they had fitted characteristic aspects of Renaissance humanism and reflected its confident spirit. They invoked both Holy Writ and the example of classical antiquity, the latter because it seemed to support the ideal of a simple, free, and dignified society. The concept of a state of nature underlying formal institutions was prominent in their thinking and was contrasted with the oppressions and disorders of the moment. (Naïvely, they were inclined to identify this pristine state of nature in England with the Anglo-Saxons and to attribute all noxious growths to the Norman conquerors.) Whatever their arguments, the Puritan critics were on the whole forward-looking rather than reactionary, and more apt to be too bold than too cautious. While emphatically and primarily religious in orientation, to a considerable degree the seventeenth-century Puritans anticipated the social vision of the philosophers of the Enlightenment. In their doctrines is to be found more than a hint of the concept of human perfectibility, and they earnestly accepted as a duty the enlistment of their faculties in the task of improving the State and society.

For all its promise, the Puritan movement culminated in failure. Although it accomplished much of permanent value, it failed in its far-reaching external objectives. It was not able to transform the Church of England, which reasserted itself with a sharp vengeance at the Restoration of 1660. More significant still, Puritanism faltered in its vision of a social order based on rational and ethical principles. Many reasons can be assigned for this defeat, among them the breach that developed between Cromwell and his radical supporters, some of whom he felt compelled to repudiate or imprison. He was a practical man, and utopia he deemed to be not within the grasp of his generation. Moreover, the military dictatorship which—reluctantly but resolutely—he fastened upon the nation provoked an indiscriminate reaction against the Puritans and all their works, whether good or bad. The most ardent reformers were not the ones who held the reins during the Commonwealth and Protectorate, and those who did wield power succumbed to the temptation to use it arbitrarily. They collected heavier taxes than the discredited Stuarts had ever dreamed of demanding; they massacred Irish Catholics to show forth the wrath of the Lord; they sought to establish maritime supremacy and helped lay the foundations of an empire which would continue to quicken the pulse of Englishmen long after the Puritan dream of a heaven on earth had faded. The "Puritan Revolution" of the mid-seventeenth century did not constitute a social revolu-

tion, although it contained the seeds of one. With considerable
justice, Quakers charged the Puritans of the Cromwellian Era with
abandoning their own avowed principles. Instead of enlarging
justice and liberty they had introduced new oppressions and, for-
getting their humble past, had striven to make themselves the
rich and powerful of the earth.

Even these circumstances do not fully explain the deflection of
Puritanism from its highest objectives and the increasing sterility
of the movement. The Puritans were not exterminated at the
Restoration in spite of the general revulsion against them. Their
edge was blunted more by contempt than by persecution, although
the persecution was real enough for a while. As they lost the
support of the country gentry they gradually adopted an acquies-
cent and narrowly middle-class philosophy and became content
to measure their success with the yardstick of material advantage.
During the ascendancy of Cromwell they had appeared—unintentionally perhaps but too clearly—in the guise of a political faction;
and now they had to suffer the unpleasant but endurable fate of
a party out of power. They learned to conform to the rules of
party politics and bided their time, finally receiving compensation
in the "Glorious Revolution" of 1688. Undeniably, something of
the Puritan tradition of resistance to tyranny contributed to that
fortunate and climactic event, which drove James II and the
divine-right dogma from the throne and established the supremacy
of Parliament. The Revolution of 1688, though it was a constitutional landmark of great importance, lacked the dynamic ideas
that had illuminated Puritan polemics in the 1640's. It was a
"bloodless" revolution in the figurative as well as in the literal
sense. Its leaders had more sophisticated and less splendid objectives than the creation of a democratic commonwealth based
on spiritual brotherhood. They were concerned with such practical matters as building a Whig political machine, protecting the
Bank of England, and halting the ambitions of France. In the
Revolution of 1688 the Puritans, who were now usually called
"Dissenters," faithfully performed an assigned and subordinate
role. They had refused the bait of James II's Declaration of Indulgence, and they were rewarded by Parliament's Toleration
Act—which gave them the right not to sit in Parliament but to sit

on Sunday mornings in their own chapels, provided they kept the doors unlocked, were properly licensed by the bishop, and continued to pay tithes to the support of the state church. Actually, through the device of "occasional conformity," Dissenters managed to obtain seats in Parliament, and they even recovered hope of modifying the Church of England as the power to appoint bishops passed into the hands of Whig ministries. (This turn of events inspired the sarcastic remark of a Tory character in one of Addison's essays: that in the entire county not a single Presbyterian was to be found, excepting of course the bishop!) But a bishop's miter was not the kind of crown that had been sought after by a Lilburne, a John Hales, or a William Walwyn. By the close of the seventeenth century Puritanism had spent most of its force. It had ceased to be dangerous; it had also too largely ceased to be challenging. However, it had performed an unforgettable service in demonstrating that religious incentives could be brought to bear upon practical problems of living and of human relationships. Moreover, its influence persisted as a subdued but significant element in the English cultural heritage (in America as well as in England) and imparted something of its ancient fervor to the philosophy of liberalism and to humanitarian projects.

REHABILITATION OF REASON AND FAITH

While efforts toward social reconstruction at the hands of English sectarians were subsiding, a program of broader scope and dedicated even more specifically to the emancipation of men's minds was beginning to be formulated in various quarters of Western Europe. It was borne on the rising tide of rationalism and reached its climax in the eighteenth century. Its social and political objectives and even its reasoning processes were not totally foreign to those of the Puritan reformers, but it started from different premises and admitted no dependence upon religious dogma or affiliation. Also, it was perhaps more directly indebted to the Commercial Revolution—positively, because expanding contacts and familiarity with distant regions stimulated a search for universally applicable principles; negatively, because materialism, imperial greed, and despotism provided fit subjects for stinging attack. The rationalist movement found expression in almost all aspects of the culture of the Age of the Enlightenment, affecting literature and art as well as philosophy. Although it was primarily a phenomenon of intellectual circles rather than of the populace at large, it was by no means confined to the realm of abstract ideas. It was concerned with the entire world of experience and had a definite impact upon problems arising from the growing complexity of society. It aimed not only to impart a sense of direction but to re-examine the assumptions underlying traditional activities and the setting in which they took place. Finally, it embodied a quest for values, for standards of measurement, and for objectives which could evoke the highest level of endeavor. Disregarding national boundaries, the concepts of rationalism engaged the minds of key individuals in most of the countries of Western Europe and also in the New World, ultimately creating a tremendous stir.

The rationalism of the Age of the Enlightenment had deep roots and might be regarded as a culmination of tendencies reaching back through the Middle Ages to classical antiquity and beyond. The judgments rendered and many of the arguments employed were not new. The thinkers of this period reaffirmed conceptions of human nature, of society, and of man's relationship to the universe which had been held at various times before. Their basic conclusions were similar to those which have been and always will be brought into play whenever there is an overwhelming desire to improve man's estate and a faith in his capacity for such improvement. The rationalist interpretation of human nature had much in common not only with the ancient classical but also, perhaps still more, with that of the late medieval thinkers; even though the rationalists regarded the Scholastics—if they deigned to think of them at all—as at the opposite pole from themselves.

In attempting to recover and firmly establish a belief in the inherent dignity of man, however, the rationalists used an approach which was fundamentally new. Instead of invoking the voice of authority they appealed to the evidence of science. Actually their philosophy was inspired by the remarkable progress of the natural sciences, which had projected a more intelligible picture of the physical universe than any previously known and which seemed to have provided a technique for the continual enlargement of knowledge. Their speculations were the first philosophical crystallization of the findings of modern science. They were vibrant with the enthusiasm imparted by the sudden widening of horizons. They reflected the confidence that with the discovery of an infallible method of acquiring truth the bondage of the past could be shaken off, leaving the mind free to build on the solid foundations of experience and reason.

Exponents of the Enlightenment attempted to apply the tools of science to the solution of every type of problem. They breathed an atmosphere of daring and imaginative experimentation. Descartes resolved to dismiss from his consciousness all opinions which had been acquired at second hand, and then to accept only those "innate" ideas which returned with the insistent force and clarity of mathematical axioms. From such pure unshakable principles he would deduce the structure of the cosmos. Others felt that Descartes had conceded too much in acknowledging any suprarational factor. Locke preferred to reject "innate" ideas. He regarded the mind as a blank tablet upon which impressions are described through the operation of the sense organs. According to Locke, sensations are the raw data out of which ideas are compounded, and upon this mechanical and empirical foundation the reason can erect an edifice which mirrors the symmetry and embodies the laws of the eternal order of things. The figurations which the rationalists, including the Lockian empiricists, saw taking shape in their minds with mathematical precision were remarkably like concepts which had formerly been anchored to faith and revelation. Typically they included such postulates as the existence of God and of the soul, immortality, and the moral perfection of the universe. But their advocates insisted (except when anxious to avoid the wrath of ecclesiastics) that these beliefs rested upon demonstrable principles rather than the authority of dogma or tradition.

Although the rationalist movement was more indebted to the distant past than its adherents recognized, it was not simply a repetition of familiar themes. Still less was it an idealized interpretation of the contemporary scene. To a large extent it was a reaction against prevailing mores and institutions. It frowned on the overcharged emotionalism of the Renaissance and the Reformation; it opposed the unreflecting materialism and the irresponsible cult of power which had followed in their wake. It aimed to liberate from oppression, especially from the oppression born of ignorance. It sought to rediscover man beneath the maze of distortion, abuse, and fear.

Because it was fed by a desire for change and intended as an antidote to present ills, rationalist thought often assumed a critical or even negative form. It was suspicious of institutionalized religion because religion had spawned fanaticism and bloodshed. It had a strong bias against despotism and its disciples usually did not warm to the tawdry triumphs of greedy kings. Impatient with provincial prejudices, it cultivated an international and cosmopolitan outlook. In contrast to the meanness, hypocrisy, and calculating selfishness of conventional European society, it glorified the "noble savage" on the one hand and the "Chinese sage" on the other; the former because he was uncorrupted by the vices of civilization, the latter because he had supposedly risen above them by following the light of reason.

Yet the prevailing mood of the Enlightenment was optimism, and its central emphasis was positive rather than negative. It was an affirmation of faith in man and forecast a magnificent future for the human race. The method of approach and the assurance of success were derived from science, but the chief interest lay not in specialized technical knowledge nor in the march of mechanical power but in the application of intelligence to human needs and aspirations. For this reason rationalism differed from much of the science-based thought of the present day, which is apt to be either highly esoteric and socially irresponsible or narrowly utilitarian. It was remarkably parallel in spirit, and even in form, to medieval Scholasticism in its heyday, in spite of an iconoclastic tone and contempt for authority. The data of science are indeed very different from the dogmas of the Church Fathers. However, the most impressive scientific advances had come in those fields which, while relying on observation, are speculative and deductive rather than experimental and inductive. Astronomy had outstripped chemistry and was far ahead of geology or biology, which were just beginning to be subjected to critical examination.

Mathematics, a purely conceptual discipline, was the new queen of the sciences, regarded as the perfect example of what a science could be and as holding the key to universal knowledge. Consequently there was a prominent strain of deductive reasoning in seventeenth- and eighteenth-century thought, of proceeding by logical derivation from infallible premise to particular instance, even in the study of such variables as human behavior and the operation of social institutions.

Aside from the question of method, rationalism in its prime objectives and guiding convictions resembled Scholastic thought more closely than has usually been recognized. Of course the rationalist movement was too broad and too varied in expression to be classified in any single category, and individual pronouncements can be found representing the most divergent attitudes and opinions. On the whole it was disinclined to erect or endorse a closed system, such as Scholasticism had striven to achieve. The Scholastic thinkers had looked to the past in search of authorities with which to fortify their arguments, and when they viewed the future it was at a great distance and from the standpoint of the ultimate and transcendental goal of the human race. The rationalists, scorning the past, pinned their hopes to a future which they believed to be close at hand and which promised release from the most intolerable burdens of man's present condition. Furthermore, the task that the rationalists saw cut out for them was a purely human one, with man, a free agent, plotting his own future and bringing it into actuality through his own efforts and the guidance of his own intellect. Nevertheless, there was substantial similarity between the thirteenth-century Scholastics and the eighteenth-century rationalists in their estimate of the potentialities of the human creature and even in their conception of what constituted his ideal state. Scholastic thinkers, for example, did not rule out the possibility of change in institutions. Although St. Thomas believed that the natural law was immutable (as did the rationalists of the Enlightenment), he raised the question of whether human laws could rightly be altered "on account of the changed condition of man"—and answered it in the affirmative. And although the rationalists were far more prone to stress the necessity of change, this was because they wished to reshape institutions in conformity with the ideal pattern of reason. The majority of them believed that there was such a pattern and hoped, if they could succeed in capturing it, to perpetuate it for all time. The great Scholastic teachers, especially St. Thomas, were synthesizers, who stood at the end of an age and viewed it from a lofty ideal summit, fitting the recalcitrant pieces into place with determined logic. The men of the Enlightenment stood—or thought they stood—on the threshold of a new age of which they were the prophets.

The rationalists proclaimed a revolt against traditional authority, and certainly owed no deference to the particular authorities that the thirteenth century had held in reverence; in fact they took not the slightest notice of them. But the rationalists were most incensed against restraints and injustices attributable to coercive agencies of fairly recent growth, whose power was concrete, formidable, and questioned only at considerable peril—especially the tyranny inherent in the union of absolute governments with authoritarian state churches. In challenging the dogmas that supported the contemporary enemies of freedom, the rationalists necessarily armed themselves with conceptual weapons forged in an earlier age. And they developed a view of man and the universe which, without any consciousness or acknowledgment of the debt, had many points in common with the reasoned judgment of late medieval thinkers. The most typical philosophers of the Enlightenment assumed that the universe is rational and purposeful and also that man is capable of understanding it through the exercise of reason implanted in him by God. They affirmed that the whole physical order is controlled by laws emanating from God, the supreme intelligence and faultless designer. The laws of nature underlie the world of living creatures, including man, and provide the basis for a beneficial community life. Human laws are dependent upon the natural law. They are, or should be, a means of applying and enforcing it within the context of civilized society. All of these precepts, so fully elaborated during the Enlightenment, had been explicitly stated by St. Thomas Aquinas. To the "Natural Law" and the "Human Law" Aquinas added also the "Divine Law" (the Scriptures), but only for the—one might almost say—professional reason that man was destined for an eternal and special kind of bliss beyond the earthly felicity which he shared with other creatures and which he was capable of achieving through his own natural endowments.

The apostles of the Enlightenment, again in agreement with their medieval predecessors, believed in the inherent goodness of man and argued that man has the ability to develop a harmonious social and political order. Here, departing most widely from theological tradition, they rejected the doctrine of original sin. The evils and injustices which abound, they affirmed, are not an inescapable sentence of fate but the result of man's failure to abide by the laws which permeate the universe and which he is fully capable of discovering and utilizing if he wishes. Actually, St. Thomas was in substantial agreement with this position. Although he of course retained the notion of original sin, it did not figure greatly in his system. Certainly it never assumed Augustinian or Calvinistic proportions. His emphasis was upon the redeemability of the creature, upon his potentialities for moral and spiritual growth. (It is significant that in referring to the primitive paradisiacal state before the Fall, Aquinas described it as a condition in which "nothing either beside or against reason could take man unawares.")

The Scholastic thinkers looked upon the cosmos as having been designed primarily for the benefit of man—to bestow blessings upon him and, when necessary, chastisement. To them the earth—man's abode and God's footstool—was the center of the universe, the hub of the whole creation. While the men of the Enlightenment generally accepted the heliocentric astronomy of Copernicus, Galileo, and Newton, they were just as positive that the earth and the starry firmament were intended to minister to human needs and to speed man's progress. They believed that by penetrating the secrets of nature and reducing them to mathematical formulas people would be brought to an understanding not only of space and matter but of the principles of justice and morality. Ye shall know the truth *of science* and the truth shall make you free, was their gospel. The findings of science were hailed as a new and final revelation, displacing all priest-concocted Scriptures. In the words of Alexander Pope:

> Nature and Nature's laws lay hid in night;
> God said, Let Newton be! and all was Light.

Thomas Paine, pamphleteering crusader for the rights of man and for Deism, the new religion of nature and reason, brought its tenets down within reach of almost everyone's understanding, expounding them with glowing enthusiasm if somewhat curious logic. In raising the question as to why God had created a plurality of worlds rather than a single sphere, Paine concluded that it was for the specific purpose of providing easier instruction for the human race in science and the mechanical arts. He looked forward to the day when all mankind would endeavor to imitate the Deity "in everything moral, scientific, and mechanical."

Essentially, then, the science-intoxicated men were returning to the belief in a consistent, purposeful, and beneficent universe, a belief which had been undermined in the attempt to break with the circumscribed world view of the Feudal Age and jettisoned in the scramble for riches and empire. Although they invoked the testimony of astronomy and physics to fortify their cause, their contribution was on the side of humane and spiritual values. The cosmic principles, the "laws" which they thought so clearly distinguishable, were not necessary and inevitable derivatives from the factual data that had been accumulated, as Hume and other skeptics were soon to point out. These principles were, rather, articles of faith, verifiable in large part in the forum of human experience, especially as spread over the pages of history, rather than in the laboratory. The vision of the philosophers was not a reflection of nature but, in Carl Becker's phrase, a "heavenly city" of their imagination. Because it was a vision, an ideal—not something to be had for the asking from the bounty of nature—it challenged its adherents all the more to heroic efforts.

Inevitably, it was when the canons of rationalism were applied to social practices and institutions that its bite began to be felt. It was distressingly obvious that European society did not conform to the pattern of reason nor to the ideal objectives of an enlightened humanity. Particularly in France, where the Enlightenment reached its highest pitch, to look in any direction was to see how unreasonable the existing order actually was. Consequently the progress of rational thought was almost certain sooner or later to produce an explosion in that sanctuary of bureaucracy and absolutism.

Aiming to liberate mankind, the French philosophers condemned, either openly or by parable and innuendo, the institutions which they considered noxious. Voltaire's defiant slogan, "Wipe out the infamous thing!" was not directed exclusively at the Church or any single instrument of injustice. Under attack were oppressive governments, the bigotry of ecclesiastics, censorship, the restraints imposed by a state-controlled economy, cruel and arbitrary penal systems, slavery, the butchery inseparable from the military sport of kings.

With their eyes upon the promotion of justice, the thinkers of the Enlightenment were quick to single out war as one of the chief props of despotism and sources of human misery, and most of them condemned it in no uncertain terms. During the seventeenth and eighteenth centuries numerous concrete proposals for the establishment of European and even world peace were put forward. Considering these proposals as a whole and the attention which they directed to the underlying causes of conflict as well as to the appropriate means for abolishing it, it is no exaggeration to say that they anticipated and sometimes surpassed the liberal thought of our own day on the subject and were ahead of the practices of governments in any day. The reproach so often leveled at the eighteenth-century intellectuals that they were abstract perfectionists and conceived of society as static is hardly justified. The ablest of them, although boldly imaginative, were more penetrating in their approach to international problems than are contemporary statesmen, and more realistic, if it be admitted that these problems ought really to be solved rather than merely juggled.

The famous *Project of Perpetual Peace* of the Abbé de Saint-Pierre was based on the dubious idea of maintaining the *status quo*, for which reason it was sharply criticized by several of the rationalist advocates of internationalism. Some of these thinkers, it is true, oversimplified the issues and produced rigid formulas which are monuments of intellectual naïveté. For example, the plan of a certain Pierre Gargaz laid down eight "infallible" means for establishing peace, which included the proposition that after proper adjustments had been made the territory of no state henceforth could ever be either enlarged or reduced. A few years later (1788) Palier de Saint-Germain called for an indissoluble, irrevocable Association of all Christian sovereigns in which these worthy potentates would solemnly agree not to take the law into their own hands any longer. (Doubtless a piece of wishful thinking, but as good as the Kellogg-Briand Pact of 1928 to "outlaw" war.) However, there were many other more trenchant and practical suggestions. The need of promoting domestic welfare to remove an incentive for aggression was stressed, to which end the curtailment of government extravagance and tax reform for the relief of the poorer subjects were recommended. Much emphasis was placed upon the economic causes of war, especially the rivalries inherent in imperialism. The Physiocrats, such as Turgot and Saintard, advocated freeing trade and industry in order to promote the greatest degree of well-being among the whole European community. Frequently discussion centered upon the distinction between "just" and "unjust" wars, with a clear appreciation of the risks in admitting the possibility of the former. The futility of competition in armaments as a security measure was pointed out, as well as the evils of secret diplomacy and the harm done by ambiguities in peace treaties. (Saintard commented: "Treaties are not the product of reason . . . but the proof of weariness.") The smaller nations of Europe were urged to form regional federations for their mutual protection, while more ambitious plans were conceived for a universal league of nations, with an international police force, compulsory arbitration of disputes, and a world tribunal.

In contrast to the pleas of such earlier idealists as Erasmus, the peace proposals of the Age of the Enlightenment were not merely recommendations for good behavior put forward in hopes that regnant princes would see fit to act upon them. They were closely allied to the mounting denunciation of rulers and to the challenging of their claims to absolute power. Many critics clearly perceived that the bases of state and society would have to be reconstructed if peace and the general welfare were to be attained. The ideas of limited government and the separation of powers, of popular sovereignty, of the origin of civil society through a contract entered into by free men were in the air. Montesquieu, who was certainly no radical, believed that the establishment of political liberty was essential for human happiness while he also believed that war was the greatest danger to liberty. Others went much farther than Montesquieu, demanding equality of rights and opportunities, and some, such as d'Holbach, Condorcet, and Rousseau, boldly argued that the creation of a democratic way of life was prerequisite to the success of any project for lasting peace. Diderot contended that a social upheaval would have to take place before these ideals could be realized. Condorcet, an aristocrat born, was one of the most unrelenting champions of equality as well as an enemy of violence. Ironically, he fell a victim not to the outraged monarchy but to agents of the inflamed populace—to whose interests he was unselfishly dedicated—when revolution had opened the gates of hatred and terror. Under the shadow of the guillotine he reaffirmed his faith in the progress of virtue and intelligence and pronounced a benediction upon the human race from which he was about to be separated.

In the light of these considerations it is obviously unfair to charge the thinkers of the Enlightenment with being oblivious to social and economic realities, wedded to abstract theory, and indifferent to the needs of the masses. When they adopted as their goal the liberation of mankind, they meant mankind, not just themselves—the educated few—and not just Europeans. They underestimated the difficulties involved; they failed to realize the complexity of social phenomena and the extent to which they depend upon nonrational factors; they were prone to assume that the methods and results of the physical sciences could be applied immediately to other fields. But they saw distinctly that the reforms which they desired could not be secured by patchwork, that they would necessitate a profound social reconstruction.

At the same time it is true that most of these reformers opposed violent commotion and mob action. They wanted revolution to come through emancipation, through enlightenment, under the direction of those whose intelligence was awakened and disciplined. They did not wish to jeopardize the gains which appeared to be within grasp or invite the risk of chaos by letting the great majority of ignorant and untrained folk suddenly take the destiny of the community into their own hands. Such an attitude does not brand the rationalists as hypocrites, snobs, or pseudo reformers who were enemies of the people's welfare. Perhaps it shows that they were in the long run the truest friends of the people. The events of the French Revolution, which ran contrary to the desires of the philosophic reformers, indicate that their caution was not unfounded. Although the Revolution shook society to the roots and released the full tide of popular energies, its accomplishments fell—not ahead of—but short of the program envisioned by the philosophers, while it intensified some of the specific evils which they had struggled against.

The final justification of civilization is the extent to which it promotes the welfare of the people who live under it—the welfare not of a few but of all. Therefore the democratic thesis is eternally valid. However, the greater the democracy the more need for disinterested and intelligent guidance; the more need for education and for the self-imposed discipline which is by all odds the hardest kind of discipline to come by. These qualities cannot be acquired overnight; we have not yet discovered how to attain them fully. The French rationalists may be chided for not embracing the democratic ideal more wholeheartedly than they did, but they are more to be commended than the demagogues of the Terror who promised an earthly paradise and bequeathed the guillotine and the firing squad.

It is unfortunate that the most famous and influential protagonist of democracy was Jean Jacques Rousseau, whose sensitivity of perception and fine intellect were marred by extreme emotional instability. The avowed champion of the feelings as opposed to cold reason, Rousseau gave full rein to his own emotions, whether petty or sublime. With his indulgence, self-pity, and self-justification, with his alternation between defiance of convention and craving for approbation, he was far from a perfect embodiment of emancipated humanity. His inconsistencies entered deeply into his writings and contributed something to the confusion surrounding the democratic ideal of which he was such an enraptured prophet. Rousseau sang the praises of the common man. Upon the unspoiled instincts of the great body of humanity, rather than through the contrivances of sophisticates, he would erect a social and political structure in which equality, freedom, and harmony prevailed. He dealt in sweeping concepts, in black and white with few nuances. ("Man is born free; and everywhere he is in chains.") Not content to cry Down with oppressive governments! he would add Down with private property! or even Down with civilization! so fondly did he long for a state of uncorrupted simplicity. But he didn't actually mean everything he uttered in his more impassioned moments. In his *Social Contract* he found room for most of the institutions which he had first looked upon with horror. While by definition the "state of nature" was the most perfect condition imaginable, through some miraculous alchemy the new order of civil society founded upon Rousseau's social contract was declared to be still more perfect. Natural liberty would be exchanged for "true liberty," which was the expression of the General Will of the entire community.

In his mystical democracy Rousseau felt that all the checks and safety devices which guard against the fallibility of human institutions could be discarded. The only requisite was to give full sway to the General Will, which could never be wrong. The individual might cheerfully surrender all his individual rights in becoming a member of the great collective body, which somehow was more and better than the sum of its parts. Thus Rousseau's political prescriptions, which took their origin in a desire for liberty, led if carried to a logical extreme to the tightest kind of despotism. Such of course was far from the intention of Rousseau. It was even more contrary to the desires and to the program of the majority of the philosophers of the Enlightenment, who placed their emphasis upon the securing of fundamental rights, believing that the public good would be advanced as individuals were afforded greater protection and wider opportunities.

THE HEADY WINE OF REVOLUTION

The climax of the Age of Reason was a tumultuous eruption that convulsed the greater part of Western Europe for a quarter of a century. The ideas of the Enlightenment contributed to the coming of the great French Revolution and provided inspiration and slogans for its leaders, but the rationalist movement in itself would never have produced this particular chain of events. The causes of the Revolution were numerous and deep-seated, an accumulation of abuses which became more and more intolerable before the growing confidence and stiffening resistance of the commercial middle class. The old regime—in society, economics, religion, and politics—had become an anachronism, which was stubbornly supported by those whose interests were tied up in it but which no one could defend with any conviction. The situation in France before 1789 is the classic illustration of the refusal of entrenched forces of privilege to give up any part of their advantages for the sake of saving the remainder, to say nothing of saving the social fabric as a whole. The remark "After us the deluge"—attributed to Louis XV—could well summarize the attitude of the court nobles, the princes of the Church, and the gang of sinecurists who fed so greedily at the public trough. The ominous rapidity with which they were approaching the bottom of the trough should have warned them that the deluge might be nearer than they had anticipated.

Many of the rationalist philosophers had seen the necessity for a reconstruction of society, but they had hoped to effect this through a process of reform. They wanted a revolution from above, not an explosion from underneath. The idea of revolution from above was inherently feasible, and if it could have been managed it would have saved incalculable agony. Many members of the nobility and of the clergy favored reform and some of them were active participants in the Enlightenment. The peasants, the great majority of the French people, were becoming impatient with their unredressed grievances, but they were moderate in their demands (in so far as they were able to formulate them at all), grateful for small favors, and innocent of any design for

The Rediscovery of Man

overthrowing the state or even the aristocracy. The *bourgeoisie* was the most dynamic and the most incensed element. But although its members were determined to better their position, their objectives were limited and specific. While they produced their quota of firebrands, as a class they were not radical. Practically all of the requisites for peaceful and gradual reform were present with one important exception: the inept and floundering administration was not capable of carrying through any consistent policy, even one of total repression. It is always difficult for any institution to reform itself, and the bureaucracy which operated in the name of the legally omnipotent but pitifully bewildered Louis XVI was more than ordinarily impervious to constructive suggestions. The weak king yielded to the pressure of parasitical courtiers and dismissed courageous ministers who gave him good advice. The inability of the court party to offer any effective leadership in time of crisis left no alternative but defiance. Defiance on the part of the traditionally snubbed third estate was revolution. Moderate as were the aims of the hastily constituted "National Assembly," its leaders had set forces in motion which as they acquired momentum proved to be impossible to control. It was an easy matter to tear down the tottering Old Regime. It was not easy to erect something durable in its place, especially with the discovery of the effectiveness of hysteria and terror as political instruments.

The French Revolution released its fury against the monarchy, the aristocracy, the economic power and monopolistic position of the Church, the system of mercantilism, and various legal and administrative bastions of privilege. It succeeded in uprooting many things which the philosophers had been attacking for the better part of a century. But at the same time it was the enemy of their methods and incorporated only haphazardly the reform program which they had visualized. To project reform while a revolution is shaking the whole of society, and especially while this convulsed society is engaged in large-scale defensive and offensive warfare, is like trying to remodel a house during a hurricane. Much debris is inevitably cleared away, but the experience will leave many people with an exaggerated fear of storms or with an aversion to future remodeling even in calm weather. Magnificent as were some of the changes effected by the Revolution, the emotional frenzy and the violence associated with it injured the prospects of social progress through the steady growth of enlightened public opinion and the application of reason.

The Revolution and its aftermath not only marked a break with the method and spirit of the rationalist thinkers but actually intensified some of the evils against which they had struggled. Instead of international solidarity the sentiment of nationalism had been inflamed until it exhibited the desperate fanaticism of a religious cult. Instead of the abolition of war, militarism had been intensified. It now drew its support not from the hired assassins of roistering kings but from the whole body of citizens, who were bound to the system by exhortation and by the surer bonds of conscription. Instead of guidance by a new aristocracy of merit and intelligence, the threat of mob rule had been followed by indiscriminate reaction and a beating down of all who dared speak out in behalf of the cowed populace. Eclipsing the triumph of reason came a riot of romanticism, seeking anchorage in authoritarian dogma, in flights of mysticism, or in rapturous adulation of the *status quo*. Above all, in place of freedom new instrumentalities of despotism had been fashioned and demonstrated. The uprising which had begun against the flabby autocracy of Louis XVI was brought to rest in the rigidly efficient tyranny of General Bonaparte. And when he was finally overthrown the European repairmen at Vienna, who endeavored to restore as much of the old "legitimate" order as possible, returned a Bourbon to the throne of France.

The changes effected by the Revolution, however, could not be undone by restoring the trappings of the ancient monarchy; and all of Europe was to feel the currents that the great upheaval in France had set in motion. Although the methods pursued by the revolutionary leaders were such as to impair the success of their program, France had served as a testing ground for potent social ideas. During the most radical (and terrifying) stage of the Revolution, even while the sanctity of human life was being trampled under foot, men's imaginations were fired by the prospect of a new and harmonious society which would benefit all future generations. To further this end, drastic but concrete reforms were inaugurated. A revision of the laws of inheritance cut away at one stroke the legal sanctions through which family pride had perpetuated great feudal estates, and substituted the democratic principle of equal division among the heirs. For the first time women's rights in property were given recognition and protection. Imprisonment for debt was abolished and an ambitious effort was made to correct and codify the whole body of law (preparing the way for Napoleon's more famous but less equitable *Code*). Through the initiative of radical reformers, France became the first of the great Western nations to emancipate the slaves in her colonies. The assertion of equality before the law, of religious freedom and other fundamental civil liberties, and even a brave attempt at providing equality of economic opportunity were essential aspects of the radical program, although not accepted unequivocally from "the Year One" (1792-93) henceforward.

Altogether, the ideals expounded during the stormy climax of the Revolution, while tinged with rationalism and embracing a faith in science (witness the adoption of the metric system of weights and measures), cut deeper than the typical formulas of the Enlightenment. They were charged with a religious fervor—dissolving too easily into the mania of nationalism, but embodying a genuine devotion to the interests of mankind. Periods of titanic conflict inevitably bring to the surface both the best and the worst in human nature. The French Revolution revealed the cruel force of mass hysteria, the deadening and self-destructive tyranny of fanaticism, and the futility of violence as an instrument for promoting brotherhood. It also nurtured humanitarian sentiments of the greatest intensity and which were not dependent for survival upon any particular form of government or social system. The radical leaders—Marat, Danton, Robespierre, and St. Just—championed the cause of the common people, poor peasants and day laborers, whose needs had hardly been met by the abolition of serfdom and the overthrow of the monarchy. Perhaps these leaders—themselves bourgeois—were not entirely sincere, and certainly their methods were questionable; but they had focused attention upon a neglected area of eighteenth-century thought. At the close of the Revolution, when the *bourgeoisie* had regained a fairly secure position, a tide of reaction set in against any further social reform.

In spite of reverses and broken dreams, the ferment of the Enlightenment could never be entirely suppressed, and the values which it had delineated remained as a heritage of the nineteenth century. The French Revolution, for all of its aberrations, had made more vivid some of these ideals, and the Revolutionary wars and the Napoleonic conquests had spread them far beyond the borders of France. The desire for national independence, for constitutional government, and for personal liberty had been implanted among the peoples of Germany, Austria, Italy, and even Spain. These objectives were temporarily held in abeyance under the backward-looking regimes established by Metternich and his colleagues at the Congress of Vienna, but they were more indestructible than the Metternichean system. In England, as elsewhere, reaction and repression set in, but here liberal concepts proved even tougher than on the Continent, capable of surviving, like the inhabitants, beneath a layer of soot and dust. And already liberal ideas had found more opportunity for unimpeded growth in the New World, where they were being woven into the framework of government. The vision which seized the imagination of the rationalists was not to be rejected as a mere fanciful illusion. It had rekindled a faith in the destiny of man.

CHAPTER TEN

THE DISCOVERY OF THE MACHINE

BEFORE the outbreak of the French Revolution, and independent of contests in politics and religion, Western man had begun to make conquests in a totally different field. A transformation in industry was underway, much less dramatic than the controversies which were exercising the European communities, but more pervasive in its effects than any of them.

The Industrial Revolution was a set of changes in an area directly subject to man's planning and control although the planning, throughout human history, has been typically haphazard or conspicuously lacking. It was not revolutionary in the sense that it immediately reoriented people's thinking or embodied radically new aspirations. In origin it did not even constitute a response to a new set of consumer demands. Rather, it sprang from the attempt to augment the supply of goods which had been staple items from time immemorial but which were not being produced rapidly enough to match the needs of a growing population. The remarkable success of the inventions devised to meet this need made it inevitable that they would be followed by others in order to fulfill desires previously less insistent, and eventually by the deliberate creation and stimulation of demands which had never existed before. Inconspicuous in their beginnings, the technological changes which were gaining momentum toward the end of the eighteenth century represented a potential for redirection and expansion such as no society had as yet experienced.

A peculiarity of Western civilization, especially during its modern phase, is that it has been subjected to a series of shocks, of increasing force and with diminishing intervals between them. Restlessness and tension are inevitable aspects of any civilization unless it is in the last stages of stagnation, but the commotions in Western society in modern times have been extraordinarily profound. To a notable degree, also, they have emanated from within the society rather than from without, although affected by external conditions and capable of altering these conditions. Toward the close of the Middle Ages the broadening of intellectual interests and the stimulus of commercial contacts with the Near East provoked a crisis in the Church and feudal order. By diligent effort it was still possible to resolve the crisis—at least on the higher intellectual level—by projecting a bold and reasoned synthesis of experience. But as the material bases of society continued to fluctuate, the medieval synthesis became more and more irrelevant. It was largely swept away by the Commercial Revolution, which took the Europeans out of themselves and gave them a scope of activity unimpeded by the restraints to which they had been accustomed in their traditional domains. The great religious upheaval meanwhile was cutting the bonds of solidarity and permitting a drastic readjustment of values. With different implications, but overlapping these other forces, came the rise of modern science, which, as interpreted by philosophers, challenged the intellectual underpinnings of the none-too-stable social order and suggested the possibility of its reconstruction from top to bottom. The unheralded revolution in technology, therefore, was one in a long line of disturbances, but destined to be more far-reaching than its predecessors. It has proved to be not an ephemeral episode but a continuous operation, with intensifying impact upon all aspects of culture. In recent times especially it has modified the character of society at such an accelerating pace that conscious attempts at social readjustment have never quite been able to keep up with the changes themselves.

MIRACLES IN THE WORKSHOP

There was nothing intrinsically new about the inventing of machines nor about their application to industry. Since early modern times experimentation had been carried on in this direction with considerable success. Complicated machinery, requiring water or horsepower, had been used since the sixteenth century in the manufacture of a few products, such as brass castings, gunpowder, glass, and paper. In England as early as Elizabethan days some establishments were actually factories, employing a considerable number of workmen. The deepening of mine shafts below water level had necessitated the perfection of the vacuum pump, and a successful method of smelting iron ore by coke instead of charcoal had been devised at Coalbrookdale in Shropshire by the early eighteenth century. Compared with the impressive and noisy contraptions which had been employed for many generations, such innovations as the flying shuttle and the spinning jenny might superficially appear to be hardly more than trifles. Nevertheless, the eighteenth-century inventions in the cotton cloth industry did in reality mark a new departure. Their application was to commodities of universal daily consumption, rather than to the limited requirements of a few specialized trades, the luxury market, or a military establishment. They could affect the living habits of almost every member of the community, either as producer or consumer, by delivering faster, more abundantly, and more cheaply items which were in perennial demand. For the first time, the machine had been called upon to take over an important segment of the normal work of mankind. By multiplying the productivity of human labor it provided a potent tool by which the environment could be transformed.

Certainly the new instruments of textile manufacture were not conceived with the conscious purpose of transforming the environment nor with the idea that they might lead ultimately to a different kind of civilization. They were contrived as practical expedients to meet specific needs arising out of the industrial process—needs which seemed to enlarge rather than diminish as success was obtained. Each labor-saving device necessitated an improvement at some other point. The flying shuttle (1733), which could be propelled by an easy motion from one side of the loom to the other, enabled a weaver singlehandedly to produce cloth of any desired width. The adoption of this simple gadget created a greater demand for thread than could be supplied by domestic spinners, even when the spinning wheel hummed briskly in every cottage. A generation later Hargreaves' spinning jenny, when improved by the inventions of Arkwright and Crompton, put spinners far ahead of the weavers until a power loom was perfected. The introduction of these large and heavy machines made it imperative to find greater sources of power than man or animals could contribute with which to operate them. When steam began to compete with, and then displace, water power, more coal was consumed and mining operations had to be expanded. Because wood was hardly suitable for the construction of the power-driven textile machinery, coal was required not only to produce steam but to furnish coke for the smelting of iron ore. Aside from the problem of marketing the finished products of the mills, to move quantities of iron and coal from one part of the country to another called for a better system of transportation. With the demonstration of the practicability of steam-propelled vehicles for both overland and water travel, a new era in transportation had been inaugurated which would bind the hemispheres more closely together and change the destiny of continents. What had begun as a modification of one of the leading industries in England had produced an interminable chain of consequences certain to alter the condition of the entire world.

In its origin and the manner of its development the mechanization of industry was so undramatic and gradual that objection has been raised to applying the term "revolution" to it. However, in its entirety the process did constitute a revolution in human activities, the most sweeping one since the even more essential discoveries of the New Stone Age had established the prime techniques of agriculture, animal husbandry, pottery-making, and hand-spinning and -weaving. Like these Neolithic legacies, its fruits were to be spread over the total area of human habitation. The power-driven machine was more than a labor-saving device. It was a means of multiplying the objects of man's desire. Something better than the dream of the alchemists had come to pass. The wheels spin, the frames vibrate, and raw material is transformed into useful consumer goods, faster than the movement of hand or eye and in quantities expansible without limit as technological refinements are added. The output of the industrial machines was real wealth, not the sterile bullion of "phantastical imaginary value" for which mercantilists had fought and bled. To produce it required skill, courage, and imagination in addition to a command of such essential ingredients as raw materials and a supply of labor. Geographic factors, including climate, played a part in the location of factories—the damp atmosphere of Lancashire, for example, was peculiarly suitable for keeping cotton fibers pliable. But no unique combination of natural resources was needed. The process of manufacture could be initiated almost any place where men were sufficiently interested and energetic. The Revolution began in England in the cotton textile industry, although cotton had to be imported from such distant regions as India and Central America. Even capital seemed hardly to be a prerequisite in the early days when looms and spindles were relatively simple and when there were in any case no great reserves of capital for inventors or entrepreneurs to draw upon. Many a successful business was begun by venturing a small accumulation of savings or a slender inheritance. Capital was supplied by the industrial system itself as it extended into a widening market. As soon as a factory began to operate successfully, its profits could be, and often were, turned back by the owner into enlarging and improving the plant.

The emergence of the factory represented not only a stepping up in the production of consumer goods but a new stage in the evolution of capitalism. The Commercial Revolution had brought a tremendous increase in wealth to Western Europeans. But this had come chiefly through exchange, and although various classes had shared in the rising standard of living the major share of the wealth had accrued to "merchant princes" and great banking houses. (Governments, of course, periodically appropriated large slices but spent money so rapidly that it again passed into the hands of merchants.) Also Europe had begun to live off the rest of the world to some extent, receiving the benefit of foodstuffs, drugs, spices, furs, and naval stores which were produced cheaply and abundantly in other continents and readily procured through oceanic commerce. In so far as the augmentation of wealth was measurable, it was related directly to the quantities of gold and silver which the Spaniards brought over from America (the amount of bullion in circulation in Europe increased five hundred per cent during the sixteenth century alone). This supply of precious metal, which helped fill the growing demand for an acceptable medium of exchange and at the same time sent prices shooting skyward, did not in itself constitute an addition to the real wealth of the European peoples. There were limits to the addition which could be made by mercantile enterprise alone, even when colonial empires were secured and direct trade established with the Orient. The revolution in technology, however, removed these limits and introduced the means by which the totality of wealth could be increased indefinitely. The industrial processes, which had already been subjected to capitalist control, now became the chief feeders to the growing reservoir of capital. The modern era of industrial capitalism had begun.

INTERNAL AND EXTERNAL EFFECTS

The advent of power-driven machinery for the production of basic commodities, halting and modest as were its early stages, marked one of the most significant triumphs in the history of man's attempt to improve his material condition. Because it occurred in Western Europe, the peoples of that region were enabled to assume a position of dominance over the earth's surface. Because it began first of all in England, this small nation became the strongest power in Europe and for a time acted as arbiter in world affairs. Equally important, however, were the effects of the machine and its appurtenances upon the social order—upon man its maker. And these effects could neither be foreseen nor directed. The more highly developed and complex the areas of mechanization became, the more relentlessly was society subjected to their pressure. The more human ingenuity succeeded in enlarging and refining the instruments of production, the more helpless did intelligence appear to be in determining the goals of community life or even the conditions under which it existed. Until in our own day the question projects itself as to whether man can command the machine to minister to his welfare or whether his inventions—more particularly the enormous masses of power which they have put into his hands—will dehumanize and eventually destroy him.

The impact of the machine upon society was both internal and external. It provoked sudden disturbances in the immediate localities where it was introduced and soon affected more distant areas and even the relationship between national groups which had hardly begun to experience technological change. The factory towns of western England and the Midlands in the late years of the eighteenth century were undergoing a more drastic alteration than any urban centers had witnessed since the decay of Roman administration in the third and fourth centuries. The urban population was growing rapidly as a result both of natural increase and of the steady influx of families from the country districts under the twin pressures of the enclosure movement on the land and the lure of wages in the mills. The increment of population in England, most conspicuous in the cities but characteristic of other regions also, was in itself a healthy phenomenon. It was abetted by progress in medicine and sanitation, in hospital and nursing care, although the overcrowding in tenements and eventually the deleterious conditions in mines and factories where the workers spent most of their waking hours made it impossible for large numbers of the population to benefit from the scientific advances.

Contradictory tides were running against each other. New skills and new opportunities were coming into recognition, while at the same time cushions of security were being ruthlessly eliminated. The fact that in the textile mills many essential operations could easily be performed by women and children seemed to offer a welcome means of supplementing the incomes of poorer families. But when the head of the household—a skilled craftsman suddenly rendered obsolete by the machine—was forced to sit in idleness, supported by the wages of those who were his nominal dependents, the situation was anything but wholesome and the family as an institution was threatened. Neither law nor custom contained protective standards to cover the hiring of women and children. The field was wide open, and wherever there was a backlog of unemployed, employers did not scruple to take full advantage of their opportunities.

Even before clouds of smoke were very heavy above the little factory towns, a dark shadow had fallen upon their inhabitants. Within a generation or two, unimagined depths of human degradation were plumbed, providing vivid although too long unheeded proof that the machine could be a force for evil unless subjected to the restraints of an alert public conscience. The demands of industry and the factory system were beginning to create a new and horrible kind of slavery, fastening especially upon women and children, and thus sapping at the vitals of society. It was a desperate compulsion which induced parents to shake little six- and eight-year-olds out of bed at three o'clock in the morning, to send them running to the mill where they might be whipped if they were fifteen minutes late; or to let them stand in the rain for hours before the locked gate so that they would be on hand when it opened. Only a terror as unpitying as steel fetters could keep these children bent and strained over their machine-paced tasks for twelve, fourteen, or eighteen hours a day—fainting or crying beneath the overseer's whip in the late afternoons—until their tender bodies were misshapen and their senses dulled. It was nothing less than slavery when apprentices were locked within their master's establishment day and night and beaten severely if they attempted to escape. And when, in the never ending night of the coal pits, girls and women struggled through pools of cold water with hundred-pound weights on their backs or crawled on all fours dragging the heavy carts to which they were chained.

Such incidents are not a figment of romantic imagination but drawn from the sober accounts of a long series of witnesses before parliamentary committees in the 1830's and 1840's. Thanks to the determination of a few undaunted humanitarians (including Tories who sincerely pitied the children but also hated the Whig millowners), the gentlemen of Parliament were finally compelled to look upon living examples of the human wreckage which the industrial areas were producing and to contemplate the nightmare of their existence as it emerged from the halting testimony of "ignorant, filthy, ragged, and deplorable-looking objects." The coal was dug, the iron was smelted, the cotton spindles whirled, to bring profits to the masters and sinews to the power of England; but in the process a race of deformed dwarfs, pallid and brutish, was being created. Almost as degrading as the slavery of children was the helplessness of men who had been deprived of the means of supporting their families and had to sentence their own offspring to a living death to prevent them from starving. The look in the faces of some of these able-bodied men, confined to the poorhouse in enforced idleness, reminded Carlyle of Dante's Hell.

These things came into being while the machine age was still young, while cities were very small by modern standards and the factory system the exception rather than the rule in industry as a whole, and while the great majority of the population was still engaged in agriculture. In the worst districts families were crowded into hovels with as many as five persons sleeping in one bed (if they had a bed to sleep in), breathing poisonous air in the midst of filth and debris, as if there were no fresh open spaces left. Actually there was an abundance of space for healthful and sunlit habitation. England was far from being overpopulated; there were large tracts of unused land perfectly suitable for cultivation and plenty of room for unplotted towns. The advance of the new industrialism was erratic, disorderly, and ruthless. As it became an irresistible movement its paradoxical effects stood out the more starkly. Suffering on the doorstep of comfort; festering disease outrunning medical progress and the science of sanitation; waste amid want; bulging storehouses barred to the penniless folk who had filled them—these were among the hallmarks of the Industrial Revolution.

It was difficult to bring effective action to bear upon the intolerable social conditions. Millowners stoutly resisted any attempt to compel them to reduce working hours, raise wages, or introduce safeguards for the health of their workers. They resented the assumption that the public authority had a right to interfere with their business on any ground whatsoever. Liberal sentiment was still directed against the remnants of mercantilism and was slow to recognize the need for a new type of regulation. The abstract principle of "freedom of contract" was upheld as more sacred than the welfare of the family or the health and education of children. With the triumph of individualist philosophy the attempts of laborers to organize for bargaining purposes were regarded with horror and prosecuted as conspiracies, while hardly anyone noticed that manufacturers acted with remarkable concert in resisting labor's demands and blacklisting the "agitators." (Adam Smith was one who had noted and commented on this habit of the masters, when the Industrial Revolution was still in swaddling clothes.) Upon the authority of Malthus, the clergyman-economist, it was asserted that any material assistance to alleviate the lot of the overly prolific lower orders would inevitably make their condition all the worse; therefore, they must remain subject to such "natural" checks as disease, vice, and poverty. (These therapeutic factors hardly stood in need of support from Malthus or anyone else, but their efficacy as checks was debatable.) The classical economists of the early nineteenth century spelled out their scientific, inflexible economic "laws," which promised that in the long run society would be prosperous and everybody as contented as he deserved to be, and that in the short run nothing much could be done about any specific unpleasantness.

Although Factory Acts were eventually passed to deal with the most flagrant abuses, legislation could not determine the course and character of industrial development nor solve all the problems which it gave rise to. At best it lagged behind the events and fixed upon isolated phenomena. Alleviation of distress seemed to come finally from the succession of economic changes itself. England's darkest hour, socially and economically, had followed the defeat of Napoleon and the collapse of war prosperity. In the severe depression which ensued, made more malignant by the repressive tactics of a stodgy and frightened Tory ministry, conditions were horrible beyond belief. By the middle of the century, railroads were being built on an ambitious scale, foreign markets were brisk, and the swelling demand for goods lifted wages and brought a vision of prosperity even to the working classes. The mills and mines had taken a staggering toll of victims during the era of unrestricted child labor, but the race has a terrific power of survival.

The external effects of the machine technology upon society were more subtle but almost as rapid as its internal effects upon the industrial communities. Even agrarian regions found their economic structure modified by the needs and output of industry. As Great Britain maintained the lead in manufacture, she became progressively more dependent upon the outer world for foodstuffs and for raw materials. The introduction of textile machinery had created an insatiable demand for raw cotton. The invention of the cotton gin by Eli Whitney of Connecticut enabled the American South to meet this demand, but it also fastened the plantation system and Negro slavery upon that section, leading to the creation of a fatal division between the Northern and Southern states. The developments in transportation which had been carried out as a necessary adjunct to the progress of manufacture in England could be, and were, introduced into countries that were still overwhelmingly agricultural. In the United States by the middle of the nineteenth century the prairie farmlands of the Middle West were linked more closely to the commercial Northeast by artificial communication lines than they were to the agrarian South by the natural waterways—a circumstance which contributed significantly to the preponderant resources of the Northern states in their struggle with the Confederacy.

Western Europe as a whole, long before the factory system had become paramount, reflected the influence of the new economic forces. The growth of large-scale manufacture was very uneven and no respecter of historical traditions or national prestige. Tiny Belgium forged ahead of every other country of continental Europe until the second half of the century. France moved determinedly into the railroad age under the patronage of Emperor Louis Napoleon; but because of the spotty character of her coal reserves and the lack of a formula for extracting the iron ore of Lorraine, she made slow headway in the production of iron and steel. Also her textile industry offered resistance to the inroads of machinery as long as silks and fine hand linens commanded a good price. Sprawling Russia, under an autocratic Tsar and benighted aristocracy, remained shrouded in feudal mists, temporarily beyond the periphery of technological progress. The segregation of Europe's natural resources by the arbitrary network of political boundaries hampered the full utilization of these resources. So did the internal political tensions which filled the period of repression between the Congress of Vienna and the explosions of 1848. The most striking example of the effects of political backwardness upon economic retardation is seen in Germany. Here the belated but effective unification of the country in 1871 led with almost miraculous speed to the replacement of an agrarian and semimedieval guild economy by a highly urbanized society with a gigantic industrial potential.

The United States was undoubtedly the chief beneficiary of the stagnation of Central Europe. Refugees from the oppressive regimes of Austria, Hungary, Germany, and Italy, as well as emigrants from more favored regions, flocked to the land of opportunity at a time when the rapid growth of transportation and manufacture there called for a supply of sturdy and not-too-expensive labor. Thus in spite of its political youth, its agrarian character, and the magnetic effect of Western frontier lands in drawing population from the East for large-scale agricultural ventures, the North American Republic was in a position to cross the threshold of the machine age more rapidly and wholeheartedly than most of the nations of Europe.

During the first century of its unfolding, the Industrial Revolution released a tide of human energy and implanted a hope of achievement beyond anything which had been accomplished before. In spite of some harsh features, its objectives were constructive and forward-looking. And its program, though inordinately ambitious, was pragmatic and realizable. Its essence was action, its time was now, its participants were everyone. It was the latent power which had been locked within the Western communities for centuries and finally had broken free. It enabled the Western nations to make their voices heard and their wills felt around the world and to imprint their characteristics upon every part of it. Distance was annihilated, barriers broken, the forces of nature routed or bent to the role of obedient servants. Disaster, whether natural or man- or machine-made, could not stay the surge of expansion. After a Civil War, more devastating than any conflict in their previous history, the people of the United States immediately projected gigantic industrial enterprises. Railways were pushed to the western edge of the continent in a few years, opening the way for lumbermen, miners, ranchers and farmers. Indians and buffalo were exterminated, together with traditions of gentility and the moral law; but the great open spaces were enclosed and sprawling villages turned into smoking cities. This in spite of the fact that valuable resources were being wasted recklessly and fortunes squandered in political corruption. The work of construction and all that went with it—organizing, capitalizing, manipulation and propagandizing—engaged the faculties of Europeans and Americans to a maximum degree. Although not extinguishable even by war, the fascinating and profitable material developments were responsible more than any other factor for the absence of a general European conflict between 1815 and 1914.

THE PERSISTENCE OF IDEALS

Many of the changes resulting from the new technology were of the sort that can be readily noted and measured. They differed in degree and in rate of acceleration from any which civilizations had heretofore experienced. They altered the balance of power among nations and the distribution of wealth within nations. They were applied to ever-widening segments of the environment. It does not follow, however, that the essential character of Western civilization was being modified in keeping with the visible changes in its equipment. Civilization is a complex of many factors, of which the material are only one aspect. At the time when the Industrial Revolution began, Western culture was already of long standing, vigorous, and possessed of well-defined forms. It had summoned the machine into being to suit its own purposes and was not to be easily diverted from these purposes. The rise of the factory system and its reverberations did bring unforeseen results, bound to affect all of society; but it was quite conceivable that they would prove amenable to and perhaps even aid the objectives already outlined but never adequately fulfilled.

For society as a whole the most tangible response to the material trends was an unprecedented growth in the number of its people. During the nineteenth century the population of Europe considerably more than doubled, while that of Britain increased nearly fourfold. In the United States, where immigration and an elastic frontier were factors, the increment was about two thousand per cent. Obviously the significance of an epoch is not to be judged by the number of persons per square mile. A rapid increase in numbers may be an advantage or a disadvantage, depending on various other considerations. In the nineteenth-century setting, the steady growth of population was undoubtedly a force promoting the advance of the democratic concept. Aristocratic traditions could not withstand the upsurge from the ranks of society. If the thesis that governments are responsible to their people were admitted at all, it could no longer remain an empty theory. The people were too much in evidence to be treated as a mere abstraction or a convenient political metaphor. Their needs became year by year more palpable and insistent. At the same time the opportunities for organizing opinion were multiplying and there was a growing articulateness on the part of the populace. Hence, it was inevitable that the whole mass of society should come to be reckoned with as a political force and also as a potent influence upon almost every aspect of culture. The progress of democratic thought and democratic institutions was very largely a reflection of demographic statistics.

The Discovery of the Machine

The ideal of democratic control, involving direct participation by the citizens in the process of determining public policy, has rarely been in evidence in the history of human societies. Furthermore, in most times and places it could hardly be carried into practice even if the ideal were conceived. As recently as the Age of the Enlightenment, in spite of the prevailing optimism as to man's capacities, it was generally assumed that the structure of society would remain aristocratic although no longer based on arbitrary distinctions and hereditary privilege. Not only Montesquieu but Rousseau, archprophet of the modern democratic faith, believed that actual democracy was almost unattainable—theoretically feasible in a small community if the citizens were poor and approximately equal, but out of the question in a large state like France. The rise of modern industry changed the picture radically. While it stimulated population growth, it provided the means for integrating the population. Urbanization, ease of communication, and facilities for disseminating reading matter cheaply made possible at last the attainment of likemindedness among the members of a large community. The role of the printing press in bringing about this situation could hardly be exaggerated. The art of printing from movable type had indeed been known in Europe since the fifteenth century; but far more significant for its effects upon society at large was the invention of power-driven and rotary presses in the nineteenth century, together with papermaking machinery. Now a voluminous output of books, periodicals, and newspapers came within reach of manual laborers and permeated the rural areas. The mechanization of industry, together with the modern mass-production printing press, created the setting in which the democratic thesis could be given an unlimited application.

This does not mean that the Industrial Revolution was the progenitor of the democratic ideal nor that it was necessarily a force ensuring the triumph of the ideal. It simply provided the means whereby, society willing, democracy could be made operative over extensive and heavily populated areas, not only in the political sphere but in the cultural, social, and economic as well. However, the instrumentalities which the advance of technology yielded could just as readily be used to produce results entirely contrary to the ends of democracy. This has been all too vividly illustrated in the twentieth century by the emergence of totalitarian states, which buttress themselves with technological efficiency and bend every effort to stimulate a numerical increase of their members.

Technological changes in themselves are neutral factors, lying outside the area of value, neither elevating nor lowering the standards which govern community life. A remarkable characteristic of man is his adaptability to different types of environment, and the trait remains even when the environment has been artificially modified by his own agency. A person who travels by airplane may still believe in witchcraft, like his medieval ancestor who plodded on foot. A professor of philosophy who lectures in an air-conditioned hall, dictates letters to a recording machine, and commutes twenty miles by subway may be a more ardent admirer and emulator of Plato than a fourth-century Athenian who could stroll into the Academy to hear a discourse of the master. Nuns who "fret not at their convent's narrow room" may now enjoy the advantages of central heating, and aesthetic or spiritual ideals can be (although they usually aren't) propagated by television. Machines neither create nor destroy culture, although they have made it very easy for people to lose sight of cultural values, accommodating their aspirations to the objects and sensations which the machine can most readily supply.

The onset of modern industrial technology, with parallel transformations in commerce, agriculture, and so on, undeniably entailed social effects both staggering and sordid. Nevertheless, it would be erroneous to define nineteenth-century culture in terms of material forces, great as was their impact. The distinctive qualities of Western culture were still the reflection of elements only indirectly related to technological change.

Political developments during the nineteenth century revolved around three dynamic ideas, which in varying proportions remodeled the institutional life of the Western world. These were liberalism, democracy, and nationalism—all abstract concepts, intangibles, a projection of the will and imagination; their influence illustrates the power which ideas can exercise over human events. Each of the three concepts antedated the Industrial Revolution, and only the second of them was intrinsically related to the sweep of material forces. All of them, however, were ultimately invoked to deal with the problems arising from a competitive industrial regime.

Attempts to work out a better political order were essentially a continuation of the efforts begun during the Enlightenment. They had been distorted by the tyranny of Napoleon and then opposed and almost choked out by the conservative reaction which followed the overthrow of his Empire. But they continued to pulsate throughout the era of reaction. In Western Europe during the first half of the nineteenth century an Hegelian struggle was in process, with the organized agencies of repression ranged against liberal and revolutionary tendencies. Basically the struggle was between opposite ideals, although it was enacted on the material plane and division among the participants was largely along class lines. Where the reactionaries were routed, the triumph was one for the middle class, the group which was steadily being strengthened by the incidents of industrial expansion. In this battle, however, the middle class was the heir to liberal, humanitarian, and reformist ideals that had been propounded in the eighteenth century. This was true in England of the philosophic radicals, the Benthamites, the free traders, the advocates of penal, municipal, and parliamentary reform. It was true on the Continent of the champions of constitutionalism and of the rights of assembly, discussion, and the dissemination of ideas. A passion for freedom was at the bottom of the whole revolutionary movement. In the early years even nationalism was frequently an ally of liberal or democratic forces. Patriotic spokesmen of frustrated national groups preached independence and unification as a prelude to the achievement of genuine self-government. A Europe composed of true nation states, it was also argued, would be a Europe living in harmonious peace. Mazzini, the high-minded apostle of Italian nationalism, assumed that when Italy was freed from the Austrian yoke she would become a democratic republic and that, moving "as an angel of light," she would assist other peoples toward the same shining goal. He intended his propaganda society "Young Italy" to be the forerunner of an internationally based "Young Europe."

Not only in the political sphere but in all the major fields of thought and expression the nineteenth century bears testimony to the power of imagination and the toughness of aspirations, to their ability to withstand the corroding acids released by a rapidly shifting material order. In its entirety the century presents a paradox. Mechanization and urbanization proceeded ever more swiftly. The life of the ordinary man was separated by a widening gulf from the world of nature and the members of industrial society were also being separated more widely from one another in function and status. A class of unskilled and propertyless laborers and a bourgeois class holding title to the instruments of production were coming into being. Because of their strategic position, the owners of factories and other industrial resources increasingly set the tone of society. The mid-nineteenth century in Western Europe (a little later in the United States) was the Bourgeois Age. Unscrupulous greed and callous materialism were certainly a part of it, but the more earnest attempts at interpretation and expression which it witnessed can hardly be explained in these terms.

It was during the period of the early Industrial Revolution that Romanticism reached its height—the glorification of sentiment and spirit—in poetry and prose and the fine arts. By no means a logical response to the tempo of a machine age were the classical and the Gothic revivals in architecture, the latter of which was glaringly inappropriate to the building requirements of an industrial society. A widespread phenomenon was the quickening of interest in religion, especially in its emotional forms of pietism and evangelism. Some of the most typical and influential philosophical movements were a direct negation of the claims of the world of sense, matter, and machinery.

The Romantic Idealists sought to define reality in terms of Idea, World-Soul, Will, or Absolute Spirit. This school of philosophers stemmed from Kant, who had summoned the imperatives of the moral law, intuitively perceived, to supplement the cold mathematical deductions of eighteenth-century rationalism. Depressed by the conviction that the cause-and-effect route of pure science led to an inescapable determinism in which value judgments had no place, Kant affirmed the co-existence of a spiritual realm where the eternal verities—God, freedom, and immortality —could be approached through the door of faith. (Being still so largely under the spell of the eighteenth century, he chose to call it, not faith, but "practical reason," thus confusing the issues incalculably.) His nineteenth-century followers broke even more completely with the rationalist tradition of the Enlightenment. Curiously enough, in an age which was becoming both more mechanized and more scientific, there was a tendency to recoil from the thought of the preindustrial seventeenth and eighteenth centuries because it seemed too impersonal, too rigidly objective, too mechanical.

Several of the German Idealists, in search of something tangible to fix their loyalties upon now that the revelations of astrophysics no longer intrigued them, found their quarry in the sentiment of nationalism, and celebrated the folk or nation as a spiritual entity and object of devotion. Hegel regarded the nation state (especially the Prussian) as the consummation of destiny for his generation and the medium through which man, by a process of identification, could realize true freedom. To Hegel, however, the state was not the convenient hub of mechanical progress but the embodiment of divine intelligence revealing itself through the successive stages of historic development.

It is true that German Idealist philosophy was to a considerable extent a natural reaction against French ascendancy (which had produced not only philosophers but Bonapartes). Also, it may be objected, the industrialization of Germany had not yet begun, and where the Industrial Revolution was under way, especially in England, the currents of thought echoed its influence unmistakably. Romantic Idealism had little vogue in England in the early nineteenth century. Far more typical were the down-to-earth ideas of the Utilitarians and the individualistic doctrines of the classical economists. But these complementary philosophies, which certainly bore directly upon the problems of contemporary society, had roots in the preindustrial age and embodied the general objectives of the rationalist thinkers of the Enlightenment. The Utilitarians cherished the pragmatic humanitarian maxim of "the greatest happiness of the greatest number." The classical economists grounded their system on "natural law"—no matter how shockingly unnatural its implications proved to be in action. The persistence of these empirical and individualistic schools of thought illustrates not so much a direct response to physical changes in the environment as the fact that the conservative reaction was less pervasive in England than elsewhere.

Although the English liberal creed somewhat too complacently allowed itself to be geared to industrial capitalism, it did not entirely renounce its own underlying principles. On the contrary, to many adherents it offered the correctives which could be applied to redress the evils of the factory system, overrapid urbanization, and other injurious aspects of social change. Bentham's dictum that the community was a "fictitious body," amounting only to the aggregate of its members, was perhaps a healthy antidote to Rousseau's lyricism or the fantasies of Romantic Idealists; but it was hardly adequate in the light of the growing interdependence of society. By mid-century the most wide-awake liberals were turning to the problem of how the general welfare might be secured with the minimum sacrifice of individual liberty. Some of their spokesmen were quite prepared to use the power of the state to regulate economic relationships for the purpose of salvaging humane values. John Stuart Mill, by training and inclination one of the stanchest of individualists, said bluntly that even communism would be preferable to the sufferings which abounded under a regime of unrestrained competition. He did not want communism, but he refused to believe that the only alternative to it was "the trampling, crushing, elbowing, and treading on each other's heels, which form the existing type of social life."

Undeniably, there were significant cultural movements which directly reflected the impact of the machine upon the individual and society. By the middle of the century a number of trends gave evidence, sometimes rather shocking evidence, of such an impact. In literature, romanticism was displaced by realism, which projected vivid and unflattering pictures of contemporary characters. The fine arts, also, showed disturbances of a similar nature. The impressionist painters were resolute antiromanticists, who aimed at the objectivity of the scientist in capturing isolated but precise moments of the passing scene. They opened a breach in the academic tradition which proved to be irreparable, as impressionism yielded to postimpressionism and to various other experimental and dissident tendencies.

To a large extent the postromantic literary and artistic movements were a protest against the superficialities of contemporary sentiment and opinion. The literary realists sounded a somber warning that vacuity or degradation might lie beneath the smooth hard surface of the bourgeois order. They often attacked specific abuses, ugly by-products of the industrial system. Much of their writing was in the nature of an exposé, or reformist propaganda. It aimed to shake comfortable people out of their complacency and make them look upon the harried, hungry faces of the poor. Far from glorifying the machine age, it served a brusque notice that humane values were in danger of being extinguished. By implication at least—except in the works of a few cosmic pessimists—the situation could be corrected by restoring reason to a position of supreme command. In fact, some of the later realists rejected pessimism and became enthusiastic proponents of the idea that scientific progress, joined with an awakened social intelligence, could banish the evils peculiar to the Industrial Revolution and also all the other ills to which mankind had been perennially subject.

THE CONCEPT OF EVOLUTION

Although less obtrusive than the progress of technology, developments in science had a more pervasive effect upon thought. In contrast to the process of mechanization, the scientific movement was not of recent origin. It had already proved to be one of the most potent factors in the Western culture complex, and the

achievements of the nineteenth century were built upon foundations already laid. However, the character and implications of
these achievements differed not only in degree but in kind from
the scientific discoveries of earlier centuries. The most impressive
results of the preceding period centered around a description of
the physical universe, typified by the concept of the Newtonian
world-machine. Now investigation was directed more determinedly to the life process itself. Biology and geology—the study
of organic life and its habitat—emerged from the mists of vague
conjecture in which they had been hidden; and the consequences
were startling. The concept of biological evolution, documented
by the relentless research of Darwin, was a revolutionary idea.
Besides providing the key for all subsequent biological study, it
overflowed into every other channel of inquiry. At first, the Darwinian hypothesis arrested attention by its challenge to the traditional view of creation and to the notion of an unbridgeable gulf
between man and other animals. In the long run, however, its
most significant effect was to rule out the belief in a static order of
nature, of a static society, or of a static universe. It postulated
change as the one constant and unfailing characteristic of the
cosmos.

After a brisk but relatively brief skirmish between scientists
and theologians, the evolutionary concept was accepted by intellectuals—just as the Copernican hypothesis had been after the passions of the Reformation cooled, and as the Saracenic-Aristotelian
rationalism had been in the twelfth and thirteenth centuries. The
new concept was not only accepted, even by theologians, but was
embraced with an enthusiasm hardly consonant with the judicious
caution of Darwin. Enthusiasm was kindled as in discussion and in
the popular imagination emphasis shifted from man's slimy sub-
vertebrate origin to his admirable present stature—so far in advance
of his nearest organic rivals—and to the prospects of his still more
glorious future. Change began to be identified with progress, and
man was looked upon as the custodian of progress. A new gospel,
"survival of the fittest," seemed to promise continuous human
improvement, the elimination of all maladjustments, and the com-
forting assurance that this happy state would be attained without

special contriving on anybody's part because the laws of evolution operated automatically through some indwelling and infallible compulsion.

The concept of evolution was tremendously fruitful, but it was applied carelessly and loosely, sometimes with unfortunate results. It provided inspiration for a vigorous school of historical scholarship which sought to uncover the roots of the present in the past. It suggested the genetic approach to the study of jurisprudence, social institutions, and economic systems. At the same time it was also caught up into highly fanciful philosophies and linked to dogmas no less arbitrary for bearing the label of "social science." The audacity of the budding pseudo-Darwinians knew no limits. Herbert Spencer spelled out the laws of cosmic evolution and then managed to deduce from them the proposition that any extension of governmental activity was a back eddy in the universal current. Nietzsche saw in the evolutionary struggle the ultimate emergence of Superman, rising majestically beyond good and evil, freed from the shackles of herd morality. But the doctrine could be used to bolster collectivist as well as individualist creeds. Inevitably such an overpowering force as nationalism seized upon the evolutionary formula as grist for its mill. Fervent exponents of nationalism argued that competition among nations is part of the eternal order of things; war is a proving ground, and victory denotes fitness for survival.

The theory of evolution owed nothing to the advent of the machine. As a scientific hypothesis in the hands of Lamarck, Darwin, De Vries, and Weismann it was based upon the analysis of organic evidence. As propagated by many special pleaders it was a romantic principle, easily blended with Idealist philosophies or epic visions of human destiny. Nevertheless, as it passed into the public consciousness it was bound to be associated with the mechanical developments so much in evidence. Assuming that evolution applied not only to structural changes in biological organisms but to modulations in society as well, it was tempting to go a step further and regard the advance of technology as a typical manifestation and confirmation of the theory. (Actually, Darwin's thesis, when applied to the field of industry and invention, was turned inside out. Darwin emphasized the selective influence of the environment in producing a gradual modification of the species. The stream of mechanical progress represented a modification of the environment by action of the species, without any organic change in the latter. This is the opposite of natural selection.) Particularly in England, during the middle years of the nineteenth century, mechanical improvement and prosperity appeared to be inseparable and also limitless. The eighteenth-century doctrine of human perfectibility had been revived; but now it meant not so much increase in mental and spiritual stature as in the capacity for creating and enjoying wealth.

THE MACHINE AS SAVIOR

The intellectual and aesthetic programs of the nineteenth century were not born of nor really dependent upon the technological transformation of the modes of livelihood. There is one outstanding exception to this general observation, but even the exception cannot be adequately understood without reference to the preindustrial heritage. The two most powerful intellectual influences of the last century were those which stemmed from Charles Darwin and Karl Marx respectively. The Darwinian hypothesis, which in rudimentary form can be traced back to the ancient Greek thinkers, was compatible with many different climates of opinion, but it was a concept least likely to arise from a machine-conditioned mentality. It challenged even the benevolent theistically softened mechanism of the philosophers of the Enlightenment. It underlined the irrepressible, assertive character of the life process, which uses the material environment as a ladder on which to climb rung by rung but which continually transcends the limitations of its own nature. Marx (and his collaborator Engels), on the other hand, while incorporating the evolutionary concept into his philosophy, believed that the machine would determine the future course of human development. It would provide the means of man's ultimate escape from injustice and oppression; it held the key to society's salvation. Marxian thought was the first resolute and systematic attempt to weld a reasoned philosophy of human nature and social destiny to the potentialities of the machine and the modern technological apparatus. Science had frequently been heralded as the liberator of the race (even by Francis Bacon, who didn't understand the scientific discoveries of his own century), but Marx was only incidentally concerned with science. It was the application of science to the economic process, the machine—science's working model—that was indispensable to his scheme of things.

Marx, of course, did not praise the machine directly nor celebrate the industrial regime which he saw taking shape inexorably around him. Quite the opposite. He held that the capitalist system rested upon force and exploitation. He considered it a form of perpetual and legalized robbery, whereby the owners of the instruments of production appropriated to themselves the wealth which had been created by the workers and which the workers were not permitted to enjoy. Believing as he did that the institutions and culture of every age are a reflection of its economic base, he condemned the whole contemporary bourgeois order, including its governments, whether they were organized democratically or not. In his view the state was necessarily an instrument of force, employed by the dominant minority to subjugate and exploit the majority. It was the typical implement in the class struggle which has operated, with shifting alignments, throughout all history. Therefore, in a bourgeois capitalist society the state was bound to serve the interests of the capitalists at the expense of the workers. No mere theorist, Marx buttressed his arguments with solid facts and statistics. His huge *Das Kapital*, regardless of the implications of its argument, offers an impressive indictment of the evils of the early Industrial Revolution. No one had described more earnestly the privations of the unskilled proletariat, who had no property, no cushion against starvation when their labor ceased to be in demand, no protection in the courts of law—"nothing to lose but their chains."

But while Marx was relentless in denouncing the present state of things, he was equally firm in believing that it would be overthrown, and by means which he could foresee. The modern industrial system, increasingly mechanized, standardized, and monopolistically organized, would eliminate freedom of choice and action more and more ruthlessly. A dwindling number of capitalists would climb to the top, where they would be held prisoners by the exigencies of their own position, never able to relax the drive for larger profits and markets. Meanwhile, the great majority of the population would be reduced to the proletarian level, deprived of any control over the economic structure upon which their sheer bodily existence depended. The mounting concentration of wealth, accompanied by the relative impoverishment of the laborers (the doctrine of "increasing misery"), would culminate in the most clear-cut separation of classes ever known to man. When the process of separation was complete, the proletarian masses, driven to desperation, would rise up and displace the small squadron of their oppressors in a revolution to end all revolutions. The workers would seize the industrial apparatus and destroy the state—the citadel of exploitation—replacing bourgeois dominance by a dictatorship of the proletariat. In Marx's prophecy, however, the dictatorship was to be a brief episode, necessary only to effect the liquidation of the capitalist system. As soon as its mission was accomplished, terror and coercion would be anachronisms because the subjection of one man to the advantage of another would no longer be possible.

Marx's thesis was predicated upon the evolution of material forces. The class struggle was the connecting link in the succession of civilizations and the essential formula in his interpretation of history. The peculiarity of the struggle in the contemporary era was, he believed, the fact that it was becoming simplified to the point where it could resolve itself completely and for all time to come. Society was approaching its final convulsion, beyond which lay perfect peace. What had brought about this climactic situation and what would allow it to reach a happy conclusion? Simply the machine. The machine made it possible for the capitalist system to perfect itself and to dominate the whole economy. But capitalism contained the seeds of its own dissolution. The inherent contradictions in capitalism—exhaustion of natural resources, dwindling returns from investments, competition between capitalist states, and the refusal to allow the working population to consume the wealth which it produced—bespoke its ultimate collapse. Also, it was only as the victims of the machine were reduced to a common level of despair that they would achieve the necessary solidarity of interests and purpose to enable them to cross over into the Promised Land. Finally, after the socialist revolution (which would destroy capitalism but would abolish neither *capital* nor technology) the machine would become at last the ministrant of human welfare.

While Marx excoriated the shams, shibboleths, and professed ideals of the bourgeois regime, it is obvious that his conception of the future of mankind was equally, or even more, boldly imaginative. His program transcended the limitations and the achievements of the contemporary liberal creed. Although he broke sharply with the utopian socialists, whom he viewed with contempt, his avowed goal was about as utopian as anything ever propounded. It embraced the most perfect democracy, a classless society, the disappearance of war and all forms of organized violence under the universal reign of brotherly love. His intention was certainly not to subordinate human mentality to the machine. On the contrary, he charged that capitalism was doing exactly that, blunting the finer feelings, prostituting family relationships, sapping the most precious values. His passion was to liberate mankind and to restore its dignity. While he denounced religion as soothing sirup—the "opiate" of the masses—Marx was no cynic. He had great confidence in human nature, even to the point of assuming that after the agencies of exploitation were broken man's natural goodness would make it possible to dispense with the state altogether.

This optimistic prediction was not in itself new. Its original feature lay in the fact that it was entrusted to the operation of mechanical devices. It was an eschatology, climaxed by an apocalyptic vision, but based on the bedrock of technology. It incorporated the faith that unregulated capitalism, including all of its worst features—the distortion, brutality, and stultification— would open the door to a free society. Here was an extreme kind of homeopathy. It proclaimed that the sufferer must drink his poison to the dregs so that he might emerge miraculously into a state of unbounded health. And it induces the terrifying reflection that humanity might go deep into the valley of the shadow without ever finding the sunlit hills beyond, which Marx had promised.

The Marxian creed was hammered out during the years when the teachings of the classical economists were in the ascendancy, and it was fashioned so as to constitute a direct challenge to this school. Actually, Marx drew freely upon the thought of these orthodox economists and invoked some of their own principles (that labor is the source of wealth, for example) to overthrow their conclusions. Both Marx and his philosophical opponents were engrossed with the incidents of an industrial society. The latter regarded it as the manifestation of progress; the former as the painful but necessary prelude to a future redemption. They deduced opposite precepts from their observations—inescapable collectivism on the one hand, untrammeled individualism on the other; but the advancing industrial order was equally essential to the economic liberals and to the Marxian socialists. Also, although they held contrary notions of society, they came close together in their views of human nature. To the eternal question, What is man? they had an answer. It was not the answer of Aristotle, of St. Thomas, of the Renaissance humanists, nor of the eighteenth-century rationalists. Man, they affirmed, is primarily neither a reasoning nor a sentient creature; he is an organism engaged in the production, distribution, and consumption of wealth.

Any attempt to compress the mainsprings of human personality into a formula does violence to reality. Living organisms are complex; man most of all. But the concept of Economic Man, which became so prevalent in the nineteenth century, is one of the meagerest and most superficial anthropological clichés ever devised. It extracted one essential but commonplace behavior pattern and disregarded most of what is unique in the human species. It is noteworthy that it could be credited only in a period of unprecedented economic activity, when the means of multiplying wealth seemed to be boundless and impinged upon every facet of experience. Although hastily abstracted and no more than a hollow fiction, the doctrine of Economic Man was a convenient shorthand symbol, which fitted smoothly into descriptions of, or prescriptions for, an industrial regime. Because it tended to equate man with his own creation, it was far more dangerous than the overly mathematical view of human nature such as had appeared in a Paine or a Bentham.

Neither the orthodox economic theorists nor the Marxians deliberately proposed to reduce man to the level of his material activities. They did not maintain that the economic function is the whole of human nature and the only concern of the individual or society. But they believed that it is fundamental to the rest and that the conditions under which it operates determine the totality of accomplishment. If man is an economic animal, it follows that human progress and happiness depend upon discovering the perfect economic system. If it could be obtained, then "all these things"—art, philosophy, intellectual stature—would automatically be added unto it. On this point the laissez-faire apologists of capitalism and the Marxian collectivists were in accord, even though each group viewed with horror the other's definition of what constituted the ideal economic arrangement which was to bestow perpetual blessings upon the race.

Human beings are so constituted that they cannot argue with any satisfaction unless there is a substantial area of agreement between the opposing sides. In the early centuries of the Church when heresy hunting was rife, the splitting of heads was sometimes a consequence of the splitting of hairs. Catholics and Protestants who fought so bitterly against each other during the Reformation shared a multitude of assumptions in common; in fact they were competitors for the same territory, instruments, and authority. The mutual recrimination between the Nazi and Soviet totalitarian states in the 1930's obscured their underlying similarities; and many persons were astounded to find that these giant rivals could easily change into allies and then again to mortal enemies without any internal dislocation. It is almost a rule that whenever the invective becomes most intense between two rival philosophies or power systems they are most alike underneath the surface—opposite sides of the same coin.

Thus the conflict between the Marxians and the orthodox economists detracted attention from the fact that the area of controversy was a limited and artificial one. A victory for either side would mean the vindication of a dehydrated, streamlined view of man and his functions, and abandonment of the arduous attempt to see life steadily and see it whole. The machine, invented to assist man, might come to serve as the measure of his achievement and even to assign its limits.

CHAPTER ELEVEN

EXPANSION AND RIGIDITY

THE spirit of the nineteenth century—in so far as such an intangible quality can be distinguished—was not alien to the preceding centuries but rather the culmination of what they had engendered. At the same time, however, the great increase in potential and in the range and rate of movement ruled out the likelihood of attaining stability at a stationary level. The nineteenth century marked the climax of the modern Western era not in the sense of completing or perfecting the work underway but, rather, in that it created new possibilities for the projection of this work. By its enormous impetus to the available supply of physical and social energy, it demanded a rethinking of all programs of community action. Either these programs would have to be readjusted and given wider application than ever before or they would be swept away in the flood tide of material change.

All of the necessary ingredients for a successful civilization were present in the Western lands. There was an abundance of material resources which, in spite of shocking waste, was continually added to by discovery and research. The vigor of the human species was improving, as evidenced by a rapid increase in population and a lengthening of the average life span, even though deplorable living conditions and privation still took their deadly toll. Energy, initiative, daring, and a lively imagination were much in evidence. More important still, there were definite social and political objectives to contend for, expressed in programs which were fairly clear-cut, challenging, and viable. Finally, there was confidence in man's ability to realize his aspirations. Evolution was accepted as the law of the universe—the key to the mystery of humanity's feverish striving and the assurance that a better type of society was attainable.

With all of these factors in their favor it would be inexplicable if our very recent ancestors had failed to produce a significant culture; they did produce such a culture. It would be unnecessary to stress the fact if it were not for the strange circumstance that our own society—so close to them in time and dependent upon their contributions for its most salient features—is foreign to theirs in spirit. The contrast is so marked that we can hardly believe that our world did actually grow out of theirs. We sense an atmosphere of unreality about the culture of the past century, especially in its overbeliefs and motivating principles. We are repelled by irritating strains of romantic sentiment, and perhaps most of all by the note of confidence and self-assurance that runs through it. Yet our distaste is not devoid of a touch of envy. The comfortable dwelling of the nineteenth-century intellect has been shattered, but the memory persists of the security which a dwelling can provide. And the contemporary search for security has taken forms more questionable than the illusions of the nineteenth century. If twentieth-century man had, through greater maturity, burst the limitations of the preceding era (as of course he .has in many specific undertakings), his attitude toward the seedtime of his own harvest might be one of grateful appreciation. But instead, he has broken with the goals which so recently caught his imagination. The ideals of the nineteenth century were undoubtedly inadequate and provisional, but they promised a richer fulfillment than was actually attained either then or since. They were not sucked dry or superseded by a fuller dispensation. But because they have been largely laid aside, the expressions in which they found utterance frequently excite repugnance instead of a sympathetic response.

Few would deny that the visible effects of nineteenth-century culture were splendid, however irrelevant this culture may seem to our own day. The physical and technical changes which underlay the transformations of the age were a tremendous achievement in themselves. True, they have now been far outstripped, but they surpassed the collective efforts of all previous societies. The revolution in technology was carried in a hundred years to such a high pitch that it metamorphosed itself into a Second Industrial Revolution, still more gigantic. While facilitating mechanical change, science swept ahead of it and for the first time was unreservedly accepted as a universal tool for enlarging knowledge and implementing social objectives.

Equally virile were other products of intellect and imagination. The temper of the nineteenth century was elastic enough to accommodate both romanticism and realism and then find room for such iconoclastic movements as impressionism, expressionism, and symbolism. Currents and crosscurrents swelled against one another. The voices raised were often strident, but they never betrayed satiety. In the market place of ideas as well as of worldly goods the demand seemed to outrun supply, although the supply was prodigious. Nor was response to the heightened appetite of the Western mind merely quantitative. English literature came into its greatest age since Milton, perhaps since Shakespeare; on the whole it surpassed the product of the Elizabethans. Not only in the English-speaking world but in practically all of the European countries there was a rare literary harvest, encompassing the witchery of the romanticists' nature-magic, gusty full-bodied humor, psychological probing, ruthless caricature, and brooding pessimism; but, however varied in mood, richly saturated with life.

The Story of Our Civilization

In the fine arts also this century of smoke and bustle was hardly impotent. While not equaling the splendor of Renaissance or Baroque, the artists of the early industrial epoch proved that creative talents were still supple and vigorous. Painting was freed from the aristocratic traditions which had dominated it, so that it began to speak more directly of and to the common man. The music of this period is one of the crowning glories of the entire span of Western genius. These literary and artistic products were no ephemeral excrescence nor the limp residue of a vanishing tradition. They were a natural although an exalted expression of the society out of which they sprang. They breathed its life and its longings, while their finest examples transcend the limits of period and locale.

The nineteenth century also witnessed substantial progress in the area of political and social relations. Selfishness and cruelty were not uprooted, and a greedy industrialism made them more virulent. But in spite of dark spots in the picture the forces of reform enlisted a growing public support and acquired almost irresistible momentum. The century began under the cloud of the Napoleonic wars and Metternichean reaction, typified by censorship and savage penal codes, by Carlsbad Decrees, Peterloo Massacres, and the hanging of Spanish liberals. Before its close the whole political scene had been transformed. The strongholds of special privilege were under attack. Although nationalism was still powerful and increasingly militant, international machinery for arbitration had been instituted and the hope was dawning that the scourge of war could be eliminated.

In Great Britain the political structure was converted from an oligarchy into a democracy and buttressed with ampler guarantees of individual rights. Parallel developments took place not only in the United States and the British Dominions but in most of the countries of Europe. The shrewd Bismarck founded his *Reich* upon universal manhood suffrage even before this device was incorporated into the constitution of the resolutely democratic Third French Republic. Switzerland and the Scandinavian countries pioneered with radical applications of the democratic thesis, such as the initiative and referendum and recall. Even the frozen soil of Russia was shaken by democratic tremors in the early years of the twentieth century, and, although the Revolution of 1905 was suppressed, the Tsar felt compelled to put on exhibition a plausible facsimile of a parliament.

Before they had run their full course in Europe the currents of liberalism had spread into Asia, where they exerted a stronger influence than was perhaps intended by their Western exponents. Indian nationalists, exposed by the British to a "literature of revolt," began to demand self-rule for their own land. The imperial government of Japan, after allying with democratic Britain in 1902 and defeating autocratic Russia in 1905, was bombarded by reform proposals from progressive factions within its own society which had so recently emerged from feudalism. When revolution came to a head in China, in spite of the anti-Western demonstrations which preceded and accompanied it, the political ideals of the West were a source of inspiration. Sun Yat-sen, "Father of the Republic," paraphrased Abraham Lincoln's "government of the people, by the people, and for the people." He confessedly longed for a Lafayette from America to help China inaugurate her new era of popular rule. (In spite of expressions of sympathy, no Lafayette from America arrived; which partly explains why Dr. Sun in the 1920's accepted a Borodin from Russia.)

The vision of a brighter day reached beyond mere political reform, however necessary and successful this might be. Much has been said, sometimes sarcastically, about the American Dream. To Americans who cherished the tradition of Jefferson and Lincoln, this was neither a mere catchword nor a chimera. Actually, not only in the United States but all over the Western world the dream of humanity's finest hour had begun to take form and motivated some of the most influential figures of the age. The vision enhanced the dignity of man. It called for the acceleration of sympathy, understanding, and humaneness. It insisted that material resources should no longer remain the plaything of ruthless adventurers but should be harnessed to intelligence and good will to serve the larger interests of society. They should be used to abolish disease, poverty, and ignorance, until "alabaster cities gleam undimmed by human tears" and an awakened sense of world community makes possible the "Parliament of Man."

The social patterns of the nineteenth century were rough-hewn, its ideals impetuous, its judgments often indiscriminate. But it held the seeds of promise in a soil sufficiently rich to augur a good harvest. The soil of the twentieth century is even richer; material resources are more fully developed; the variety and extent of available energy have been multiplied many times. And yet, as the means for its realization have increased, the dream itself has grown dim. Western civilization in the twentieth century has not only failed to bring to actuality the plans outlined and earnestly begun during the preceding century; it has abandoned the plans and repudiated many of their underlying ideals. One of the supreme riddles of our day is why there has been such a change in the vital tone of civilization, a defection of purpose, a shrinkage of values. For either there has been a slackening in motivation and a weakening of conviction regarding man's superlative destiny, or else the most impressive achievements and heroic struggles of the past century will have to be written off as fictitious, a mirage, or sheer caprice.

POLITICAL FRUSTRATION AND INTELLECTUAL RETREAT

The decline is most readily apparent in the political developments following World War I. The steady advance of the democratic process, which had seemed incontestable, was halted and turned into a retreat in important areas of Europe. Not only did democracy give way to dictatorship, but the ideal was excoriated, turned upon with scorn and jeers—forsaken by the middle classes which had been its most devoted adherents. At the same time there was a disintegration of social and economic philosophies. The creed of liberalism, which had been the backbone of nineteenth-century reform movements, lost its force. In England the Liberal Party practically disappeared. Reactionary nationalists took the helm in France. In the United States a wave of opposition set in against every form of liberalism; against Woodrow Wilson's New Freedom at home and against his democratic world order abroad. Proletarian socialism fared no better than bourgeois liberalism. Having succumbed to militant nationalism in violation of their sworn principles, the socialists emerged from the war in such a demoralized state that they were impotent to stem the tide of dictatorship; and some disillusioned radical leaders in Italy and Germany actually assisted in establishing the totalitarian regimes. The White and Red terrors in Russia and the Bolshevist dictatorship which grew out of them dealt the cause of international cooperation a blow in a most vital spot, the associations of trade unionists. There could be no genuine fraternity between workers who were striving to preserve democracy and those who considered it a noxious bourgeois growth to be plowed under and replaced by the monolithic unity of the Party.

Equal in extent to the political debacle has been the demoralization of the higher forms of creative activity. There has been no diminution of such activity, nor is it devoid of interest and energy. But its manifestations convey a sense of groping bewilderment, of being isolated from the main stream of human experience. Especially symptomatic is that medley of odd phenomena which constitutes a considerable segment of modern art. The significant point is not whether or not we like it—obviously many people do. Regardless of the skill, subtlety, or ingenuity which it embodies, it is not, in the main, what art has always been in periods of mediocrity or of superb excellence. The function of art throughout the evolution of cultures has been to interpret experience, to reflect or embellish aspirations. It is not necessarily idealistic, but it is impregnated with the vital tensions that grip society and seeks to make them more comprehensible. Modern art, with some very notable exceptions, seems to be an attempt to avoid the imperatives which rest upon the artist. It is an escape, not so much from reality as from responsibility. It is ephemeral, schizophrenic, a welter of dreams, atomic particles of thought and feeling. It abandons all pretense of being a universal language and ceases to be even the language of superior intelligence and insight. Instead of trying to rise to a full view of man and see life whole, it meticulously limits itself to fragments.

In caprice and aimlessness—in their sedulous attempt to avoid all purpose other than to indulge individual fancies—the abstract and surrealist schools contrast with the art of almost every previous era. This does not imply that contemporary craftsmen are inherently meaner than their predecessors. In defense of the artists it may be said that they have reflected all too faithfully the confusion and incongruity of their cultural environment. The pathological character of contemporary art, music, and poetry is an appropriate reflex of the sickness of society. But it is self-delusion to imagine that cacophony, bizarre distortion, primitive affectation, and psychoanalytical puzzles are the harbinger of new and splendid conquests of the creative impulse. The modern cult of esoteric art has its devotees and its apologists. Great art needs no apologists. Nor does great poetry require a specially indoctrinated school of critic-initiates to support it.

Philosophy has been no more successful than art and literature in maintaining its sense of direction. It has failed to digest and to put into perspective the multifarious tendencies of the contemporary world. Philosophy began to show signs of distress long before the close of the last century. It tended to flounder partly because it was being overtaken (and largely taken over) by science, and partly because it was cluttered with the vestigial remains of outworn systems. During the past seventy-five years there has been a plethora of "new" schools—"New Idealism," "New Realism," "New Cyrenaicism," and so on, down to modern Existentialism (a kind of new nihilism). These movements are essentially revivals, warmed-over pieces which, although freshly garnished, fail to satisfy the appetite.

Modern philosophy succeeded in emancipating itself from theology only to fracture itself upon the sharp stones of science. With the successful invasion of science into one field after another, philosophers have inevitably been forced to re-examine their assumptions against the continually shifting background of scientific discovery. They have been unable to agree among themselves as to whether science is their prime source of raw materials, a rival system, or the enemy of ultimate philosophic truth. To make it more humiliating, the scientist is sublimely indifferent to the philosopher's dilemma. Although philosophy is the mother of science, the parent has lost control over its lusty and sure-footed offspring. The accumulation of verifiable and useful data measures the advantage which the modern apparatus of organized research holds over any competing intellectual enterprise. It is emphatically true that many scientists are genuine philosophers, but science as such is not responsible for the implications of its findings; it need not be concerned with their emotional impact or their bearing upon the scale of values. Yet at the same time the pronouncements of science go far beyond the limits of sensory experience. They deal with the succession of changes, with relationships, with causes and origins. In their more esoteric form they seem to provide a comprehensive and multidimensional description of the universe, more reliable than any offered by theologians or metaphysicians. To those who are capable of grasping the pertinent mathematical equations, the Einsteinian physics can be taken to represent "all ye know on earth and all ye need to know." However, the scientist's delineation of reality is one in which the concerns of man, or even his presence, appear to be quite incidental rather than of central significance.

The reaction of philosophers to the challenge of science has been varied and contradictory. At one extreme are the Pragmatists, who warmly accept the scientific method and criteria and regard all ideas not as final truths but as hypotheses to be tested in operation. If empiricism is the final arbiter, they insist on a *radical empiricism* which embraces the realm of will and aspiration as well as quantitative fact. They deny that the laboratory routine is the only valid means of establishing proof and hold that proof itself is relative to the totality of experience. Proclaiming that the *will to believe* has always been a decisive factor in what people, under any given set of circumstances, actually do believe, they open the door to an uninhibited readjustment of concepts with utilitarian objectives. This attitude, while avoiding the pitfalls of dogmatism and mysticism, puts the quest for values squarely in the center of the stage again. But it subjects all established beliefs to a searchingly critical examination and assumes the necessity of continually retesting new beliefs. Hence, in an age haunted by insecurity, its appeal has been limited to incurably adventuresome spirits.

In contrast to the Pragmatists are the groups which look upon the revelations of modern science as opening a wide breach in all

spiritual interpretations of reality. To some of the most penetrating and sophisticated of contemporary thinkers these revelations present a starkly pessimistic picture. They see the universe
as unfriendly and alien, indifferent or hostile to our highest aspirations; the theme of human striving is "Man against darkness."
To avoid the paralysis of despair man must assume an attitude of
heroic defiance, beating his wings against the cliff. He may bend
nature to his bidding but he can count on neither support nor pity
from the cosmos. The veil of mystery has finally been torn away,
revealing no beneficent deity, nor even a Grecian goddess, but a
mechanical monster without purpose and without soul. It is one
of the intellectual paradoxes of our time that an unparalleled advance in the most recondite areas of knowledge, which would have
been the envy of every previous epoch, has brought anguish rather
than serene satisfaction to so many sensitive minds. Their pessimism is not inherent in the data themselves. Undoubtedly it is
engendered by other aspects of the environment, aspects which
are related only indirectly or not at all to scientific hypotheses.

As a matter of record, cosmogonies far more constricting than
that offered by the scientist today have proven compatible with
attitudes of optimism and confidence. Disregarding the crude
world views of the ancients and of medieval Europeans, the "starry
firmament" which moved the eighteenth-century rationalists to
admiring wonder was no more splendid than what can now be described. In comparison with the latter it was almost drab, monotonous in its regularity and its transfixed, static symmetry. Even
the assurance that it was infinite and eternal could hardly compensate for the subtle interrelationships, the rhythms and trans-
mutations which are now discernible. Eighteenth-century specu-
lators beheld the universe as a machine, but this prospect did not
depress them. On the contrary it seemed to lift a weight from
their shoulders, and for most of them it by no means ruled out
belief in God or the moral law. The simple clocklike orrery which
they took to be the image of reality was sufficient to kindle their
enthusiasm for improving the understanding and the moral condition of mankind. Philosophers of the Enlightenment seized
eagerly upon the materials of science to fortify their arguments

and bolster their incentives. They took the world of nature and man in their stride and audaciously discovered the purpose and the values which they felt must somehow be there. Again, nineteenth-century thinkers appropriated the concept of evolution and from the marvelous panorama of living forms which biology revealed they abstracted meaningful interpretations of man's destiny. Undoubtedly they fell into errors and absurd exaggerations, but they met the swelling flood of knowledge head on and tried to channel it. In contrast to this courageous approach, contemporary philosophy is sicklied over with the pale cast of doubt.

FATEFUL SYMPTOMS

The deterioration in climate of contemporary civilization was not caused by any catastrophic change in the natural environment, nor was it an inescapable response to the brittle realities of science. Biological vigor, expanding resources, and all the other necessary ingredients for continued cultural growth were still present. Where, then, did modern Western man get off the track? How did he lose the way which seemed to be so clearly marked out ahead of him? Apparently his stumbling block was the usual one on which civilizations have faltered—infatuation with material acquisition. Gradually he succumbed to the temptation to put the pursuit of things, wealth, and power above more abiding and exacting goals. His temptation was stronger than any which had beset earlier societies because he had at his disposal far greater potentialities for producing things and creating wealth. In knowledge, skill, and agility he was superior to any of his predecessors. But the members of Western communities are only men like unto other men, and when they make the false choices which have led to the downfall of other cultures they must expect to risk similar consequences.

Western peoples had brought the machine into being to satisfy genuine needs, to be the ministrant to a fuller life. They were the masters of the machine and they are still its masters. But they have allowed themselves to be dominated, not by the machine directly, but by the superstructure which has grown up around it. They have yielded on the one hand to the enticements of material progress — indulging an elastic appetite for pleasure and power—and on the other hand to the harsh demands of an industrial order dependent upon large-scale mechanical production. Social relationships have been profoundly altered in keeping with the spread of industrialism, but in directions which were neither foreseen nor intended. The technical equipment itself represents the acme of intelligent planning. The institutional patterns which have developed around it do not reflect the same intelligence. The factory system began as a small growth in the midst of society. Now the industrial complex reaches out to encircle and mold the character of society, not in isolated communities or individual nations but over the globe.

Before the close of the nineteenth century the intricate and artificial environment resulting from the Industrial Revolution was creating serious stresses. One of the first symptoms of the intensity of the gathering pressure was the revival of imperialism. Beginning about 1870, the struggle for control over the territories and economic resources of distant lands became a major concern of the great European powers and, to a lesser degree, of the United States also.

During the preceding half-century there had been comparatively little interest in colonial ventures and the logic of free trade had gained ascendancy. The progress of the early Industrial Revolution had focused attention upon the rich rewards to be gained by remaking domestic economies with the aid of technology and a more efficient division of labor. The prospects of internal development offered, for a time, sufficient challenge to engage the energies of whole populations. But as the advance of industrialism led to tighter competition for markets, a growing scarcity of raw materials, and a declining interest rate on capital accumulated for investment, eyes were turned hopefully to the still undeveloped regions of the world. Western nations began to vie with one another for the right to exploit Africa, Asia, and tropical islands. Soon the competition was producing a series of international crises as well as repercussions among the natives of these colonial areas. Little wars and the threat of big wars became endemic to the process. Nevertheless, the drive for rubber, copper, oil and tin, for markets and concessions, grew hotter and hotter. Reinforced as it was by national pride, the fever seized hold even of states which had little chance of success in the unequal contest, while those which secured the largest stakes were still unsatisfied.

The new imperialism differed significantly from that which had been manifested during the age of discovery and the Commercial Revolution. It did present many similar features—imperialism inevitably does. Once again explorers, traders, and missionaries spearheaded the drive for dominion; mercantilist doctrines and practices were revived; governments threw up the usual naval and military fences around their preserves; and economic warfare threatened constantly to turn into the bloodier kind. But in the sixteenth and seventeenth centuries the discovery of potential colonies was accidental and incidental to the inauguration of oceanic commerce. The states of Western Europe were just becoming conscious of their strength and were eager to try it out. When areas inviting colonization were found, they challenged European energies and stimulated rivalry among the powers, the keener as the proceeds of successful exploitation began to be apparent. The American settlements (and some others) did prove to be tremendously valuable, but they were not absolutely necessary to the welfare of the controlling countries. When the early modern age of colonization first began, the objectives of the movement were hazy. Justification came later, along with the sweat and toil and bloodletting. The dogmas of mercantilism, spun out to rationalize the whole undertaking, were embraced so firmly that it required revolutions to discredit them; but after the scramble for empire had worn itself out in the wars of the eighteenth century the peoples of Europe found themselves relieved of a heavy burden.

With latter-day imperialism the circumstances were reversed. Internal pressure within the leading industrial nations had reached such a point that relief had to be sought somewhere. The whole economy was in danger of breaking down. To make it sound it needed to be drastically overhauled, but a temporary respite seemed to be offered through enlarging the physical scope of its operations. Imperial ventures were projected deliberately and cold-bloodedly to succor business interests from the threat of depression and to allay the incipient class conflict within European society. Domestic problems, it was hoped, would be forgotten when national energies were directed toward exotic exploits in distant lands. An avalanche of argument was released to enlist the favor of public opinion and to convince doubting Thomases that the call was for something far nobler than a sordid traffic in cacao beans, gum rubber, or the stout backs of half-savage black men.

Although the earlier imperialism brought a flood of evils and failed to yield the anticipated rewards, it did no irreparable damage to the European states. It was not adopted as a desperate last resort but was, in itself, a symptom of vitality and overflowing confidence within these communities. By contrast, the later imperialism was an indication of decadence. This does not mean that there was a decline in expendable energy. On the contrary, the states were far more powerful and their peoples more numerous (and stronger) than they had ever been before. But they refused to face squarely the problems which their power and their industrial potential had brought into being. They chose instead to seek a temporary alleviation by transferring the problems to the periphery. The solution which they hit upon was no solution. It merely postponed the day of reckoning and actually magnified the dangers. It made it inevitable that the crises of capitalism would no longer be local disturbances but world-wide catastrophes.

There is no need to expatiate on the lurid incidents of modern imperialism. They have been publicized widely, documented, deplored, and frequently—after the deed was done—officially repudiated. The field of impact was much vaster than that of the earlier European and all of the ancient empires; and the armory of medical science as well as improved means of communication and transport made it possible for white men to carry on in regions previously closed to them. The tremendous margin of advantage which Western methodology possessed over primitive techniques encouraged the rapid extension of an economy of exploitation, lulled by an attitude of contempt for the unresisting lesser breeds and insensitive to its own derelictions.

Expansion and Rigidity

But in the over-all view of Western culture, the most alarming aspect of the revival of imperialism is that it put in jeopardy the liberal humanitarian traditions which were the West's most priceless possession. It debased ideals which had been an inspiration to her peoples and which had begun to be applied with spectacular success. In deference to the powerful influence which ideals had acquired, the schemes of conquest could not be announced as such or in terms of sheer economic calculation. It was first necessary to release subtle poisons into the blood stream of the body politic until a tolerance for fantastic doctrines was established. Spokesmen of the Western nations began to parade the most arrogant superiority complex since the twelfth-century crusades against Islam. Journalists, historians, scientists, clergymen, as well as statesmen declared that the hour had come when the proud should inherit the earth. To those that had should be given—whatever their strength enabled them to seize. "Colonization is for France a question of life and death." (Leroy-Beaulieu.) "Every virile nation has established colonial power." (Treitschke.) "Small states are of the past, and have no future." (Henry Cabot Lodge.) Yet it was claimed that forceful expansion was a work of moral grandeur, benefiting conqueror and conquered alike. Said Jules Ferry: "The superior races have a right as regards inferior races. . . . They have the duty of civilizing the inferior races." And so the *mission civilisatrice*, the spread of *Kultur*, "Manifest Destiny" and "the Big Stick," "philanthropy plus five per cent," and "shooting men into self-government" were all part of the white man's burden, undertaken for the good of humanity and even in fidelity to the divine plan.

The apologia of budding imperialism was a strange medley of the glorification of raw power, oozing sentimentality, and rancid piety. It sometimes gave vent to boasts almost as brutal as those which were to haunt the world during the years of Nazi ascendancy; and, surprisingly enough, some of the most extreme statements came from America, where there was as yet no plea of economic necessity and the country as a whole was unaware of the "strange destiny" in the offing (although an American editor on the eve of the Spanish-American War thought he could detect "the taste of Empire in the mouth of the people even as the taste of blood in the jungle").

Theories of racial supremacy were widely propagated, closely linked to swaggering nationalism. Cecil Rhodes, harvesting gold and diamonds in South Africa, saw in his dream of empire the fulfillment of the purpose of history, which was to give the Anglo-Saxon race, as the highest type of life on earth, command over the greater part of the earth's surface. Joseph Chamberlain agreed that "the Anglo-Saxon race is infallibly destined to be the predominant force in the history and civilization of the world." Andrew Carnegie, who had prospered so exceedingly in his adopted country, looked hopefully toward the day "when five hundred millions, every one an American, and all boasting a common citizenship, will dominate the world—for the world's good."

John W. Burgess, an eminent American professor of history and political science, proclaimed that only the Teutonic nations were endowed with the capacity for establishing true national states and that the future belonged to them. The politically capable, he said, should "force organization by any means necessary" upon the "unpolitical populations." They "may righteously assume sovereignty over, and undertake to create state order for, such a politically incompetent population." Alfred T. Mahan, the indefatigable apostle of sea power, urged his fellow Americans to prepare for mastery of the world's essential water routes. To Captain Mahan the growth of the British Empire had been a process of bestowing blessings upon mankind, so much so that it transcended the reaches of mere human wisdom: "One marvels whether incidents so widely separated in time and place, all tending towards one end—the maritime predominance of Great Britain—can be accidents, or are simply the exhibition of a Personal Will, acting through all time, with purpose deliberate and consecutive." But now, it seemed, the sublime Personal Will was turning from Britain to North America in search of a still mightier navy than Britain's to execute His benign purpose.

Science as well as religion was called upon to support the claims of the Western races to world mastery. The Darwinian theory of evolution proved particularly amenable. The great naturalist himself had suggested that natural selection might lead to the emergence of superior national types and had cited the progress of the United States, whose citizens were drawn from the more courageous and energetic European stocks, as a case in point. Enthusiastic disciples of Darwin easily convinced themselves that the beneficiaries of natural selection should go forth to illuminate the dark places by acquiring dominion over them. Benjamin Kidd, an English sociologist, argued that the establishment of Anglo-Saxon control over Africa and other areas of "social inefficiency" could not fail to promote the common good because the English had developed such a high degree of altruism and social responsibility. (He forgot that the English people had developed these qualities in their struggle to emancipate their own society from the domination of a self-righteous paternalism.)

Even if the new imperialism had proved to be only a temporary aberration instead of the inauguration of a long era of unreason, the extent of its damage would be incalculable. The reckless forces which it set in motion could not be easily halted. The racism which it inculcated became more and more blatant and made fiercer the waves of intolerance which swept over civilized peoples in time of stress. International insults were embodied in treaties or enacted into statutes, such as the Oriental exclusion laws in the British Dominions and the United States. And when the "superior" Western powers came to loggerheads with one another, they were caught in their own net and had to revise hastily their theories as to where leadership properly belonged. During World War I, for example, the projected re-publication of a book by John Burgess was suddenly abandoned when someone pointed out that its underlying thesis—the unique political capacity of the Teutonic peoples—was not quite the point which it was desirable to stress at the moment. (The situation was not entirely dissimilar at the beginning of World War II. A British spokesman, Lord Londonderry, proclaimed: "There is only one *Herrenvolk*, in spite of Germany's claims. We are the *Herrenvolk*. The Almighty put us outside Europe so that we could rule better.") In addition to stimulating national and racial arrogance, imperialism necessitated the aggrandizement of military establishments and prepared the ground for wars and revolutions. It saddled the governments even of successful colonial powers with debts, responsibilities impossible to discharge, and nerve-wracking crises. What Jules Ferry, in 1890, said would happen *unless* imperialistic policies were adopted was a far truer prophecy of the results of these policies: "European powers of consumption are saturated. New masses of consumers must be made to arise in other parts of the globe, else we shall put modern society into bankruptcy and prepare for the dawn of the twentieth century a cataclysmic social liquidation of which one cannot calculate the consequences."

Unfortunately, imperialism did not prove to be a temporary episode, although it has changed its form from time to time. As an economic proposition it has been pretty thoroughly discredited. Reluctantly it is found that imperialism does not "pay" in anything like the degree anticipated. Still, the habit, so deeply ingrained, persists; and the corpse, to which last rites have so often been administered, has a way of reviving. The renunciation of imperialism was prominent in the peace aims of Woodrow Wilson, but under the guise of mandates the victor nations obtained the substance of the spoils they coveted. During World War II innumerable commentators, both liberal and conservative, insisted that imperialism was doomed—was in fact already dead. It is true that since the close of the war some empires have been partially or substantially liquidated, despite the famous announcement in which Mr. Churchill sought to dispel any hopes raised by the Atlantic Charter among Britain's colonial subjects. But obviously the great powers have not renounced whatever influence they possess over adjacent or remote areas; they are, on the contrary, fighting to retain it. Could anyone argue that the world has returned to a policy of live-and-let-live, with international trade flowing freely and voluntarily, and with emphasis upon disinterested and spontaneous forms of co-operation? The old-fashioned word "imperialism" is no longer in good standing and is now reserved as an opprobrious epithet to be hurled back and forth between ideological enemies. Power politics has finally introduced a third phase of the expansionist mania which was first exemplified by the conquistadors of the sixteenth century and then resurrected in the 1870's. In its third and current phase the struggle has become more completely global, more "total," while its objectives dissolve into a haze of uncertainty. Financial stakes in the contested areas are no longer the main consideration. No one could "sell" imperialism today as a profitable investment; it is a liability; its romantic glamour has entirely faded. But equally effective is the doctrine that action must be taken to fill a "power vacuum." Power, instituted to support a program, becomes the program itself. Power for the sake of power symbolizes the dead end of international diplomacy.

BETRAYAL AND ACQUIESCENCE

Of the many contrasts which separate the civilization of the twentieth century from that of the nineteenth, there is one which overshadows all the others; so much so that it may be said the real terminal date of the nineteenth century was not the year 1900 but 1914. The preceding century could perceive, dimly but more and more surely, a vision of perpetual peace. The present century lives with the vision of perpetual war. This change did not come about abruptly or fortuitously, but it is one of titanic proportions.

World War I was the climax of some forty years of rivalry, maneuvering, and jockeying, the almost inevitable outcome of a long chain of circumstances. Nevertheless, in spite of the tensions and the armaments race; in spite of militant nationalism and rampant imperialism; in spite even of the enthusiasm of a few individuals for the conflict when it came, the outbreak of war in 1914 stunned the entire world. It seemed incredible that such an event could occur. It could not be reconciled with the things that had been fervently believed and hoped for. To reflective persons it was immediately apparent that this was not just one more war in the gory annals of European statecraft. The great civilized and industrialized nations which had been extolling their leadership and political sagacity had suddenly released a rain of fire and death upon one another.

Soon, however, the idea took hold that the war, horrible as it was, must be endured as the necessary final blow to autocratic government and the military system. Although fed by deliberate falsehoods and perverted by unscrupulous manipulators of opinion, a surge of genuine idealism swept over the warring nations. This idealism reached its highest pitch in the inspiring eloquence of the United States President. It became a spiritual weapon which undermined the enemy's will to resist and was the most formidable asset which President Wilson carried with him to the Peace Conference. However, the idealists discovered too late that the devices—physical and psychological—essential to waging the war and crushing the enemy were fatal to a Wilsonian peace. After months of secret dickering and wrangling among the statesmen of the victorious powers, there emerged not the blueprint of a saner world but a Europe cleft with artificial boundary lines and strewn with time bombs of resentment.

At the close of the war, the air was full of charges of "war guilt." During the years of belligerency each side had proclaimed the rightness of its cause, and the group which finally defeated Germany was most adept in ringing the changes on moral issues. But after the fighting ceased, the question of responsibility for its inception came to the fore and stirred up a long controversy. Argument over the matter passed through several stages. The dogma that Germany was uniquely and deliberately guilty was the verdict of the Peace Conference and was written out in the famous Article 231 of the Versailles Treaty. This was primarily a strategic device, to justify the evasion of the Fourteen Points and to give a cover of legality to a peace of vengeance. But the question could not be disposed of by decree, and it assumed larger proportions as secret diplomatic records came to light.

The whole phenomenon of World War I has dwindled in interest before more enveloping conflicts. However, it is significant that the question of responsibility once engaged the serious attention of thoughtful people. The discussion was often partisan, distorted and bitter. Attempts to shift the blame from one group to another involved elaborate mental gymnastics and a tortuous straining of microscopic details. But underneath the shifting charges and rebuttals there was a core of truth. The quest for guilt was sound, although the idea that it could be lodged with any one nation, group, or individual was a delusion. The war was not the result of a conspiracy, nor was it merely a political or diplomatic failure; it was a moral tragedy. It was the beginning of a cave-in, a surrender to brutal tendencies which had long been combated. Europe and the things Europe stood for could never be the same again. In the welter of recrimination which followed the peace, a haunting conscience was at work, while there was a general failure to realize that the guilt was collective and lay upon the whole body of Western society.

The aftermath of World War II did not yield any such profound agitation over the problem of war guilt. Evidently the human spirit can learn to live with its vices:

> seen too oft, familiar with her face,
> We first endure, then pity, then embrace.

There was indeed no lack of denunciation and vilifying, but there has been little of the earnest self-examination which followed World War I. It is easy to assume that there is nothing to examine because all of the guilt *this time* rested upon the Axis Powers, the aggressors who were defeated. If this is true, it is strange that the nations which banded together determinedly to protect the world and root out the evil were not able to move with a clearer conviction than had been possible amid the confused issues of World War I. World War II did not produce a burst of idealism like that which swelled so dramatically during the earlier crusade. The most eloquent speakers, authors, playwrights, and journalists tried hard to incite one, but it never quite came off. Peoples went to war apathetically, resignedly, in a spirit of grim fatalism. Ironically, a better show of enthusiasm was managed by the totalitarian countries than by the democracies. The Russians seemed strangely uninspired by their communist faith, but they did respond heroically to the challenge of "the great patriotic war." The Nazi legions displayed an *élan* and a will to conquer which was not matched by the French will to resist. (The French were under the disadvantage of remembering that they had won the last war; the Germans had not yet tasted the disillusionment of victory.)

During the war there was more discussion about building a new, peaceful, and better world than ever before in history. But in spite of all the brave words it was impossible to implant the faith that anything very beneficial would actually come to pass. The realities of the power struggle spoke too loudly; idealism was not in them; against the spiritual emptiness the voice of hope sounded weak and flat. World War I had been a "war to end war." This time the securing of peace for a generation appeared as a reasonable goal. President Wilson's Fourteen Points had been precise and straightforward. They went to the heart of the problem, with the intent of cutting out the rot of militarism, imperialism and secret diplomacy. They electrified a tired world. Compared with the Fourteen Points the Atlantic Charter of 1941 was forlorn and insipid.

Woodrow Wilson's League of Nations was a pretty poor instrument, even aside from the defection of the United States. But when the architects of victory gathered at San Francisco in 1945 to frame the charter of an international organization which would "have teeth in it" and be effective for keeping peace, they carefully bound it to the dogma of the impregnable sovereignty of each of the great powers. The provision for a unilateral veto of the most critical decisions is a stumbling block to which even the old League was not subjected. It insured not only the dominance of the Big Few over the will of all other member nations but also that disputes between these giants could be resolved only by recourse to traditional and avowedly discredited methods. At the outset the great powers showed clearly that they did not trust the instrument which they had created. In spite of the tremendous good which the UN and its affiliations have accomplished, in spite of its impressively wide membership, at its vital center it enshrines isolationism.

There has been comparatively little discussion of "guilt" since the last war because there is little interest in the matter. There is no perspective from which to approach it. It has no relevance to the course which nations are now pursuing—or it has so much relevance that to raise the question in full sincerity would bring paralysis. The concept of guilt has no meaning unless there are accepted standards of right and the capacity to be shocked when the standards are violated. But standards of international morality have been liquidated in the caldron of total war. During World War I people were horrified by the torpedoing of merchant vessels and by the introduction of poison gas. They were shocked also by atrocity stories which were deliberately invented for the purpose of shocking them. In World War II there was no need to invent atrocities—there were too many well authenticated; but they did not produce the same profound reaction. In the course of this war people learned to accept area bombing, the wiping out of whole cities, and finally indiscriminate devastation by the atom bomb. Perhaps the guilt is properly lodged—and buried—with the fascist states that precipitated the torrent of destruction in 1939. But then it should be inquired how these states with their nihilistic impulses came into existence; and that inquiry would lead into many twisting lanes, back through the Great Depression and the insane economic nationalism which brought it on, back to the Treaty of Versailles and the sins of the statesmen who threw away the chance to build a genuine European community. So the question of guilt goes too deep to be of any advantage in contemporary controversy. (Also the innocent and the guilty nations keep switching their positions in confusing fashion.)

The war crimes trials, which in outward appearance bore directly upon the problem of guilt, are but another illustration of the change in moral climate between the two world wars. At the close of the earlier conflict there was loose talk of trying the Kaiser and other German leaders, but the project was dropped with the realization that it would be too embarrassing for all concerned. After the second war, however, the conquerors were not embarrassed. They proceeded to declare the law (ex post facto), set themselves up as prosecutor and judge, and passed and executed the sentence. What these trials, with their tons of testimony and argument, proved is very difficult to say, except the obvious lesson that it is risky to lose a war. The idea of outlawing international aggression is both sound and noble and was undoubtedly a motivating factor with some of the participants in the Nuremberg and Toyko proceedings. But the whole framework and staging of the war crimes trials and the fact that they were inseparable from the incidents of a military triumph made it impossible for them to arouse moral enthusiasm among either the vanquished or the victor peoples. If such was their purpose, they are among the most patent failures of the reconstruction era.

This is not to say that there has been no general revulsion against the tragedy of mass warfare or that there have been no constructive efforts to repair its ravages. On the contrary, inside and outside of the UN both public and private agencies have worked heroically to bring relief and the means of recovery to stricken populations. The Marshall Plan, while based partly upon calculations of America's political and commercial interests, was also prompted by a generous impulse to assist nations most in need, regardless of ideological differences. The Point Four program suggested almost unlimited possibilities for promoting international good will, beyond its immediate benefits in the form of technical aid to the underdeveloped areas. Unfortunately, these painstaking and unspectacular activities tend to be crowded out of view (and out of funds) by the convolutions of power politics and cold war strategy. The United States with her surplus of skill, goods, and gold undoubtedly must and will give aid from her bounty; but this is a situation which entails tremendous responsibility. The effect of a program of assistance is dependent upon the spirit in which the program is conceived and executed. If it is coupled with arrogance or if it should become a whip to compel obedience in a global power struggle, it will vitiate rather than nourish the democratic cause.

DEMOCRACIES IN GLASS HOUSES

During the period following World War I, democracy was in retreat. The rise of the fascist dictatorships not only set the stage for another war but it represented a deliberate repudiation of nineteenth-century ideals and commitments. And it occurred among peoples that had long been an integral part of European society, not aliens recently inducted. The phenomenon seemed like some weird nightmare. The world rubbed its eyes, hardly able to believe what it saw and heard coming out of Italy and Germany. Resources and skills which had been laboriously cultivated were being used to serve the ends of a regime based upon brute force. The protagonists of the new order were the sworn enemies of European traditions and of the values of civilization—*hostes humani generis.* In the scheme which they formulated industry, technology, and science would be intensified, but disassociated from and used to destroy the culture in which these things had been nurtured. The program was self-annihilative, because the magnificent techniques accumulated through centuries of evolution could not long survive when the subsoil out of which they grew was poisoned. Nevertheless, frenzied attempts were made to extinguish the past, to substitute "futurism." Hence came the burning of books, the shackling of scientific research, the prostitution of education and corruption of youth, the "co-ordination" of institutions, thought, and art, the degradation of religion.

While fascism was a morbid aberration—proclaiming a philosophy which was no philosophy but a hodgepodge of primitive impulses—it can only be understood in the context of contemporary European society. The liberal and democratic Western nations were not entirely immune to the poison themselves. Although aghast at the effrontery of the Fascists, they were assailed by doubts as to the traditions which they were nominally upholding. Liberal humanitarian ideals were on the defensive in every country before the cynical materialism and reactionary spirit that followed in the wake of the war and the 1919 peace settlements. There was more than a suspicion that perhaps the dictators "really had something."

The gravest menace confronting the West was not that the totalitarian states might eventually attack the others, but that conditions were being created in which totalitarianism could exist, be tolerated, and even appear normal. In 1919 and the years following, not only democratic ideals but the principles of decency and integrity were violated by the countries which had sworn to defend them and had sent their sons to die for them. Germany, under the only genuinely democratic constitution which she has ever had (and one of the most advanced and thoroughly democratic constitutions in the world) was treated as a pariah among nations. Four years after the Peace Conference, the French, beneath the guise of collecting reparations, seized the Ruhr Valley, the nerve center of German industry, and tried to detach the Rhineland from Germany in violation of the Versailles Treaty. It is not strange that extremists both of the right and of the left were able to capitalize on the embitterment of the German people. Had there been more intelligence and farsightedness in the post-World-War-I policies of France, Britain, and the United States, *Der Fuehrer* probably would have remained one of many briefly remembered nuisances, with unusually powerful lungs.

Fascism fed upon the disillusionment, the doubt and the moral decay which was sapping the vitals of Western society. Its sinister tendencies could be seen everywhere. In England Sir Oswald Mosley and his black-shirted followers were more ludicrous than dangerous. In France, however, the exploits of Colonel de la Rocque and the *Croix de Feu* were so formidable as to induce friends of *liberté* to seek an alignment with Communists in the Popular Front. Even in the United States, proverbial land of freedom and plenty, the Ku Klux Klan throve lustily, Huey Long's *putsch* was successful in the state of Louisiana, and Father Coughlin captivated millions of listeners. While such movements could not gain the upper hand in countries that were strong economically, placated with the trophies of victory, and enjoying a heyday of political ascendancy, they proved almost irresistible to nations whose outlook was bleaker. The judgment of the democracies upon the dictatorships should have been tempered by the reflection "There but for the grace of God go we."

The democratic powers failed to recognize or acknowledge that they had contributed to the general conditions in which fascist regimes could take root. They failed to perceive that their own societies were susceptible to the virus and that some of the most noxious devices of the dictatorships could be and actually were employed by peoples committed to democratic traditions. Racist doctrines had frequently been flaunted widely and shamelessly. The murderous anti-Semitism of the Nazis was a fiendish intensification of an ancient prejudice. Unreasoning nationalism, the cult of state worship, was a familiar theme long before the dictators discovered its efficacy for mass hypnosis. And the dream of continental supremacy, to be attained by making every citizen a soldier, is at least as old as the French Revolution. But instead of trying to isolate the evil tendencies and avoid contagion, the democracies sometimes showed themselves eager to share in or benefit from the dictators' successes. Many people found that they could, and were quite willing to, "do business with Hitler"—and with Mussolini, with Marshall Pilsudski and Admiral Horthy, and with General Franco. Only when the ruthless ones threatened the security of the democratic powers did these governments belatedly discover that they were confronting a foe without scruple or mercy and that all the values of Western culture hung in the balance. At the outbreak of the conflict in 1939 Mr. Chamberlain announced that the war was against "evil things." It was certainly the result of evil things; the fight against them has been all too timid.

Undoubtedly one reason for the complaisant attitude toward the fascist dictators in the 1930's, at least among British Conservatives, was the feeling that they could be turned to good account in checking the Soviet Union. A clash between the Nazi and Communist regimes, it was hoped, would weaken or ruin both of these dangerous aggregations and save the European balance of power for the states which had traditionally benefited from it. But, as events turned out, the crushing defeat of Germany was accompanied by a great accretion of power to the U.S.S.R.; and the Western democracies were now face to face with a totalitarian rival much more formidable than that which the Nazis had alternately baited, befriended, and finally attacked. The territorial, strategic, and diplomatic gains of the U.S.S.R. far exceeded the expectations of her allies, even though the latter had very generously contributed to this result in their eagerness to secure the maximum Russian effort for the defeat of Germany and Japan. With remarkable swiftness the wartime allied sentiment of sharing together in a common heroic task was replaced by suspicion of Russian intentions. Hardly had the enemy nations surrendered when Western spokesmen began to sound the alarm, declaring that it would be far worse for China to be dominated by Russia than by Japan and that Stalin was more dangerous than Hitler had ever been.

The democracies seemed fated to move from one baffling dilemma to another. They had defeated their fascist enemies, but in an exhausting struggle and only with the help of another totalitarian dictatorship. Now, that victorious dictatorship cast a frightening shadow over the whole "free world," placing in jeopardy all the gains of the recent ordeal. What nemesis had brought this to pass? It cannot be explained simply by describing the development of the Soviet state and the growth of Soviet power during the past thirty years. That is a remarkable story in itself, belying probabilities and predictions, but it is only a partial answer.

In so far as the Soviet system constitutes a threat to the world, it is—as was Nazism—a projection of the defects and corruption within the whole of contemporary Western civilization. This is not so readily apparent for communism as for fascism and nazism. Those were petulant, nihilistic movements which found a thrill in deliberately trampling under foot values universally cherished; because these coveted values, appearing inaccessible, had turned sour. But the Bolshevik leaders had sought to transcend the goals and canons of the bourgeois liberal tradition, sweeping them away in order to build a better social order, a "new civilization." The program which they conceived was far-reaching and imaginative; it inspired their followers with the enthusiasm of creative action. Gradually, however, the molten flux of exciting promise hardened into rigid forms of conventional design. The Russian Revolution, which announced its emancipation from the whole dead past, conjured up ghosts of the past and conformed to the normal pattern of revolutions. In contrast to the French Revolution it extended terror and dictatorship into permanent procedures, but it employed them eventually for purposes drastically opposed to the objectives of the early Bolshevik leaders.

Both the original ideals of the Communists and what was substituted for these ideals—the actualities of the present Soviet order— were derived almost entirely from the general store of Western experience. They were not exotic or Oriental, in spite of Russia's historic association with Asia and the alleged influence of "Tartar" strains. The Marxian philosophy was a distillation from Western industrial society, combining a sharp awareness of its pathological tensions with a faith in the elixir of scientific and technological progress, blended with a strong dose of eighteenth-century utopianism. Lenin and his associates aimed at nothing less ambitious than catching up with the mature industrial nations and then outdistancing them by constructing a planned economy for the future. With a backward, agricultural, and illiterate population they proposed to carry through an industrial revolution, while at the same time skipping directly over capitalism into socialism and effecting, parallel to all this, a political, intellectual, and ethical transformation. The program of the Bolsheviks was launched in the midst of the economic breakdown and demoralization which accompanied Russia's debacle in World War I, and of necessity the greatest efforts were directed to economic development—to the stimulation of industrial production and the collectivization of agriculture. It is along these lines that the Soviets, in spite of miscalculations and reverses, have achieved their most spectacular successes. They have harnessed latent natural resources; they have turned the most backward of European countries into an industrial giant. They have succeeded in their mission of overtaking their Western rivals. In doing so they have lost, or buried deeply, their vision of a freer society.

In the degradation of the Marxist-Leninist ideal, a multitude of factors has played a part. Undoubtedly a major one was the stern demands of an industrial regime which had to be created from the foundations up and largely by planners without experience. The eagerness to promote heavy industry—steel and iron, coal, oil, transportation, and electrification—involved a continuous sacrifice in the production of consumers' goods, sentencing the majority of the population to a low standard of living for decades. The fact that the struggle was carried on not only against considerable internal resistance but in the midst of latent or actual hostility on the part of surrounding states aggravated its harshness, by underlining the urgency of a program which appeared to be a race against time. Beyond these considerations, and probably even more fundamental, are the typical human failings which have marred most revolutions—an impatience avid for shortcuts; the assumption of infallibility on the part of leaders; belief that the end justifies the means, which results in the means becoming the end; and the infatuation with power, which power almost always instills in those who exercise it.

Discerning students of the Soviet Union have noted over the years the re-emergence of archaic motifs, the gradual surrender to numbing influences which had theoretically been exorcized forever. The doctrine "To each according to his needs" is belied by a hierarchy with numerous and invidious gradations in income and prestige; labor is regimented and moved about arbitrarily; the piecework system, long denounced as a vicious capitalist device, becomes a standard technique for squeezing the utmost effort from the workers. The heralded freedom of women gives way to a crusade for large families. The old visceral type of patriotism is revived. The workers of the world, whom Marx told they had no fatherland, are now taught that they have one fatherland, to which they owe unquestioning allegiance. Swashbuckling heroes of the Tsarist age, whom the early Bolsheviks spewed from their memories, are rehabilitated as inspiring examples for patriotic youth. And militarism, the scourge of bourgeois capitalism and imperialism, becomes the staff of national life. Even religion, the "opiate of the people" is pressed into service during a war for survival (opiates have their value, the Communists discovered). These changes, perhaps well suited to the ends of dictatorship, represent a reversion to old stock formulas conspicuous in the evolution of Western societies but long considered obsolete by enlightened and progressive elements. They are a proof of unoriginality, of the faltering of imagination and faith. And the more these formulas are relied upon the more surely do they leave their mark upon the national psychology.

Observers in Russia have commented on the tendency of the people to become enamored with the mechanization of their economy, succumbing to what Marx branded as a "fetish" of capitalism. The Marxian program promised to emancipate both the bodies and the minds of workers from a machine-paced existence. But apparently under the banner of communism people are no more immune to machine worship than under the banner of capitalism. Arnold Toynbee pointed out in 1933 that a "tug-of-war" was going on in Russia "between the ideals of Lenin and the methods of Ford," with the likelihood that Ford would win as the peasant was taught "to think as the mechanic thinks and to feel as he feels and to desire what he desires." He saw the Soviet leaders as working furiously "to ensure the triumph in Russia of the very civilization which they are denouncing in the World at large."

The reactionary tendencies within Soviet communism evoke a rather strange response in the strongholds of capitalism and democracy. There is a sort of grim satisfaction over the evaporating of the dream of the early Bolsheviks and in the observation that the state and party machinery have slipped back into familiar grooves. Yet the dream was not a threat to the world's peoples, whereas the lines of policy which have turned the dream into mockery are very much a threat. Quite rightly the crass and inhumane elements of the Soviet system are denounced. But these elements pertain to the areas where the Soviet leaders did not dare to be different. The evils, the false materialistic standards are the universal stock in trade of power-oriented societies, intensified of course and made all the more repulsive in a police state erected upon a population which never had an opportunity to become habituated to genteel codes of behavior. Because the most dangerous aspects of Soviet policy are not peculiar to communist ideology but are the all too easy resort of desperate men of various persuasions, the checking or military defeat of Russia would not free Western society from peril. In concentrating too exclusively on effecting a checkmate, we intensify the peril, by enhancing the strategic value of the practices which we deplore in our adversary, and even by adopting them ourselves.

In the Soviet menace the evils of our civilization are written clearly and with a large hand. They should serve as a warning to the Western peoples to look within themselves, to forsake abominations and cleanse their hearts. Instead, these peoples are inclined to relieve their feelings by pointing out that the Communists are like other men, that they have feet of clay, and worship false gods.

In the verbal battles of the cold war we seem to be saying: "You Russians are as bad as the rest of us—only much worse. You exploit the workers even more than capitalism does. You indoctrinate your youth with a fanatical nationalism which sacrifices conscience and the interest of humanity to the will of the state. You talk of peace, but you are right beside us in the armaments race; you are more militaristic than we are!"

It is frequently remarked that the Communists understand no language except force. If this is true it is one more indication of reversion to the norm. It suggests that the Soviets have learned well the lessons of international politics during the past thirty years. When Germany was weak economically and militarily, she commanded little respect, even though she had adopted a democratic form of government. After Hitler came to power and began rattling the sword, he was able to win concessions, step by step with Germany's improved military position. Force was the language which Mussolini employed in Ethiopia; and Britain and France understood it so well that they declined to place sanctions on steel, iron, and oil. Force determined the fate of Republican Spain when under the cloak of "nonintervention" the Fascists were allowed to destroy the legitimate government. It spoke in tones of authority at Munich, and again the Western democracies hearkened to the voice. Aside from these object lessons, the Soviet leaders had their own experiences to draw upon. One of President Wilson's Fourteen Points, dealing specifically with Russia, called for "unembarrassed opportunity for the independent determination of her own political development . . . and more than a welcome, assistance also of every kind." But communist Russia was not invited to the Peace Conference; and while it met, the country was tightly blockaded, and French and British armies on Russian soil were attempting to encompass the downfall of the revolutionary government. Only after the Red Armies proved capable of defending Russian territory both in the West and in the East was diplomatic recognition accorded by the great powers.

For a few years Russia was the leading advocate of collective security. Being still comparatively weak militarily, she took a prominent part in the movement for world disarmament. Maxim

Litvinov at Geneva in 1928 startled the other members of the League's Preparatory Commission by proposing a plan for the gradual and proportional disarmament of all nations. The response of the commission's president was to admonish the Soviet delegation to attend future meetings "in a constructive spirit." When the conference opened at Geneva in 1932, the Russians again suggested a universal scaling down of military forces by fifty per cent. After two years of argument, however, nothing actually came from the Geneva Conference except conclusive evidence that there was no mutual trust even among traditional allies and that each sovereign unit would rely upon its own armed strength. Finally, in 1939, when Hitler's intransigence made a conflict with the democracies imminent and the Soviets had acquired a military potential worth reckoning with, they found themselves assiduously courted by both sides. They drove a hard bargain.

Every major stroke of policy in recent years has been grounded on the assumption that force is the final determinant in the dealings of states with one another. It is the universal idiom that everyone is supposed to understand. Everyday experience, as well as the most elementary historical insight into the evolution of civilizations, shows that there is another approach and a different language —appealing to hope instead of fear and speaking in tones of reconciliation—which produces more agreeable and more enduring results. But this is not in the repertory of international politics.

When power becomes the prime objective of nations, strange things happen to the perspective, especially when the world is riven between two competing power centers. Western observers view with anxiety the success of Soviet enterprise. It strikes them as ominous that the Russians have doubled their production of coal since 1940; that their increase in steel production has exceeded the increase of all the Western European countries including Britain by almost one hundred per cent and that they may even double their present output of steel by 1960; that they have made equally impressive strides in oil and in other branches of heavy industry. But most ominous of all (in this Alice-through-the-looking-glass era), there is the prospect that Soviet economy may finally be directed toward a more generous supply of consumers' goods and thus elevate the living standards of the Russian people. A European correspondent writes: "By 1955, it appears, the average Russian will have at his disposal, statistically, more than twice as much grain as the average Frenchman. . . twice as many potatoes, more fish, more table fats, more cotton cloth, as many shoes. . . . By 1955 or 1956, according to some French economists, standards of living in France and Russia will be equal." The significant point is not the accuracy or inaccuracy of these predictions but the light in which they are viewed. The writer remarks that most European economists consider the French calculations "outrageously gloomy." He adds, however, "But no economist quibbles with the basic content of these French surveys—that the Russian economy is overtaking the west European economies one by one." The remarkable growth of Russia's industrial potential has increased her formidability as a military threat. But "the political danger point will come when this expanding basic production reaches the area of consumers' goods." In other words, the worst thing to fear is a mitigation of the grinding austerity of the Soviet regime to allow its people the physical satisfactions which are the pride and the prerogative of older industrial nations. The safety of the "free" world depends upon the continued degradation of the other half. What a sequel to the nineteenth-century vision of continually increasing productivity for the enrichment of the common life of humanity!

It is now apparent that there is nothing either racial or ideological about the application of advanced technology. The peoples of Asia, the Chinese most of all at the present moment, are appropriating them with the utmost enthusiasm. The Western democracies have entertained false premises concerning Soviet destiny, and this mistake has contributed to their extreme case of nerves. They have assumed all along that communism must fail. It has neither failed nor succeeded—its essential principles have been abandoned long since in the area behind the Iron Curtain— but the Soviet Leviathan has gone on steadily enlarging its resources and augmenting its strength. It is equally true that Soviet leaders have been wrong about the West. They have clung to the dogma, to them an article of faith, that capitalism bears the seeds of its own dissolution, and they look forward to its downfall. They note with satisfaction the towering burden of debt in the United States and the little wisps of suspicion that a slackening of the defense program would bring disastrous unemployment. Behind their wall of steel they wait for a depression which will cripple the economy and scuttle the confidence of the West. But there is no imminent prospect of collapse either in the Soviet Union or in the United States, the citadel of democratic capitalism. Each of the two antagonists is growing stronger and more resolutely prepared for an eventuality which it neither desires nor knows how to prevent.

CHAPTER TWELVE

CIVILIZATION IN CRISIS

AN attempt to predict the fate or future course of Western civilization would be both profitless and presumptuous. Even a diagnosis of the condition of contemporary society is extremely difficult, not only because the subject is complex but because there is no vantage point of distance from which to view it with a clear perspective. It is possible to be objective about ancient civilizations which have passed away (and the scantier the information the easier the task becomes), but no one can detach himself from the civilization which impinges upon him from all sides, gives him his sense of direction, and even conditions the adverse criticism which he may bring against it. Hence we cannot evaluate with complete assurance our own culture and institutions. We do not even fully understand the nature of man, the builder and wrecker of cultures. We do not know what is his ultimate role in the drama of evolution. Nevertheless, it is imperative that we should try to find our bearings and estimate, however tentatively, the resources and weaknesses of our civilization, even though there can be no general agreement in the matter.

Civilization in Crisis

Viewed in its entirety, Western civilization is undoubtedly one of the most remarkable ever to come into being. Among the civilizations still existing it is the most recent in origin; yet it has spread farther and affected a larger proportion of the earth's population than any other advanced culture, ancient or modern. The tremendous achievements of the Western peoples are explained not by biological superiority but by the numerous advantages which they have enjoyed—of climate, geographic location, and access to abundant natural resources. They have benefited not only from the spacious and varied environmental setting in which their own culture developed but also from stimulating contacts with other cultures. Finally, science, by enabling them to unlock the secrets of nature, has put almost unlimited power into their hands.

Although from its inception Western civilization was the heir to inestimable treasures from the successive Near Eastern cultures which reach back to the dawn of history, it took its rise upon the ruins of Greco-Roman civilization. It is encouraging to remember that the European peoples began to construct what was to be a distinctive type of society in a time of turmoil and harassment, when the "end of the world" seemed to be at hand. While they were still living under primitive material conditions they displayed intellectual and artistic vigor which attained ambitious and brilliant expression, marking one of the high points of the Western story.

From the end of the Middle Ages on, came rapid expansion and material improvement. What had been a poor society was transformed into a rich one. The expansion, impetuous and operating in several directions at once, ruptured social disciplines and traditional values. The Renaissance and Reformation eras were characterized by reckless individualism, fierce conflict, cupidity, and even grave doubts as to man's worth. However, the upset was not fatal. Basic values were vindicated and given fresh importance, notably during the Age of the Enlightenment, a period which represents another significant page in the Western record. It yielded the vision of a reasonable society—humane, peaceful, and progressively intelligent.

The Industrial Revolution produced a far more explosive set

of changes than any which had preceded it. But a courageous rallying took place to deal with the problems which emerged from this revolution, and bolder programs were formulated. Liberalism, democracy, and the idea of progress sparked a new idealism; science was hailed as the doorway to knowledge and as an instrument of social betterment. Along with sweeping technological innovations came a prodigious flowering of culture, which stemmed from a broader popular base than ever before. The middle years of the nineteenth century witnessed a climax of the Western creative spirit. The challenge of industrialism, of an enveloping materialism, was almost successfully met. But the technological transmutation became continually greater and more dislocating, until it presented to the twentieth century a still more staggering challenge. This challenge has not yet been effectively answered, and modern civilization is harried by forces which it has developed within itself.

Because a series of shocks and crises has characterized the history of Western peoples in modern times, the prospect of facing one more need not be unnerving. The ability to recover equilibrium and to synthesize conflicting tendencies has been demonstrated again and again. In fact, the repeated experience of having to make readjustments is a salubrious tonic which largely accounts for the dynamic quality of our society and its culture. However, the perplexities of the present are so serious that it will require a full measure of intelligence and fortitude to resolve them.

THE NATURE OF THE CONTEMPORARY CRISIS

In attempting to deal with the crisis of contemporary civilization, the first requisite is to recognize that a crisis exists and to try to understand its nature. In its most obvious form the crisis is the threat of another world war, with horrors which are clearly delineated and others which can only be imagined—a sort of mammoth genocide and suicide which might erase civilization from the earth and would almost certainly end the dominance of the Western nations.

But even the avoiding or postponing of World War III does

not remove the crisis. At the present time the world's political units are divided between two opposing power centers. Ortega y Gasset in his *Revolt of the Masses* (written about 1930) made a strong plea for the Western European nations that had been the historic leaders to resume the initiative and create a United States of Europe. The challenge of this task, he believed, would release latent energies and the project would restore confidence and a sense of direction to European and even world affairs. He dismissed the suggestion that either Russia or the United States might assume command in the event of default by Britain, France, and Germany. Neither Moscow nor New York could rule in the world, he said, because each represents a "new people"—the Russians a "child-people," the Americans "a primitive people camouflaged behind the latest inventions." Perhaps Ortega was right in arguing that these two young nations could not rule in the sense of providing effective guidance based upon understanding of needs and the ready acceptance of this guidance by other peoples (he observed that in the normal and true sense of the word, rule never rests upon force). But it has become apparent that because of their enormous power Russia and the United States can exert control over large sections of the world. They can and do compel the adoption of certain policies and the abandonment of others. They are able to determine the destinies of millions of people.

In both Russia and the United States the accession to a position of world authority has been very recent. The nations of Western Europe, damaged and disorganized by World War I, refused to merge into a union which not only would have restored their economy but might have strengthened it beyond what it had ever been before. World War II almost destroyed their economy and ended the supremacy of the West European states for the foreseeable future. The impoverishment and decline of the key European areas, therefore, conferred upon the peripheral powers, Russia and the United States, the role of dominance over a prostrate Continent. The suspicion and hostility between the two prevents a normal recovery, and neither of the rivals can lead in the task of reconstruction with complete disinterestedness. The ruthless police-state methods of the U.S.S.R. render her suspect.

The United States, for her part, has little experience in or tradition of world responsibility. It is always unhealthy for any nation to be able to impose its will upon others, all the more so when there is a great disparity of strength between the parties. And for the most heavily populated and most highly developed areas of the world to be caught in the cross fire between two rival superstates is exceedingly dangerous.

To go a little deeper into the matter, one of the most ominous factors today is the increasing militarization of society. It represents the reversal of a trend, traducing the logic of the evolution of Western communities. Social stability and cultural progress have since the Middle Ages been associated with the growth of a productive middle class, the *bourgeoisie*—citizens and civilians. With the rise of the modern nation states, fighting was relegated to mercenaries and professionals, commonly regarded not as honorable members of the body politic but as the "regimented assassins" of European princes. The reversal of this tradition began with the French Revolution, which contributed the concept of "the nation in arms" and the citizen-soldier. During the nineteenth century a sinister aspect of the growth of technology and of democracy was that these two developments in combination created the basis for the modern type of mass warfare. World War I demonstrated its frightful possibilities and World War II did so on a much grander scale, ushering in what is now frankly and properly called a military age. Whatever the causes of this development it is an indication of decay in the innermost fibers of the social organism. For a mature civilization to move in the direction of militarism marks the beginning of decline, and one which heretofore has always proved fatal. It is one of the few clearly recognizable factors in the disintegration and collapse of the Assyrian, the Egyptian, and the Roman empires.

As the process of militarization continues, it becomes a pervasive phenomenon, permeating all phases of life and thought. The cloud which at first was no bigger than a man's hand grows until it blacks out the sky. Inevitably a military bureaucracy develops, which obtains the final word in the foreign policy of nations and ultimately determines domestic policies as well. The military organization reaches out—it is already doing so in the United States—to gain control over education. With funds at its disposal it can hire a significant portion of the brain power of colleges and universities. It subsidizes scientific research, prescribes its course, and clamps the lid of secrecy upon its findings. The armed forces now serve as a colossal training ground for youth in their formative years. In the words of an Army officer, "The military establishment has become the greatest educational institution in the United States today." It is illusory to think that the chief purpose of this training ground is to develop mental and moral character. The qualities most desired in a well-disciplined combat army are directly opposite to those inherent in the liberal, democratic, and humanitarian tradition.

Obsolete Instruments

The roots of the contemporary crisis extend into the area of beliefs, attitudes, and values, where subtle changes which can alter the entire complexion of society and of human behavior are taking place. Even the surface phenomena, however, are sufficiently formidable to engage the faculties of anyone genuinely concerned with the fate of mankind. The economic and social disciplines of the principal nations have been subjected to military inroads which rob them of spontaneity and regiment them into impersonal instruments of mass action. In the abnormal state of international politics peoples are locked in the vise of two opposing powers. Overhead hangs the threat of a war of annihilation.

Granting the existence of perils which could prove disastrous, the important question is whether or not they can be successfully met. What are the prospects for resolving the crisis of our age and moving on to new levels of achievement with restored confidence? On the basis of the record of the past fifteen hundred years, the answer to the question is that the prospects are excellent. But on the basis of current trends and policies—on the basis of what is being done to meet the crisis—the answer is less reassuring.

An unfortunate circumstance is that the directive agencies of contemporary society are not equipped to deal with the kind of crisis which confronts it. Foremost among Western institutions is the state. The history of the state is the connecting thread through the progressive movements of recent centuries. This political vehicle has served well in facilitating transition from an agrarian to an industrial and urban economy. But the radical transformations effected by science and technology have rendered the state, in its present form, obsolete. The nation state presupposes distinct, significant, and more or less permanent differences among communities and their geographical separation from one another. It was invented at a time when the barrier of distance was effectual and the task of welding together people with diverse dialects and customs, even within such small areas as France, Spain, or Germany, seemed overly ambitious. It was demarcated by puny natural boundaries like rivers and mountain ranges. It was adorned with legends, provincial symbols, and slogans in the attempt to awaken a sense of community and to integrate social resources efficiently. Most of the conditions that were relevant to the genesis of the state have passed away. Nations are not separate from one another; there are no more geographical boundaries; national legends have been outgrown; social resources have passed the point of efficiency and threaten to explode.

The modern state is by no means an unmitigated evil; but it is fundamentally an instrument of power and is by tradition and design bent upon perpetuating and enlarging its power. And power, expanding and more and more uncontrollable, is the source of the perils which overshadow mankind; it is the enemy at the gate.

The modern nation state has become an anachronism. It opposes the realities, even the bare physical realities, of present-day existence. It attempts to isolate peoples and freeze their attitudes into molds of the past, while their experience is revealing to them new opportunities for communion and the need for a new integration. It opposes the idea of One World, even though it is clear that the world has become one in destiny and can enjoy a productive future only on this basis. But while the state is an anachronism

—so far as its competence to recognize and meet the urgent needs of the moment is concerned—it is also the strongest of institutions, tending to lock all others within itself and to prescribe their operation. Such a situation is not unprecedented. Feudal rituals and loyalties became most elaborate when their usefulness was vanishing. The absolute royal despotisms of the eighteenth century were remarkably tenacious and required more than the shock of the French Revolution to unseat them. The ancient Roman imperial bureaucracy was most resolute when it was unwittingly directed toward the liquidation of the really vital elements in Roman society. Institutions have a way of hardening when they are no longer the channels through which supple and creative forces are flowing. The task of reconstructing the anachronistic nation state in the light of international realities is perhaps no greater than other reconstructions which have been accomplished; but there is not unlimited time and the penalty for failure threatens to be uncommonly severe.

The prevalent economic institutions are also obsolete. They are not worthless; they are probably better than most societies have known. Undeniably, economic progress constitutes one of the really impressive and solid achievements of the modern Western era. But the economic organization no longer works in such a way as to satisfy the requirements of society. It does not satisfy even the basic material needs of the members of society—for shelter, nourishment, and remunerative activity. Throughout human history the primary economic problem has been how to produce enough goods. That problem was solved by the invention of power-driven machinery and the scientific technology of the industrial age. But the rise of industrial capitalism introduced a new problem which has been central ever since—how to distribute the goods which are produced. Whatever success modern economic theorists have had, the problem has not been solved in practice.

Under a system of private profits, industry prospers only when there is an "effective demand" for its goods, and this means a condition in which there are not enough goods to go around. But with the spur of "effective demand" there is a tendency to produce a supply of goods which exceeds the "effective demand" and approximates the real demand. This brings lower prices, declining profits, curtailed production, and scarcity. Industry can produce sufficiently to meet the real demand but has no incentive to do so. In fact it is perilous for it to do so because of the risk of bringing the whole industrial apparatus to a standstill, in which event capitalists, laborers, and consumers all suffer, although not in equal degrees. The invention of mechanized technology, which makes it possible to create wealth abundantly, has not been paralleled by an invention for distributing the wealth—that is, for getting it consumed. And when wealth accumulates, not only men but the means of producing wealth also decay. The more the productive potential increases the more severe the problem becomes; every mounting surplus of unconsumed goods is matched by an area of deficiency or privation somewhere in the population.

Various attempts have been made to induce the economic system to function more smoothly—to wean it from the "boom and bust" cycle of high production plus poverty and low production plus greater poverty. The most conspicuous direct attempt in the leading industrial nation was embodied in the New Deal program of the early 1930's. The New Deal had many facets and enacted reforms of permanent value; to a large extent it succeeded in relieving the groups which were suffering most acutely. However, pragmatic and experimental as the program was, it incorporated the general principle of curtailing production as a means of stimulating demand. It subscribed to a philosophy of scarcity—created artificially if need be by plowing under rows of corn and killing baby pigs—as a requisite incentive to arouse the economy from stagnancy.

The New Deal, the reforms of the Popular Front government in France, and similar schemes for beating the depression did not resolve the basic economic dilemma of how to make it profitable to keep the productive mechanism running in high gear while at the same time distributing its output to the people who actually need it and can consume it. These reforms relieved, but they did not remove, the phenomenon of mass unemployment, which is the embarrassing exposed surface of the dilemma. However, after several lean years of depression the Western economies were given an unprecedented lift and a new lease on life by the adoption of a program of armaments expansion, first by the fascist states and then by their democratic rivals. Perhaps neither the dictatorships nor the democracies adopted a rearmament policy for the deliberate purpose of salvaging their economies; but it is true that no one of the industrial nations which had been severely struck by the depression discovered any way to restore a high level of productivity and full employment except by diverting industry to the requirements of a military establishment. Obviously, the situation has become much more extreme than it was in 1939. The dependence of heavy industry—steel, metallurgy, rubber, aircraft, to say nothing of atomic projects and similarly subsidized research—upon military demands has grown and will probably continue to grow. The highest degree of prosperity ever reached in the United States, measured by the annually rising national income, is accompanied by and is the direct result of the most gigantic military expansion in our history. It was this unexampled prosperity that President Truman was referring to when he said that if his administration had brought ruin to the country, as his opponents charged, it was "a wonderful ruin" and he was glad to be a part of it. But the policy, whether ruinous or not, is not the work of any one man or administration; it marks a trend almost universal in the contemporary Western world.

Thus, after tinkering with the economy, the more potent course was adopted of releasing it from the vagaries of consumer demand and harnessing it to the requirements of a government-directed enterprise which can be expanded indefinitely. The critical state of international affairs elicits popular support for such a program, and its benefits are immediately felt. Because it promotes maximum employment of the population and high wages, it eliminates the difficulty of disposing of the consumer goods which, in decreasing quantities, are manufactured. But no one would argue that such an "emergency" regime is a real solution of the economic dilemma. It makes profit—not for "warmongers" and "profiteers" only but for whole nations—out of war and the fear of war. It rests upon the insane premise that the only way to keep the industrial order functioning efficiently is by letting it produce the instruments which will destroy it utterly. Sooner or later the accumulating weapons will inevitably be used in the manner for which they were designed. Even short of that dramatic finale, the program has grave disadvantages. It wastes irreplaceable natural resources. It directs the energies of society to unproductive ends. It forces a decline in the standard of living the more drastic as the program accelerates, until people find themselves working harder and harder to have less and less. Relevant to this inescapable result are the difficulties which the United States has encountered in implementing the N.A.T.O. arrangements. Essentially we have been trying to persuade our European allies to divert their shaky economies into military channels. Having already gone farther down these treacherous sluices than we have, they are reluctant to comply. Thus we run into a contradiction. If militarization is beneficial to the economy of the United States it is damaging to the economy of each of our allies and also to most of the rest of the world. (The U.S.S.R. might possibly gain proportionately to our success in committing the West Europeans to a guns-instead-of-butter program.)

In the political field, in the economic field—and even, it must be admitted, to a considerable degree in the areas of the physical and social sciences and education—the paramount institutions of modern society are not coming to grips with the contemporary crisis. Their total effect is, rather, to heighten it.

THE PARALYSIS OF DOUBT

It is true, as so often remarked, that the real crisis of our age is a spiritual one. Unfortunately, spiritual crises cannot be resolved by material means. If they could be, our problem would be simple because never before has our material store been so ample. Spiritual values are in jeopardy, and they must be defended if our civilization is to survive. But they cannot be defended by being buried in a vault nor by being replaced, even temporarily, by principles and practices which are the antithesis of these values.

Civilization in Crisis

The spiritual crisis is more profound than is generally recognized. A popular notion is that defense of such priceless things as personal liberty, democracy, and religious freedom is a matter of maintaining the independence, well-being, or supremacy of the nations which by definition (and a rather elastic definition) are the custodians of these great principles. This will be of little help if the values have evaporated among the people who are supposed to be preserving them. Ever since World War I the Western adherents of the democratic Christian heritage have been struggling against the spoilers of this heritage. While they have won most of the battles, they are losing the war. They are losing it because they have relinquished their faith in the efficacy of their own ideals, because they have adopted the habits and attitudes of the enemy, and because they are using methods which intensify the evils they are fighting against.

At bottom the trouble with contemporary Western civilization is that it is immoral. This is not to say that everyone has become immoral or that there is a larger percentage of immoral persons than in earlier times. Evidence points to the contrary. Over the general period of the last two or three centuries moral sensibilities have undoubtedly grown stronger. Progress has been made in charting areas where improvement is desirable and in setting up agencies to promote such improvement. Psychology and psychiatry, using scientific techniques, have helped to ferret out the causes of the quirks and aberrations in human behavior and to devise correctives. The developments along this line and the interest which they have aroused are a splendid and heartening achievement, holding great promise for the future. But society is confronted with a paradox. While efforts are directed to salvaging human wreckage and to promoting better personalities the climate of the larger social environment is becoming less favorable to the growth —or even the survival—of such personalities. There are countless numbers of moral individuals, but they must adapt themselves to a civilization which is becoming immoral because its directing units are morally irresponsible and it is succumbing to irrational forces. Accordingly, people are beset by irreconcilable loyalties which can lead to a state of schizophrenia. The soul of contemporary man is a house divided against itself.

The basis of the contemporary moral crisis is that, while standards of right and wrong have applied to individual conduct and have been cultivated with a deepening understanding, they have not applied to the paramount institution of modern times—the state—and still less to the relations between states. The modern state is the most formidable institution which mankind has ever known, and it is entirely secular in purpose and function, divorced from ethical imperatives. It is nurtured in the Machiavellian tradition that statecraft is a law unto itself and that the only limits upon what a state can or cannot do are the external restraints and internal resistances which happen to be effective at the moment. Throughout the modern era governments have in the main followed policies consonant with this doctrine, but never before our day have they had such power at their disposal. Power separated from moral responsibility is fatal; it can destroy the whole moral fabric of society. Yet the belief persists that there is one code of conduct for the state and another entirely different for the individual. A prominent American political scientist recently expressed the opinion that any great power which based its foreign policy upon moral considerations was doomed. To judge from the realities of international politics his advice is superfluous, but for that reason doom is all the more imminent. It is useless to argue that the state is neither moral nor immoral but *amoral*. States do not exist in a vacuum; they are composed of people and they operate through and upon people. In the nature of the case a state acting in important and controversial areas, affecting the destiny sometimes of millions, is acting either in a moral or an immoral way. And if it engages in acts of wanton barbarity, its people— even though unwilling participants—are degraded.

When there is so much anxiety over the fate of the basic values embedded in Western civilization, it is well to consider the question of just what these values are. What are the indispensable, most priceless elements which should be saved at all cost in a time of upheaval when it is plain that not everything can be held intact? If we are not clear on this, our policies will be confused and ineffectual. The basic values must be those beliefs and attitudes which have been vindicated again and again in the tortuous evolution of Western societies, although usually obscured and never given complete support. They must be those precepts and convictions to which men return after spasms of waywardness, as to a fresh spring after wandering in the desert; the flashes of insight which have provoked the most sustained efforts, illuminated the most enduring achievements, and restored hope in time of despair. They are epitomized in the ethical teachings of the Hebrew prophets and in the ethics of Jesus: charity, tolerance, compassion; faith in the inherent worth of man and reverence for the sacredness of individual personality. These are the supreme values, without which Western culture is "sounding brass or a tinkling cymbal"; and they must be sought after and clung to if modern man is to regain a state of confidence and well-being.

In recent years moral sensibilities have been subjected to a process of blunting. They have suffered attrition from constant exposure to collective acts of injustice and rapacity. At the close of World War II the expulsion of millions of people from their homes in Russia, Poland, Czechoslovakia, and Germany—literally a death sentence for thousands, especially women, children, and the aged—was carried out not as a military necessity but to satisfy a pent-up flood of hatred and revenge after victory had been won. Accompanied by epidemics of disease and slow but systematic starvation in the occupation zones of Germany, the deportations were crueler and more flagrant than all the vindictive barbarities that followed upon the collapse of Germany and Russia in 1918. Yet these atrocities, perpetrated so recently, hardly kindle the indignation. They are dismissed as mere incidents in the termination of a war or forgotten amid preparations for the next war. It is an ominous symptom that today there is such widespread indifference to the simple palpable fact of human suffering. There is not indifference to all suffering; floods, cyclones, and other natural disasters bring quick and generous efforts to help, and isolated examples of pointless cruelty arouse pity. But there is a cold resignation to the suffering inflicted upon human beings by other human beings who are acting in an official and accepted capacity, especially if it is done on a large and systematic scale. The nervous system of the organized community seems to be atrophying. The reason is partly that we can become accustomed to almost anything and horrors repeated daily cease to be horrible, and partly is due to the habitual use of semantic cushions. The brute facts are translated into abstractions and statistical summaries. When we reckon the score in terms of "personnel" (there are now "anti-personnel" weapons), D.P.'s, P.O.W.'s, G.I.'s, and R.O.K.'s, it is possible to forget that we are actually dealing with flesh-and-blood human beings.

The strength of any civilization derives in large degree from its underlying beliefs. The beliefs may be unverifiable by objective tests; they may be illusions or a bizarre collection of folklore. The cherished ideas of one age are likely to be derided by the next, but they are serviceable while clung to if they give the individual a sense of direction and provide a rationale for community effort. One major reason for the confused condition of contemporary society is that its accepted and motivating beliefs have begun to give way. The evaporation of faith is not purely or even primarily a religious manifestation. Religion may gain, at least in terms of the number of adherents, as other supposedly more solid dispensations become perforated with doubt. In spite of the impact of science and material engrossments, religion is perhaps as powerful a force as it ever was, and some prophetic minds look to it as the redemptive influence which will lead the nations out of the quicksands onto firmer ground.

Certainly antidotes to the pathological addictions of contemporary man can be found within the orbit of religious thought and experience—and more fully here than anywhere else. The difficulty, however, aside from the fact that religious groups are myriad and frequently competitive, is that organized religion is tightly interlaced with the secular institutions which are most in need of reform. It has become an accepted part of the existing order of things, while its logical function is to transform that order. When omnipotent force is proclaimed as the safeguard and chief objective of civilized communities, all the agencies which nourish the intellect and the spirit are called upon to bow to its omnipotence.

The churches are urged, not to oppose the tide but to swim with it. The next decade may prove to be the most crucial period in the history of the Christian churches, as they are compelled to decide where their loyalties ultimately lie.

A more remarkable collapse than any in religion has taken place in the secular ideals which accompanied and abetted the evolution of modern industrial and political institutions. The assumptions, the articles of faith, the myths and the folklore—if that is what they really were—have lost their hold upon large segments of the population. The "folklore of capitalism" has been discredited; but so has the folklore of socialism, and even the folklore of liberalism and of democracy.

The creed of liberalism and the creed of socialism were each intended to eliminate the flaws which are so conspicuous in present society. In spite of their opposite connotations, the two ideals are complementary and necessary to each other. The logical solution to the economic dilemma of modern times is a welfare economy designed to provide abundance and the maximum of opportunity and freedom for the individual, coupled with an enlightened individualism (a socially conscious liberalism) which inspires the individual to seek his personal fulfillment through enriching his society. But the incentive to strive for such a goal flags as the philosophical bases of both liberalism and socialism disintegrate.

The trouble with the gospel of liberalism or individualism is that it has had the misfortune to be identified with a corpse—laissez-faire capitalism. A regime of *laissez faire* is as incongruous to our intricate and closely interconnected economic order as would be the medieval merchant guilds. Enlightened capitalists, who value freedom and respect human dignity, no longer believe in *laissez faire*. Unenlightened capitalists who advocate *laissez faire* (with modifications in the direction of protective tariffs, legalized monopoly, and reserved seats on what is left of the public domain) do not believe in freedom. The intelligent and conscientious liberal is caught between the devil and the deep sea. Treasuring personal liberty as a supreme good, he must oppose the claims of the state to omnipotence. He is not deluded by the argument that it is necessary to surrender individual freedom so that the state can protect the collective liberties of its members. He recalls that this argument was the stock in trade of the totalitarian destroyers of liberty. (It was Gentile, philosopher of fascism, who said, "The maximum of liberty always coincides with the maximum strength of the State.") He knows that freedom creates power; that power does not and cannot create freedom; and that through most of history power has been the enemy of freedom. Yet when the liberal opposes statism, as he must, he is likely to be claimed as an ally by those who condemn any form of public regulation or any modification of economic practices. He runs the risk of being made a stalking horse for selfish interests which, while denouncing the villainies of government, would like to replace it by an "invisible government" under their own control.

Socialism, the other secular program of emancipation, has also suffered the buffets of fortune, the cruelest one being its perversion into tyranny in the U.S.S.R. and her satellites. But aside from that, socialism has degenerated from an ideal into a technique. In Great Britain and Western Europe it is not much more than the necessary procedure for stretching out short rations. The scarcity of essential commodities is so great that publicly controlled distribution is essential to prevent social collapse, especially when haste in military preparation is being urged upon the population. The stringencies in these countries are not actually the result of socialism; rather, they made imperative the dismal kind of socialism now operating there. An even more fundamental disadvantage of socialism is that, since Marx, it has been associated with a materialistic interpretation of history and the dogma of economic man, both of which ideas have turned stale. In a materialistic environment where the individual tends to be an economic cog, he wants his dreams at least to be spun of different stuff. He may succumb to nationalism or to a "Strength-through-Joy" program; but an international association of working men will leave him cold.

Ideals and values have not by any means been exterminated. People still believe, deep in their hearts, that truth is stronger than falsehood and will triumph over it; that integrity is better than expediency; that right is greater than might. They want to believe these things; but they are bewildered, and grope falteringly for the spiritual landmarks which have been covered over by externals. Ideals to be effective demand more than intellectual assent; they must be felt spontaneously and intensely. When they seize hold of a people or an individual, the whole plane of experience is transformed. The paralyzing hesitancy vanishes; there is a consciousness of coming to grips with reality. It is futile to try to recover values by returning to the order of the past; because, in the Western context at least, the most challenging incentives always look to the future rather than to the past. To prove themselves they must be brought to bear actively in the sphere where man's interests and engagements lie. There is every reason to believe that the peoples of the world are still capable of responding to nonmaterial stimuli; they are hungering for them. But there are other dispensations than those which the West proffers, and it will take the utmost sincerity and singleness of purpose on the part of the Western nations to ensure the perpetuation and wider acceptance of the ideals they cherish.

INDUSTRIALISM—THE WAY OUT OR THE WAY DOWN?

Some analysts of the contemporary scene advance the thesis that the industrial complex holds the key to the future and that the particular problem confronting us is to produce a true "industrial civilization." "That is tomorrow's great creative task," writes C. Hartley Grattan. "The job of creating an industrial-based civilization—a civilization that is more than an accumulation of the cultural debris of past civilizations differently based—is still very much in process." The suggestion is constructive in spirit but it involves a confusion of terms and raises a number of questions. Just what is meant by an "industrial civilization"? Our civilization is already industrial-based, and by far the greater part of the crisis of our day stems directly or indirectly from this condition. Presumably it means an industrial order which will function more smoothly than the present one and without the periodic dislocations which have heretofore accompanied its development. But if the problem is to reduce frictions and inequalities, eliminate the threat of depression and war, cultivate better social habits and a wiser employment of leisure, it extends far beyond the area of economics and technology.

If the hope of the future lies in creating an industrial civilization, the United States is certainly best fitted to undertake the task, in view of her resources, technical skills, the favorable disposition of her people toward experiment and innovation, and the tremendous strides which she has already made. Even the philosophical groundwork for such a civilization has been at least partially laid. American capitalism has modified its practices and its point of view very significantly during the past thirty or forty years. Representative business leaders are able to point justifiably and proudly to a growing sense of social responsibility within their own ranks and to constructive ways in which the influence of corporate wealth is being applied. Personal and financial support has been given increasingly not merely to projects for scientific and technological research but to cultural endowments of a broad and humanistic nature, including liberal arts colleges whose educational program has no immediate bearing whatsoever upon the industrial processes.

And while capital has become broader and more liberal in social outlook, organized labor has become less rigidly proletarian in its orientation. Because bourgeois standards and ideals have permeated so deeply among all classes—clerical, professional, academic, and laboring—the transition to a technicized society could probably be accomplished in the United State with less friction and greater popular enthusiasm than anywhere else in the world.

Granting the possibility of such a transformation and admitting that it offers certain attractive features, foreshadowed by the rise of modern functional architecture and by the progress of city planning, would it solve the basic economic problem of distribution? Would it successfully meet the challenge of maintaining prosperity and full employment under an economy of peace? Even more fundamental is the question of the goals and values to be fostered in a society which is primarily directed to industrial expansion.

The glorification of technical efficiency and high productivity in the United States is somewhat ironic, in view of the general condition of mankind. The industrial revolutions have been tremendously successful in the West. But for the rest of the inhabitants of the globe it is doubtful if they have bestowed more blessing than bane. The fact is that after two centuries of scientific and industrial progress at least half of the world's population does not have enough to eat, and very little share in the fruits of modern industry. Judged by purely material standards Western industrialism has failed to provide abundance for the human family, and it has depressed some areas below their previous level. Economic progress has widened the disparity between the haves and the have-nots; the world is a land of rich men, poor men, beggarmen—and, inevitably, thieves.

Because there is already a definite movement toward more intense industrialization, in the United States and elsewhere, it is not difficult to foresee some of the changes most likely to appear if creating an industrial civilization is chosen as the conscious and primary goal of society. One almost inevitable trend would be for standards of value and judgment to become increasingly materialistic. Absorption with the process of turning out goods can lead to a pathological attachment to the goods, as has happened to a considerable degree in our society. When people become infatuated with machines and mechanical agencies, they drift in the direction of having no cultural standards, only technical ones. This is well illustrated in the field of popular entertainment, which has been revolutionized by the perfecting of media for the wholesale dissemination of impressions. In these enterprises the prime effort is to reach the masses rather than to encourage them to reach out for themselves after worth-while satisfactions. The ordinary person if he happens to be fond of the drama as entertainment seldom actually selects a drama. He "goes to the movies" or he "watches television." The film industry, spurred by the potential loss of customers since the advent of TV, has come up with ambitious promises of sumptuous and startling effects, apparently confident that these technical flourishes are what will hold the movie-going public and that theme, plot, artistic validity and imagination are of minor importance.

In themselves all the remarkable new attractions and techniques are admirable. Each represents a triumph. Civilization begins in the attempt to conquer nature and win a mastery over material forces. The utmost contriving, resourcefulness, and persistence are required to carry the process on even moderately well, and there is a delicious satisfaction in realizing success. But then arises a proclivity to become enamored with the devices that have been produced and with man's skill in producing them. The appetite keeps demanding more objects and services, more release from effort or from the limitations which man's relatively puny physical endowments impose upon him when he is separated from his implements. His goal becomes the automatic unlimited; he would construct a push-button world in which he can insulate himself from all annoyances. But eventually he finds that he has also insulated himself from the stimuli which by their irritation had forced him to exercise his full faculties. He has thrown away the oars by which he directed his course and is drifting in the currents. By sanding down all the rough edges of his environment he has made it difficult to hold a grip on any part of it. Theoretically, the achievement of a mechanized, streamlined, semiautomatic pattern of existence should bring release from strain and a feeling of serenity. Actually it does not. The elaborate apparatus of a superbly technicized society is so complicated that it requires constant vigilance to keep it functioning properly or even to keep it from getting badly out of repair. Its demands are as relentless as those which nature imposes upon primitive societies. And it is so enveloping that it intrudes into every avenue of experience. It pounds the individual at every turn until, nervous and harassed, he feels the need of escaping from the well-modulated but unrelenting turmoil. Then he finds that the means of procuring a respite are also built-in features of the environment, standardized and marketable; and an escapism however refreshing is not an escape.

Various other consequences, not all of them predictable, ensue from making the machine or factory or even a global supermarket the model for human society. The increasing mechanization of the ordinary routines of living induces a decline in intellectual interests. People are too hurried to want to give serious attention to matters requiring careful study. They insist on brief and pointed explanations, simple directions. The tempo of the age breeds an impatience with whatever is not easily accessible; and the continual impact of slogans, exhortations, and deftly condensed parcels of information upon the individual—the incessant competition for his attention—renders him incapable of fixing his attention upon anything for very long, robbing him of the power of concentration.

An inescapable effect of the simplification and standardization of public tastes, and one which is very much in evidence, is an insistence upon conformity—in pursuits, motives, affirmations, and ideas. A hundred years ago John Stuart Mill, in his essay *On Liberty*, noted that the pressure was even then ominous and growing. He wrote: "In our times, from the highest class of society down to the lowest, every one lives as under the eye of a hostile and dreaded censorship. . . . Thus the mind itself is bowed to the yoke." And he added the counsel: "In this age, the mere example of non-conformity, the mere refusal to bend the knee to custom, is itself a service. Precisely because the tyranny of opinion is such as to make eccentricity a reproach, it is desirable, in order to break through that tyranny, that people should be eccentric. . . . That so few now dare to be eccentric marks the chief danger of the time."

A mania for orthodoxy, with its fear of the slightest deviation, not only penalizes the individual but cheats society of fruitful discovery and intrepid leadership, consigning it to a state of suspended animation. That is the greatest danger in the crusade of intolerance into which a commendable concern for American ideals has degenerated. The current persecution, not only of opinion but of chance and temporary affiliation, can hardly be set down as hysteria. A wave of hysteria is dangerous, but it can be forgiven because of the volatility of human nature under the stress of excitement. The present campaign for conformity, however, is phlegmatic and cold-blooded. The whole affair, with its mock investigations, calumnious jargon, and studied innuendoes, is not in the least exciting. It is so indiscriminate, vague, and clumsy that it could not occur at all if the public mind and conscience were alert. The heresy hunters are intolerant not only of unorthodox ideas; worse than that, they are intolerant of ideas—of any ideas which are really alive and not empty cocoons.

Between the twin pressures of a physical and a social environment which tend to grow more encompassing and inflexible, a stereotyped, assembly-line species of individual is taking form. *Homo gregarius* is easily manipulated (although never convinced). He is almost entirely dependent upon stimulation from outside himself. He lacks resiliency, self-reliance, an inner core of resistance. He is dully contented or dully discontented. When he is conscious of problems he looks for them to be handled by a machine or by some external authority. Whatever happens, "they" (not "I") will know what to do about it; at any rate "they" will tell "us" what to do. This sterile type of person, becoming more numerous, seeks escape from his own nonentity by merging as completely as possible with his fellows; but he finds no serenity in doing so because he has no anchorage. He is one of "the lonely crowd," doomed to spiritual hunger.

The attempt to construct an industrial civilization involves an exaggerated emphasis upon a single aspect of man's capacities. It represents the kind of overspecialization that in the biological world has frequently caused a species to be defeated and eliminated in competition with more adaptable organisms. Mr. Grattan is right in rejecting the notion "that industrialism is inherently hostile to civilization and must be eliminated entirely if civilization is to be developed." Industrialism in itself is not hostile to civilization, but neither is it friendly. If rightly used it can be an instrument for attaining the objectives of a civilized society more completely and universally than would otherwise be possible. But the tone of a civilization depends on the attitudes, beliefs, and personality traits of its members; it is not a matter of mechanics. The concept of "industrial civilization" is as empty as the concept of "economic man" or "industrial man." Man can be helped or degraded by the machine; he cannot be equated to it nor evaluated in terms of it.

Nor can the machine take over man's unique responsibilities—even when he has invented an electronic "brain" to think for him.

ASSURANCE OF THINGS HOPED FOR

Western civilization may fail, or it may not only weather the present crises but advance to more splendid achievements. If the latter alternative prevails, it will probably be through rediscovery and utilization of the values which are now being tested by fire. In that event the character of the civilization will undoubtedly undergo drastic changes. If it succeeds in casting off the stultifying and suicidal tendencies which have defeated most civilizations, it may well assume a form hardly recognizable to the man of the mid-twentieth century.

Perhaps it would be more accurate to say not that values are being tested but that Western peoples and their institutions are being tried in the fire against the standard of these values. The moral and spiritual insights which have given the Western societies their most consoling moments and their noblest personalities have a validity beyond the environment in which they were made manifest. They are not only the most irreplaceable elements in the Western tradition; they contain the seeds of a better society than has yet been plotted. The precepts which they affirm go beyond logic and calculation, opening the door to a more rewarding life than man has yet experienced.

In the light of the proved variability of human behavior, it is conceivable that a very different kind of civilization from those of the past might be projected. The history of civilizations to date is monotonously repetitious. Rome repeats Oriental theocracy; modern nations revive imperialism, despotism, and slavery. Techniques and locale vary constantly, and there are always magnificent episodes; but again and again people have been confined within the same narrow horizons. A really new civilization would be one which utilizes the unrealized potentials within man and, by fostering changes in human nature, opens up new horizons.

The unrealized potentials within man cannot be certainly determined, but they must be factors which are related to the continuing process of human evolution. Some predict that man's intellect will increase in the future. They picture the average citizen of several millenniums hence as having a balder but more domelike cranium and a larger brain than ours. This prediction of a heightening intellectual stature is dubious. Obviously, man has not made the best use of the brains he already possesses or history would not be the chronicle of blunders and stupidities that it is. Actually, there has been no appreciable change in the size or character of the brain of Homo sapiens during the past 25,000 years. Cro-Magnon man was equal to us in brain size and psychological equipment. If we wait for a greater mental endowment to help us out of our difficulties, we shall probably have to wait for at least tens of thousands of years.

In addition to his intellectual capacities, man has still other potentials that have not been completely utilized or even sufficiently explored. These are the resources, closely related to the intellect but not identical with it, which for lack of a more scientific term are called spiritual. Within this intangible and vaguely defined area the most satisfying achievements of every civilization have been centered. The indispensable core throughout Western history has not been technological proficiency nor scientific aptitude—these are relatively recent acquisitions. It has been, rather, a faith in man's importance and destiny. This faith was operative from the beginning, when the prospect of improving the physical condition of society seemed very remote. It postulates as the central task the improvement of man himself—his redemption, his triumph over the universal brute in him—rather than the transformation of the environment, although this latter objective has been prominent also.

The most memorable periods in Western history have come when a lively awareness of evils to be attacked was joined to an irrepressible confidence in the ability of man to rise to a higher level; when the Olympian scorn of a Voltaire or a Carlyle was matched by the reforming diligence of a Beccaria, a Bentham, or a Robert Owen. The achievements of these constructive periods, often carried out against a background of general discouragement, were made possible by a consciousness of spiritual reserves too tough to be gainsaid.

Human history is largely a record of faltering effort, of complacent surrender to circumstance. But the farther man emerged above the brute level, the greater became his capacity for fellow feeling, co-operation, and compassion. He began to recognize that there is a distinction between good and evil; he acquired a conscience and discovered that it could rob him of peace of mind even when he had obtained what he thought he wanted. He came to feel that there was a power not himself which operated through him and beyond him and which lay at the root of his most insatiable longings. He was troubled because he repeatedly had to deny the promptings of the inner voice in accommodating himself to the established requirements and routines of daily living. Most of the time he did accommodate; he surrendered to the immediate demands, until the still small voice became smaller and stiller.

Once in a while, however, there have appeared individuals who cut clean through the entangling webs of tradition, conventional standards, and prudence, and dared the impossible, to the amazement of their contemporaries and the gratitude of posterity. These indomitable men and women, perceiving deeper values and swayed by higher motives than the prevailing ones, acted upon the assumption that the world was ready for these values and motives. They seized upon the future and lived as if the time had arrived when the ideal could become the actual. A Socrates, a St. Francis, a Gandhi, an Albert Schweitzer are indeed rarities. Few mortals have attained the breadth of vision or clarity of insight of a Condorcet, a Thomas Jefferson, a Theodore Parker, or a John Stuart Mill. But perhaps such figures can be interpreted as mutations in the human stock, indicative of the type of personality which may develop (altering the institutions of society accordingly) if human evolution is not cut off in midstream.

The real task ahead is not to create an industrial civilization but to create an ethical one. The ultimate rationale of civilization is the promotion of fuller, richer and more abundant life. If, instead of being devoted to this end, its resources are subverted to the gratification of the meaner impulses or to the constriction of life, then civilization becomes a predatory organism, a monstrous usurpation on man's part. And nature has a way of dealing with usurpers.

INDEX

Index

Index

Index

Edward I, King of England, 124
Egypt, civilization of, 30, 31, 36, 37-41
Einstein, Albert, 253
Engels, Friedrich, 238
Engineering, development of, 31, 38
England
  Bank of England, 196
  Barebone Parliament, 194
  Christianity in, 105
  Church of, 195, 197
  civil wars, 192
  colonial empire, 180-188
    India, 182, 186-188
  government, 121, 123-125, 196
  Industrial Revolution started in, 186, 219-244
  peasants, 118
  Puritanism, 191-197
  Reformation, 160, 161
  Restoration, 196
  Stuarts, 192
Enlightenment, Age of the, 198-209, 229, 234, 238
Environment
  influence on cultures, 94, 114
    Egypt, 42
    Greece, 47-48
    Western Europe, 281
  technological changes affect, 230
Epicureanism, 76
Equality of rights, 207
Erasmus, 169-170, 206
Ethics
  classical Greece, 59
  personal and social, 34
Ethiopia, 276
Euripides, 67
Europe
  balance of power, 227, 271
  barbarian invasion, 91-92
  early Middle Ages, 91-108
  latter Middle Ages, 109-146
  post-medieval conflicts, 46-47
  unification of, 168, 206, 231, 283
European history, Roman influence on, 68
Evolution of Man, 13-17, 246, 255
  Darwin's theory, 28, 235-238
Existentialism, 252

Expansionists of 1898 (Pratt), 10
Exploration and discovery, voyages of, 149-150
Expressionism, 247

Factory Acts, 224-225
Factory system, 217, 219, 223, 225-226, 228, 263
  condition of workers in, 221-227
Family life, Egypt, 39
Far East, European colonies, 180
Fascism, 269-270
Fear, effect on cultures, 95, 277
Ferry, Jules, 259, 262
"Fertile Crescent" of Asia, 30, 31, 32, 33
Feudalism, 97-98, 113, 114-116
  "arts of war," 115-116, 128-130
  church and, 125-130
  decline of, 148
  economic and social arrangement, 116-122
  form of government, 122-128
Force, use of, 276-279, 283
Ford, Henry, 275
France
  Carolingian state, 123
  colonial empire, 180-188
  enmity between Germany and, 97, 101
  geographical exploration, 181
  government, 122, 248, 288
  Industrial Revolution, 226
  peasants, 118, 210-211
  Popular Front government, 288
  rationalist movement, 205-207
  Reformation, 161
  religion, 181
  Revolution; see French Revolution
  seized Ruhr Valley, 269
  testing ground for social ideas, 212-213
  World War I, 250
  World War II, 265
Franco, General, 271
Franks, conversion of, 103-104
Frederick the Great, of Prussia, 182
Free trade, 256

310

Index

311

Index

Index

Index

Index

Index

Religion, *continued*
  Protestant Revolt, 158-174
  Puritanism, 191-197
  rationalism versus, 200
  Renaissance, 151-158
  U.S.S.R., 274
Renaissance, 47, 111, 147-174, 281
  art, 152-156, 248
  emotionalism of, 199-200
  Italian, 150, 152-158
  religion, 151-158
  science, 171-174
  significance of, 155-158
Reporter, The (periodical), 10
Research, subsidized, 284-285, 289
Resources
  discovery and research, 247
  to serve good of society, 249-250
  waste of, 246, 290
Revolt of the Masses (Ortega), 283
Revolution, rationalist movement and, 208, 210
Rhodes, Cecil, 260
Rights of man, 204
Robespierre, Maximilien Francoise, 213
Rocque, Colonel de la, 270
Roman Catholic Church; *see* Church, Catholic
Roman Empire
  administration of, 73, 83-86
  basis of culture, 44
  barbarian invasions, 44, 91-92, 96-97
  bureaucracy under, 83-85
  disintegration of, 83 90, 91-94
  organizing and development of provinces, 78-79, 80-81
  vitality of, 82
Romantic Idealism, 233
Romanticism, 232-235, 247
Rome
  agriculture, 81
  art, 69, 74-75
  Carthage and, 71, 72, 76
  Christianity and, 87-90, 102-103
  cities organized by, 78-79, 81-82
  class struggle, 85, 116
  cultural origins, 68-69, 75-77
  decadence under Republic, 74
  early government, 70-74

Rome, *continued*
  German barbarian invasions, 69, 96-97
  Greek civilization in, 68-69, 72, 96
  imperialism, 72, 73-74, 76
  influenced culture of Western Europe, 111
  laws codified, 78, 88, 98, 111, 157
  literature, 74-75, 153
  militarization, 84
  Pax Romana, 77, 82
  Republic, 70, 74, 80
  slavery, 80
  status of citizens, 79, 83
  trade and commerce, 81
  virtues exalted by, 72
Rousseau, Jean Jacques, 207-209, 229, 234
Russia; *see also* Union of Soviet Socialist Republics
  Bolshevist dictatorship, 251
  government, 248, 249
  industry, 226
  World War 1, 273

St. Augustine of Hippo, 106-108, 162, 164
St. Benedict, 117
St. Francis, 305
Saint-Germain, Palier de, 206
Saint-Just, Louis, 213
Saint-Pierre, Abbé de, 205
St. Thomas Aquinas, 46, 126, 133, 146, 147, 201, 202-203, 242
Sainthood, 139
Salamis, victory at, 63
San Francisco, United Nations meeting at, 266
Saracenic Empire; *see* Mohammedan Empire
Savonarola, Girolamo, 155
Scandinavians, 184-185, 248
Scarcity, philosophy of, 288
Schenk, Wilhelm, 9
Scholasticism, 126, 133, 135, 146, 149, 157, 166
  rationalism and, 198-203
Schweitzer, Albert, 305

316

Index

317

Index

Index